CASE STUDIES for INTERPRETING the MMPI-A-RF

CASE STUDIES for INTERPRETING the MMPI-A-RF

Daniel L. Davis
Yossef S. Ben-Porath

UNIVERSITY OF MINNESOTA PRESS

Minneapolis | London

Published by the University of Minnesota Press
111 Third Avenue South, Suite 290
Minneapolis, MN 55401-2520
http://www.upress.umn.edu

ISBN 978-1-5179-0532-3 (pb)

Library of Congress record available at https://lccn.loc.gov/2021025923

Printed in the United States of America on acid-free paper

The University of Minnesota is an equal-opportunity educator and employer.

30 29 28 27 26 25 24 23 22 21   10 9 8 7 6 5 4 3 2 1

CONTENTS

LIST OF TABLES

LIST OF FIGURES

ACKNOWLEDGMENTS

The first acknowledgment is to the youth whose stories are the basis for this work. May each of them find the kind of life that every young person deserves. To my wife, Vickie, who always provides me loving support, guidance, and wisdom, as well as careful editing and proofreading of the initial manuscript. You are the center of my life. To my son, Joshua, I am proud of you beyond words; and my stepchildren—Tabitha, Katie, Mark, and Rickie—you each have been additions to my life for which I am forever grateful. To my grandchildren—Aria, Aiden, Avery, Fitz, Evelyn, and John (as well as to those I hope to come)—I see with wonder the great promise of your futures. Thanks to all of you for that which really matters in life. I would also like to express my thanks to James Worling, PhD, and Terrance J. Kukor, PhD, ABPP, for their helpful comments. And to my aunt, Ann Decker, whose career with children inspired and guided my own. Last, I wish to acknowledge the late Professor Larry E. Cox, a teacher, a mentor, and an inspiration.

—DLD

To my MMPI-A-RF coauthors—Bob Archer, Rick Handel, and Auke Tellegen—whose collaboration made the test possible, and to my family, whose love and support make this and all my work worthwhile.

—YBP

PART I

Introduction to the MMPI-A-RF

The Minnesota Multiphasic Personality Inventory-Adolescent Restructured Form (MMPI-A-RF) is a 241-item test that was derived from the Minnesota Multiphasic Inventory-Adolescent (MMPI-A; Butcher et al., 1992). The 241 items are a subset of the 478-item pool of the MMPI-A. The test is composed of 48 scales: 6 Validity, 3 Higher-Order, 9 Restructured Clinical, 25 Specific Problems, and revised versions of the MMPI-A PSY-5 Scales. Also, 14 critical item sets are provided, including 7 Depression/Suicidal Ideation items. The MMPI-A-RF, although a subset of the MMPI-A item pool, was developed in a manner similar to that of the MMPI-2-RF (MMPI-2-RF: Ben-Porath & Tellegen, 2008/2011; Tellegen & Ben-Porath, 2008, 2011).

The MMPI-A-RF has a number of options available for interpretation and scoring, all of which are available from the test distributor, Pearson (www.PearsonClinical.com/MMPIARF). These options are computer scoring via web-based Q-global, on-site Q Local, and mail-in services; as well as hand-scoring keys, answer sheets, and profile forms. Given the complexity of the instrument as well as the possibility of making clerical errors, we recommend using the computerized scoring options, especially in forensic cases. The MMPI-A-RF Score Report provides raw and standard (T) scores for all the MMPI-A-RF scales, as well as item-level information, including the number of unscoreable and critical responses. The MMPI-A-RF Interpretive

Report for Clinical Settings provides all the information included in the MMPI-A-RF Score Report as well as a narrative interpretation and item-level test findings. Similar to the MMPI-2-RF reports, the MMPI-A-RF reports provide the test user with the option of plotting the examinee's results with comparison groups (including forensic, outpatient, inpatient, correctional, medical, and school settings). Additional information about the Score and Interpretive reports is provided in the *MMPI-A-RF Users Guide for Reports* (Archer et al., 2016b). Finally, using the computerized scoring options, MMPI-A data can be easily converted to MMPI-A-RF protocols.

Development of the MMPI-A-RF

In addition to the test manual, Archer (2017) provides a detailed history of the development of the MMPI-A-RF, as will be summarized in this section. The original MMPI (Hathaway & McKinley, 1943) was developed to improve the assessment of the symptomatology of patients who came to the University of Minnesota Hospital for medical treatment and who seemed to have problems that were more psychological in nature than physical. The first research studies on the MMPI with adolescents were done in 1941, before the publication of the test. Capwell (1945a) found that MMPI Scale 4 (Pd) accurately differentiated delinquent from nondelinquent girls. The stability of these findings was demonstrated in a 15-month follow-up study (Capwell, 1945b). Hathaway and Monachesi (1953) sought to expand the use of the MMPI in identifying or predicting delinquency in adolescents. They conducted a longitudinal study of associations between the MMPI Clinical scales and delinquent behavior in a combined sample of approximately 15,000 adolescents from urban and rural Minnesota, the largest such data set ever collected on adolescents. This research resulted in a study addressing the relationship between MMPI findings and delinquent behaviors, which identified MMPI variables serving as risk factors for involvement in delinquent and antisocial behaviors. The data set also served as a source of clinical correlates of the test scores of adolescents, contributing significantly to research on use of the MMPI with adolescents.

As use of the MMPI with adolescents continued, research turned to the development of adolescent norms. The norms most frequently used were developed by Marks and Briggs and first published in Dahlstrom et al. (1972). These norms were developed from the responses of approximately 1,800 males and females ages 17 and below. One of the more noteworthy modifications introduced by Marks and Briggs was discontinuation of the

K-correction procedure used in the assessment of adults with the original MMPI. Marks et al. (1974) published the first set of actuarial personality descriptors using 29 MMPI code types developed from clinician ratings of approximately 1,250 adolescents. This was the first use of code types specifically for adolescents.

Although the MMPI gained widespread acceptance after the development of adolescent-specific code type correlates and the test became widely used with adolescents, some of the limitations of the original Clinical scales also hampered its use with adolescents. Some adolescent-specific limitations also emerged. These included clinicians persisting in the use of adult norms even when adolescent norms existed, concerns over the adequacy of the existing adolescent norms, outdated language and inappropriate item content for adolescents, the unavailability of items specific to the experiences of adolescents or scales developed specifically for adolescents. In 1992, the Minnesota Multiphasic Inventory-Adolescent was published (Butcher et al., 1992). This version of the test had a number of advantages: It was shorter (478 items compared to the original 566 MMPI items); it contained items with uniquely adolescent content; standard T scores were based on a contemporary normative sample of 805 boys and 815 girls from eight states; and it included additional Validity scales as well as Content scales specific to adolescents.

Despite the considerable advancements introduced by the MMPI-A, it carried over the limitations inherent in the original MMPI Clinical scales, which was also true of the MMPI-2. These shortcomings were a product of the heterogeneous content, resulting in multidimensionality and extensive item and thematic overlap between the Clinical scales, which in turn produced excessive intercorrelation of the MMPI-A Clinical scales and substantially limited their discriminant validity. This was reflected in the higher-than-expected correlations with external correlates unrelated to the basic constructs targeted by the MMPI-A Clinical scales. Last, and not insignificant, the length of the test (478 items), though considerably shorter than the MMPI and MMPI-2, was a major challenge because it often exceeded the attention span, concentration, and interest of some adolescents—particularly the very youth for whom assessments were required.

Many of the problems just discussed had been similarly observed with the adult version of the instrument, the MMPI-2, and addressed with the MMPI-2-RF. Using the MMPI-2-RF development as a template, the authors of the MMPI-A-RF addressed the problem of overlap and heterogeneity.

They first dealt with the assessment of demoralization, the broad construct of emotional distress measured to varying, substantial degrees by each of the MMPI Clinical scales, thus contributing to the excessive correlations between the Clinical scales. Using exploratory factor analysis enabled the test developers to differentiate the major distinctive components of the Clinical scales separate from the demoralization factor. In doing so, the Restructured Clinical (RC) scales address the target concept without the contamination of a factor common to all the scales. In addition, Substantive scales covering other areas in the item pools, some specific to adolescents, were developed. The Validity scales were updated for assessment of overreporting and underreporting as well as non-content-based responding. Finally, the MMPI-A-RF contains revised PSY-5 scales. The PSY-5 model (McNulty et al., 1997) represents major dimensions of personality pathology and was originally adapted for the MMPI-A following its introduction with the MMPI-2 (Harkness et al., 1995). A total of 48 scales were developed for the MMPI-A-RF, composed of 241 items. Standard scores are based on the 1,610 MMPI-A normative sample of boys and girls.

The MMPI-A-RF Scales

Following is a brief description of the 48 MMPI-A-RF scales. More detailed information is provided by Archer (2017) and in the test manual. Table 1 provides a list of the 48 MMPI-A-RF scales, including full and abbreviated scale names. As would be expected given that the MMPI-A-RF development was modeled on the MMPI-2-RF, the structure of the instrument is quite similar. The structure of the MMPI-A-RF Substantive scales represents three levels of breadth versus specificity. The three Higher-Order scales (H-O) are at the highest level, the Restructured Clinical scales (RC) are at the middle level, and at the third level are the Specific Problems (SP) scales, the more focused, narrow-bandwidth third level of assessment. Interpretive statements based on the scales are intended to apply to T scores of 60 or higher, which correspond to the 85th percentile or higher in the normative population. In a number of these scales, low scores can also be interpreted.

VALIDITY SCALES

As with all versions of the MMPI, the adolescent restructured form includes a comprehensive set of Validity scales designed to assess the quality of the information provided by the test taker and identify content- and non-content-based threats to protocol validity (Ben-Porath, 2013). Non-content-based responding refers to nonresponding, random responding, or fixed indiscriminate responding. Random responding can be intentional or unintentional (e.g., resulting from reading or language comprehension deficits). Indiscriminate fixed responding can be acquiescent or nonacquiescent. Content-based invalid responding involves overreporting or underreporting.

TABLE 1
The MMPI-A-RF Scale Labels and Abbreviations

The MMPI-A-RF SCALES	
Validity	
CNS	Cannot Say (reported as a raw score only, not plotted)
VRIN-r	Variable Response Inconsistency
TRIN-r	True Response Inconsistency
CRIN	Combined Response Inconsistency
F-r	Infrequent Responses
L-r	Uncommon Virtues
K-r	Adjustment Validity
Higher-Order (H-O) **and Restructured Clinical (RC)**	
Higher-Order (H-O)	
EID	Emotional/Internalizing Dysfunction
THD	Thought Dysfunction
BXD	Behavioral/Externalizing Dysfunction
Restructured Clinical (RC)	
RCd	Demoralization
RC1	Somatic Complaints
RC2	Low Positive Emotions
RC3	Cynicism
RC4	Antisocial Behavior
RC6	Ideas of Persecution
RC7	Dysfunctional Negative Emotions
RC8	Aberrant Experiences
RC9	Hypomanic Activation
Specific Problems Scales	
Somatic/Cognitive	
MLS	Malaise
GIC	Gastrointestinal Complaints
HPC	Head Pain Complaints
NUC	Neurological Complaints
COG	Cognitive Complaints
Internalizing	
HLP	Helplessness/Hopelessness
SFD	Self-Doubt
NFC	Inefficacy
OCS	Obsessions/Compulsions

(continued on next page)

The MMPI-A-RF SCALES

STW	Stress/Worry
AXY	Anxiety
ANP	Anger Proneness
BRF	Behavior-Restricting Fears
SPF	Specific Fears
Externalizing	
NSA	Negative School Attitudes
ASA	Antisocial Attitudes
CNP	Conduct Problems
SUB	Substance Abuse
NPI	Negative Peer Influence
AGG	Aggression
Interpersonal	
FML	Family Problems
IPP	Interpersonal Passivity
SAV	Social Avoidance
SHY	Shyness
DSF	Disaffiliativeness
Personality Psychopathology Five (PSY-5)	
AGGR-r	Aggressiveness-Revised
PSYC-r	Psychoticism-Revised
DISC-r	Disconstraint-Revised
NEGE-r	Negative Emotionality/Neuroticism-Revised
INTR-r	Introversion/Low Positive Emotionality-Revised

The MMPI-A-RF Validity Scale Variable Response Inconsistency (VRIN-r) assesses for random responding; True Response Inconsistency (TRIN-r) measures fixed responding; Combined Response Inconsistency (CRIN) identifies the overall level of inconsistent responding; Infrequent Responses (F-r) assesses for overreporting; and Uncommon Virtues (L-r) and Adjustment Validity (K-r) measure the individual's level of underreporting. In addition, a Cannot Say (CNS) raw score is obtained by counting the number of items either left unanswered or answered both True and False.

HIGHER-ORDER SCALES

The MMPI-A-RF Higher-Order scales are: Emotional/Internalizing Dysfunction (EID), which measures dysfunction in the domains of mood and affect; Thought Dysfunction (THD), assessing manifestations of disordered thinking; and Behavioral/Externalizing Dysfunction (BXD), which identifies undercontrolled behavior. The Higher-Order scales provide a broadband assessment of whether, and to what extent, an adolescent likely presents with significant dysfunction in one or more of these broad domains. As illustrated throughout the cases included in this book, the H-O scales also serve as anchors of the MMPI-A-RF interpretive strategy.

RC SCALES

The starting point for developing the MMPI-A-RF RC scales were the MMPI-A items appearing in the MMPI-2-RF. This item set was used to form seed scales and other MMPI-A items, including items with adolescent-specific content, which were found to have optimal convergent and divergent correlations when these seeds were added to the MMPI-A-RF RC scales. Of the 58 items unique to the MMPI-A, 19 were added to the RC scales. The MMPI-A eliminated items that were inappropriate to adolescents and this change was continued in the MMPI-A-RF. Thus, while the MMPI-A-RF RC scales measure the same constructs as the corresponding MMPI-2-RF counterparts and have the same names, their content is sometimes very different from the corresponding MMPI-2-RF scales.

Demoralization (RCd) assesses nonspecific emotional distress that can be found in some types of internalizing psychopathology such as anxiety and depression, but also reflects a general level of distress, unhappiness, and dissatisfaction. Somatic Complaints (RC1) is a measure of somatization, general preoccupation with somatic functioning, and anxiety about health. Low Positive Emotions (RC2) measures the lack of positive emotional responsiveness or anhedonia, which is a distinct core vulnerability factor in depression. Cynicism (RC3) reflects misanthropic interpersonal beliefs that others cannot be trusted and are generally out only for their own self-interest. Antisocial Behavior (RC4) is a measure of rule-breaking and irresponsible behaviors. Ideas of Persecution (RC6) addresses self-referential beliefs that others pose a threat to the examinee in some manner. Dysfunctional Negative

Emotions (RC7) assesses manifestations of maladaptive anxiety, anger, and fear. Aberrant Experiences (RC8) identifies unusual thoughts or perceptions associated with thought dysfunction. Hypomanic Activation (RC9) measures behavioral overactivation, aggression, impulsivity, and grandiosity.

SP SCALES

The Specific Problems (SP) scales are the more focused, narrow-band MMPI-A-RF measures of symptoms and traits that assess facets of the RC scales, Clinical scales, or Content scales. The scale labels convey the constructs assessed by these scales, which, as seen in Table 1, are grouped into four thematic domains of Somatic/Cognitive scales, Internalizing scales, Externalizing scales, and Interpersonal scales. Of these 25 scales, 19 have direct MMPI-2-RF counterparts (although the latter scales often do not have exactly the same items). There are five scales that are specific in label and content to the MMPI-A-RF. These scales are: Obsessions/Compulsions (OCS), Negative School Attitudes (NSA), Antisocial Attitudes (ASA), Conduct Problems (CNP), and Negative Peer Influence (NPI). The MMPI-A-RF also does not have a specific scale for suicide risk (SUI in the MMPI-2-RF). Rather, as will be later illustrated, risk can be assessed through both the MMPI-A-RF scales and the critical items. Additionally, the Specific Fears-Multiple Specific Fears scale (SPF) differs in name and item content from the MMPI-2-RF because the phobias addressed in the MMPI-A item pool are different from those in the MMPI-2 item pool.

PERSONALITY PSYCHOPATHOLOGY/ FIVE (PSY-5) SCALES

The PSY-5 scales are revised versions of the MMPI-A PSY-5 scales. They represent a dimensional model of personality-disorder-related psychopathology, each scale representing a dimensional trait associated with specific manifestations of personality disorders. Aggressiveness (AGGR-r) addresses instrumental goal-directed aggression of the type found in Cluster B disorders. Psychoticism (PSYC-r) is a measure of disconnection from reality found in Cluster A disorders. Disconstraint (DISC-r) assesses undercontrolled, impulsive behavior characteristic of Cluster B disorders. Negative

Emotionality/Neuroticism (NEGE-r) measures anxiety, worry, insecurity, and fear. The last scale, Introversion/Low Positive Emotionality (INTR-r), is a measure of social disengagement and anhedonia. Both INTR-r and NEGE-r assess for manifestations of Cluster C disorders.

MMPI-A-RF RESOURCES

Two primary sources provide guidance for MMPI-A-RF users: the *MMPI-A-RF Manual for Administration, Scoring, and Interpretation* (Archer et al., 2016a), which contains detailed information on test construction as well as the interpretive strategy recommended by the test authors. The second, highly recommended resource is the 4th edition of Archer's (2017) book, *Assessing Adolescent Psychopathology: MMPI-A/ MMPI-A-RF*. This essential reference extensively reviews research, provides an interpretive strategy, and illustrates how the MMPI-A-RF can be used in forensic settings.

Administering the MMPI-A-RF

TESTABILITY OF THE ADOLESCENT

The MMPI-A-RF norms are based on the responses of 14- through 18-year-old boys and girls. There is some evidence that younger adolescents may be able to respond adequately to the MMPI-A items (Butcher et al., 1992; Ehrenworth & Archer, 1985; Janus et al., 1998; and Oldenburg, 1997). Because persons who are 18 are included in the normative samples of both the MMPI-A-RF and the MMPI-2-RF, either test can be used. The decision regarding which test to use is made on a case-by-case basis. A good rule of thumb is the adolescent's level of independence. For example, if she or he is 18 and still living at home, the MMPI-A-RF would be more appropriate. But if the youth is in the military, married, or living away in college, the MMPI-2-RF would likely be the better choice. Another illustration would be a case of bindover or waiver to the adult court. The forensic examiner may wish to use the MMPI-A-RF to compare the youth's results with the various forensic reference groups available to the MMPI-A-RF.

A variety of conditions may impair the ability of the adolescent to complete the MMPI-A-RF. Often, a youth may have difficulties with concentration and focus owing to conditions such as Attention Deficit Hyperactivity Disorder (ADHD), or they may be oppositional and unwilling to complete the test in one session. In such cases, it is permissible to administer the test in segments. However, this should be done within a short time period. Given the reduced number of items in the MMPI-A-RF, the majority of adolescents will easily be able to complete the test in 30 to 45 minutes. Finally, the examiner should be alert for interfering conditions of drug or alcohol intoxication or a thought disorder.

READING ABILITY

Most MMPI-A-RF items range between fifth- and seventh-grade reading level. The test manual and Archer (2017) provide a thorough discussion of readability of the items and how care should be taken to ensure that the adolescent has the required reading skills. When these skills are in doubt, it is good practice to administer a standard test of reading ability. The MMPI-A-RF can be administered using an audio CD, but care should be taken that the youth has the requisite listening comprehension. There may be times when administration of a measure of auditory comprehension is needed.

Because of the need to adhere to standardization, we strongly recommend that the examiner never administer the test by reading the items to the examinee. A similar question arises about explaining items to the adolescent. Although this approach may seem appropriate, it is not. The test was not standardized on individuals who had items explained to them. The test manual does allow for the use of a simple dictionary definition of words (p. 63) but does not recommend an extended discussion of the meaning of the items. Any approach that differs from only using the standardized test instructions deviates from the standardization procedure of the test and is not appropriate.

SUPERVISION OF TEST ADMINISTRATION

The adolescent must be provided with an environment that is adequately supervised. If the examiner delegates administration to another person under their supervision, this individual needs to be appropriately trained, supervised, and well-informed in standard test administration procedures. Although the examiner does not need to remain in the same room as the adolescent throughout the testing, it is recommended that individuals administering the test be able to monitor the testing. It is never appropriate to send the test home with the adolescent or allow administration in a setting where adequate supervision cannot be assured.

TESTING CONDITIONS

The setting for test administration should be comfortable and as free from distractions as possible. It is well worth the examiner's time to spend a few moments making the adolescent feel comfortable and helping the adolescent understand the value of the testing process. Although good rapport is important, it should be developed and maintained without providing a too-casual environment that might actually diminish cooperation and attention.

Although the MMPI-A-RF is considerably shorter than the MMPI-A, some adolescents will not be able to complete the test in one session. It is permissible to administer the test over one or two days. This may produce a valid test as contrasted with requiring a single session that may result in carelessness or disengagement. Administration of the test should take about 30 to 45 minutes using the booklet and about 20 to 30 minutes using computer-based administration. Computer administration can be accomplished with Pearson's software.

Scoring the MMPI-A-RF

The MMPI-A-RF can be hand scored or scored with the aid of computer software. Hand scoring can be time consuming and is more prone to produce error. Pearson's software can be used to produce the MMPI-A-RF Score Report, which provides raw and T scores for all MMPI-A-RF scales as well as information about item responses. The MMPI-A-RF Interpretive Report for Clinical Settings includes all the elements of the Score Report, augmented by a computer-generated interpretation, on the basis of the interpretive guidelines provided in the test manual. The available comparison groups and their use are described in the *MMPI-A-RF User's Guide for Reports* (Archer et al., 2016b). Both reports can also include user-selected comparison groups that provide descriptive information about MMPI-A-RF scale scores and item responses in samples of adolescents representative of settings (clinical and forensic) in which the test is commonly used.

Interpreting the MMPI-A-RF

Table 2 outlines a basic structure for interpretation of the MMPI-A-RF. This model uses the hierarchical approach developed for the MMPI-2-RF. The first step, as always, is the determination of interpretability using the Validity scales. If the protocol is deemed valid for interpretation, the Substantive scales can be examined next.

The MMPI-A-RF differs from the MMPI-A in that interpretation of elevated scores on the MMPI-A-RF are intended for T scores of 60 or higher, which corresponds to the 85th percentile or higher in the normative population. In addition, for many of the Substantive scales, low-score interpretations are made that are distinctive from average or normal range scores. In general, T scores of 40 or less (15th percentile) are interpreted in those scales for which low-score interpretations are provided.

If interpretation of the Substantive scales is warranted, then the interpretive section of the report will address the following areas: Somatic/ Cognitive Dysfunction, Emotional Dysfunction/Thought Dysfunction, Behavioral Dysfunction, and Interpersonal Functioning. Interpretation focuses on the relative prominence and importance of a scale in these areas. To illustrate, if the test findings show that symptoms related to behavioral dysfunction are most prominent, that section is addressed first. The other scales addressed in order of prominence follow. If in a valid protocol, no problem is identified in a particular area, this is also reported but with the awareness that such a finding should always be cautioned in light of existing data as the lack of reporting of a problem does not always mean that it does not, in fact, exist. It is important to note that if the MMPI-A-RF findings indicate a safety risk, this finding can be the first reported or may be in boldface or some other font variation to focus attention on the immediate problem.

TABLE 2
Basic Structure for Interpretation of the MMPI-A-RF

	Topic	MMPI-A-RF Sources
I	Protocol Validity	
	a. Content Nonresponsiveness	CNS, VRIN-r, TRIN-r, CRIN
	b. Overreporting	F-r
	c. Underreporting	L-r, K-r
II	Substantive Scales Interpretation	
	a. Somatic/Cognitive Dysfunction	RC1, MLS, GIC, HPC, NUC, COG
	b. Emotional Dysfunction	1. EID
		2. RCd, HLP, SFD, NFC
		3. RC2, INTR-r
		4. RC7, OCS, STW, AXY, ANP, BRF, SPF, NEGE-r
	c. Thought Dysfunction	1. THD
		2. RC6
		3. RC8
		4. PSYC-r
	d. Behavioral Dysfunction	1. BXD
		2. RC4, NSA, ASA, CNP, SUB, NPI
		3. RC9, AGG, AGGR-r, DISC-r
	e. Interpersonal Functioning	1. FML
		2. RC3
		3. IPP
		4. SAV
		5. SHY
		6. DSF
	f. Diagnostic Considerations	Most Substantive Scales
	g. Treatment Considerations	Most Substantive Scales

The last sections of the interpretation include diagnostic and treatment considerations. These may or may not be necessary depending upon the purpose of the report. For example, it is not always the case that a diagnosis is needed in certain types of forensic evaluations such as competency to stand trial. When a diagnosis is needed, the MMPI-A-RF can provide very helpful information but should never be used as the sole basis of a diagnosis. Similarly, treatment recommendations may not be needed depending upon the purpose of the report.

An important consideration for the MMPI-A-RF, and any other personality assessment of adolescents for that matter, is that many characteristics and behaviors seen in adolescents are transitory given their continued development. Therefore, although a test finding or diagnosis may accurately portray the youth's current functioning, these findings are not always predictive of long-term functioning. They can describe traits or factors that require intervention to prevent future problems and assist in the development of optimal future psychological functioning. Finally, there is not a consensus in research regarding the applicability and validity of diagnostic classification systems such as DSM-5 to adolescents.

USE OF THE MMPI-A-RF IN RISK ASSESSMENTS

A good illustration of the principle of structuring the interpretation to the referral question is risk assessment in adolescents. Risk assessment focuses not only on factors that act as a risk for violence but also on those factors that are protective against future violence. The MMPI-A-RF can identify not only possible risk factors such as impulsivity and conduct-disordered behaviors but also, for example, protective factors such as willingness to engage in treatment, intact reality testing, and lack of cynicism. When risk assessment of adolescents was first developed, primary attention was placed on factors identifying problems or risk-increasing factors. Beginning with risk assessment models such as the Structured Assessment of Violence Risk in Youth (Borum et al., 2006), assessment of the protective factors that mitigate against risk has become a critical part of understanding and managing risk in adolescents.

In many cases, strengths or protective factors (what we term "treatment assets" in our reports) can be identified with the MMPI-A-RF. For example, in a valid protocol the absence of certain elevations (like antisocial attitudes or cynicism) or evidence of factors (such as distress) that can motivate treatment can also be identified. Most individuals, especially adolescents, do better when treatment approaches are strength- rather than deficit-based. Although the MMPI was not designed to be a measure of normal or optimal functioning, the test data can help to identify strengths and assets.

TEST SECURITY

The *Standards for Educational and Psychological Testing* (American Educational Research Association, 2014) state that users have the responsibility to protect the security of psychological tests. Users of the MMPI-A-RF are required to safeguard the security of test materials including booklets, audio recordings, manuals, scoring templates, profile forms, software, and report guides. Test users must restrict dissemination of test materials only to other appropriately qualified professionals. In a forensic context, users can sometimes be compelled by court order to release test information, but courts will usually provide protective orders for this material. The test distributor, Pearson Assessments, has a detailed letter available online as well as other guidance for responding to litigation demands. Finally, all of the test materials are copyrighted. It is never appropriate to photocopy or reproduce materials without the permission of the test publisher, the University of Minnesota Press.

PART II

The MMPI-A-RF Cases

The 16 cases that are the focus of this book were selected to provide a broad representation of youth evaluated in two primary areas: clinical and forensic practice. For purposes of confidentiality, the names of the youth have been changed and any identifying information has also been modified. In addition, although the scoring and interpretive programs provided by Pearson Assessments contain a list of critical items, for purposes of test security, they are not reproduced in the cases presented here.

We have grouped the cases into clinical and forensic sections. Since its publication in 1992, the MMPI-A and now the MMPI-A-RF are extensively used in both outpatient and inpatient clinical settings and in forensic practice with juvenile courts. The clinical cases were chosen to illustrate how the MMPI-A-RF can be used to provide meaningful assessments to shape diagnosis and subsequent treatment in both outpatient and residential settings. The cases represent problems seen in a typical clinical practice but also some considerable societal challenges that youth face today. We include a case of human trafficking victimization as well as a case of opioid addiction, as an illustration of the depths and types of problems now confronted by clinicians.

The majority of states today have laws addressing juvenile competency and much of the work of a juvenile court psychologist is that of competency assessments. Another substantial trend is the increase in bindover or transfer evaluations in which a juvenile's case jurisdiction may be transferred to the adult criminal justice system. Although once uncommon, youth as young as 14 are evaluated for potential transfer to the adult system. During the 1990s, the juvenile court became increasingly "adult-like" and one of the consequences of this change was an increased focus on due process rights such as waiver of *Miranda* rights. Our knowledge of sex offender assessment and treatment has substantially increased and now juveniles may be required to register in some manner after being adjudicated for a sex offense. Courts and clinicians now confront once unthought-of offenses such as threats of or actual school mass violence. Juvenile courts have also evolved. Many juvenile courts have specialized dockets for substance abuse and mental health treatment. Each of these circumstances results in highly specialized and focused forensic evaluations.

The MMPI-A-RF can play an important role in such assessments. We will present forensic cases that illustrate both the psycho-legal assessment question and how the MMPI-A-RF can be used in these increasingly complex evaluations. Some of the exemplary cases contain relevant research citations concerning the forensic issue. However, these cases are an illustration of how to apply the MMPI-A-RF to forensic assessment in juvenile court and are not intended to be a comprehensive illustration of forensic assessment.

The cases are described in a standard format. The reason for referral and general background information are presented first, followed by as much historical information as we can provide in a manner that does not risk identifying the youth. If there was additional testing, it will be briefly discussed. In the forensic cases, specialized forensic instruments are used and discussed. When possible, each case is concluded with the outcome information as well as a discussion of the contribution of the MMPI-A-RF in responding to the pertinent forensic question.

The MMPI-A-RF interpretation included here may be more detailed than what might be typical in clinical or forensic practice. We do this to illustrate how to go about building an MMPI-A-RF report. Interpretations in the clinical cases section generally cite the relevant scales interpreted as an illustration of our interpretive model. Typically, citing specific elevations is not done in clinical interpretation in actual practice. In the forensic cases, we may not cite specific scale elevations but do show how MMPI-A-RF data can be integrated into answering the specific forensic referral question. The majority of the forensic case examples are longer than the clinical case examples and are also more detailed than what might actually be provided to the court because the *Specialty Guidelines for Forensic Psychology* (American Psychological Association, 2013) state that only information relevant to the forensic issue be provided. We take this broader approach to illustrate how the MMPI-A-RF might be used in a forensic formulation and to provide an appropriate degree of illustrative background rather than simply providing the report. In this way, our intention is to illustrate the process of profile interpretation not just the product of the final report.

Because the MMPI-A-RF is a more psychometrically advanced instrument and is more efficient in both administration and interpretation, the reader will probably note that our interpretations may be more focused than could be achieved with the MMPI-A. Finally, the reader may also notice that certain of the cases presented have Validity scale concerns. We made the choice to include such protocols because they represent the realities of clinical practice in which the examining clinician must interpret and integrate difficult data. In so doing, we seek to illustrate how to approach challenging cases.

The Clinical Cases

Betty
A Victim of Human Trafficking

BACKGROUND

Betty is a 15-year-old female who was referred by her residential treatment center therapist for diagnostic assessment and treatment recommendations. Betty was identified as a victim of human trafficking after substantiation of her having been sexually abused by a family member at the age of 11. She had nine other substantiated experiences of sexual and physical abuse, including incidents in which she would be given alcohol and forced to have sex with adult men. When living with her mother, Betty was often very oppositional and when challenged would become threatening and aggressive. Her problems with aggression and anger continued in treatment settings, to the extent that she was removed from treatment foster care and placed in an open residential treatment center. However, she continued to be physically aggressive and frequently ran away. Her first residential placement was terminated by the center and she was transferred to a secure, intensive treatment residential center where she was evaluated.

Interview With Youth

During her interview it was quickly noted that she appeared to present herself as more mature and capable than her age would suggest. As an illustration, she denied that any of the negative things experienced in her past were troublesome to her and indicated that she "knew" the system and did not require assistance from helping adults. She began the interview by spontaneously stating "I'm not stressed—I don't have PTSD—it's what the system thinks about me." This defensiveness and minimization (which is not atypical for traumatized youth) was also seen in findings of the psychological testing that specifically addressed trauma-related symptoms. Accordingly, the information she provided should be viewed with considerable caution, given these tendencies.

Asked how she would describe her childhood, Betty reported a good relationship with her mother. She said that her father and mother separated when she was 5 and that she has had little to no contact with her father and "misses" him. She described her childhood as "both bad and good" and would not elaborate. She said that she is the second of five children born to her mother and that she has a good relationship with all siblings, except one sister. She said that she has no close friends and indicated that she is unaware of any early childhood medical or developmental problems.

Betty reported that she was in the ninth grade and was not in special education. She indicated that she had a lengthy history of disciplinary problems in school and has been suspended and expelled for fighting and "doing what I want to do." Betty also mentioned that her career goal is to become a social worker.

Betty denied any history of substance abuse. She acknowledged a history of being sexually abused; however, when asked about it, she became emotional and said that she did not want to talk about what had happened to her and the interviewer did not press her further.

Betty reported that she has received outpatient and home-based therapy for anger problems as well as family conflicts. She also indicated that she had been placed at another residential center and said that she completed the program. She alleged that the staff there "did sexual stuff" with the residents and that she was physically assaulted. Betty said that she told authorities, who "did not care." She also said that she has been placed in shelter care, which she liked and was admitted to the current residential placement about 2 weeks prior to her current interview. She said that she did not like the facility or staff.

Betty indicated that she has never been suicidal or self-injurious. She has never been psychiatrically hospitalized and is unaware of any family history of mental illness. She said that she is not currently taking any psychiatric medication and that she needs "Seroquel for sleep." This youth denied any history of serious medical concerns. She denied any history of head trauma, seizures, loss of consciousness, or other neurological involvement.

COLLATERAL INFORMATION

Children's Services records substantiated extensive sexual abuse, as detailed previously. They also documented a history of having been diagnosed with Attention Deficit Hyperactivity Disorder (ADHD) in third or fourth grade. These records indicated further that Betty would leave home in the middle of the night and appeared to be drawn to a high-risk lifestyle that included high-risk sexual practices such as associations with older men and negative peers. She was often aggressive at home and would frequently run away. The assessing clinician noted the potential of an underlying mood disorder, substance abuse concerns, and criminogenic risk factors. Records also documented a history of having been diagnosed with ADHD in the first grade.

Current Behavioral Status

Betty was appropriately dressed and groomed in street clothing. She appeared to be about her stated age. Her hygiene and grooming were adequate. There were no overt indications of loosening of associations, flight of ideas, or tangentiality. Her psychomotor activity was nonremarkable (that is to say, she was not hyperactive or agitated nor was she lethargic or nonresponsive). Her speech was normal in tone, pacing, and volume. Her attention span was adequate. Her manner of social interaction was generally friendly, polite, and cooperative. Subjectively, she would present as quite childlike at times, yet at other times she presented as far more sophisticated and mature than expected for her age.

Betty presented with appropriate and expressive affect (emotional expression) to a stated "frustrated and aggravated" mood related to her being placed at the residential facility. When asked to rate her subjective level of distress (SUDS), she described her present degree of emotional upset as being a 5 out of a possible 10, saying that she is upset because "staff—they don't care."

Betty exhibited no overt behavioral indications of hallucinations, delusions, or paranoia. She reported feeling depressed and anxious in reaction to being placed. She reported problems with her sleep, saying that she "has nightmares" but denied problems with her health. She reported good appetite. She also denied other symptoms typically associated with depression such as loss of interest and pleasure, poor concentration, or irritability.

In response to a specific inquiry, Betty reported a history of rapidly changing moods, mood swings, agitation, racing thoughts, irritability when angry, but denied other symptoms such as periods of extreme energy and restlessness or grandiosity or other symptoms typically associated with bipolar disorder or other mood disorders in adolescents. None of these symptoms was observed during her interview.

Betty denied present suicidal or homicidal ideation, intent, plan, or access to means. She expressed a sense of hopelessness about her future, which can be associated with suicidal risk in adolescents, but did report support from her mother, which can be a protective factor. She did not present with symptoms of phobias, obsessions, or compulsions. As noted, she reported nightmares but said she does not have "flashbacks" of her abuse victimization, saying, "I've had bad things happen, but you have to live life."

Betty's memory functions were clinically intact. She was oriented to time, place, person, and situation. She showed adequate concentration by her ability to correctly perform simple mental arithmetic calculations and serial subtractions. She was capable of abstract thinking as illustrated by her ability to identify similarities between common concepts and to interpret commonly understood proverbs. Her insight and judgment were seemingly very limited, as demonstrated both by her history as well as her responses to situational questions.

Betty's cognitive functioning was assessed using the Kaufman Brief Intelligence Test, Second Edition (KBIT-2). She obtained a Vocabulary score of 79 and a Nonverbal score of 84. Her overall Composite IQ score was 79.

Betty was also given the Slosson Oral Reading Test—Third Edition Norms. This instrument is a measure of word recognition and pronunciation that correlates highly with measures of reading comprehension and diagnostic psycho-educational instruments. Her score indicated that she reads at the eighth-grade level.

MMPI-A-RF

Betty's MMPI-A-RF protocol was valid. There were no unscoreable items, she responded appropriately to item content, and there were no indications of either over- or underreporting. In addition to the normative sample, her responses were compared to a group of 114 girls in residential treatment in the Midwest.

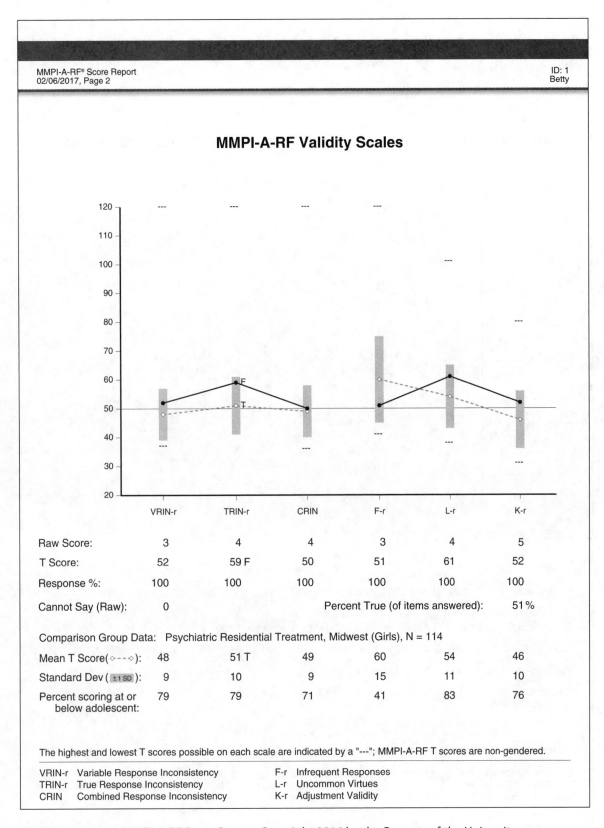

MMPI-A-RF Validity Scales

	VRIN-r	TRIN-r	CRIN	F-r	L-r	K-r
Raw Score:	3	4	4	3	4	5
T Score:	52	59 F	50	51	61	52
Response %:	100	100	100	100	100	100

Cannot Say (Raw): 0 Percent True (of items answered): 51%

Comparison Group Data: Psychiatric Residential Treatment, Midwest (Girls), N = 114

	VRIN-r	TRIN-r	CRIN	F-r	L-r	K-r
Mean T Score(◇- - -◇):	48	51 T	49	60	54	46
Standard Dev (±1 SD):	9	10	9	15	11	10
Percent scoring at or below adolescent:	79	79	71	41	83	76

The highest and lowest T scores possible on each scale are indicated by a "---"; MMPI-A-RF T scores are non-gendered.

VRIN-r	Variable Response Inconsistency	F-r	Infrequent Responses
TRIN-r	True Response Inconsistency	L-r	Uncommon Virtues
CRIN	Combined Response Inconsistency	K-r	Adjustment Validity

FIGURE 1 Betty's MMPI-A-RF Score Report. Copyright 2016 by the Regents of the University of Minnesota. All rights reserved.

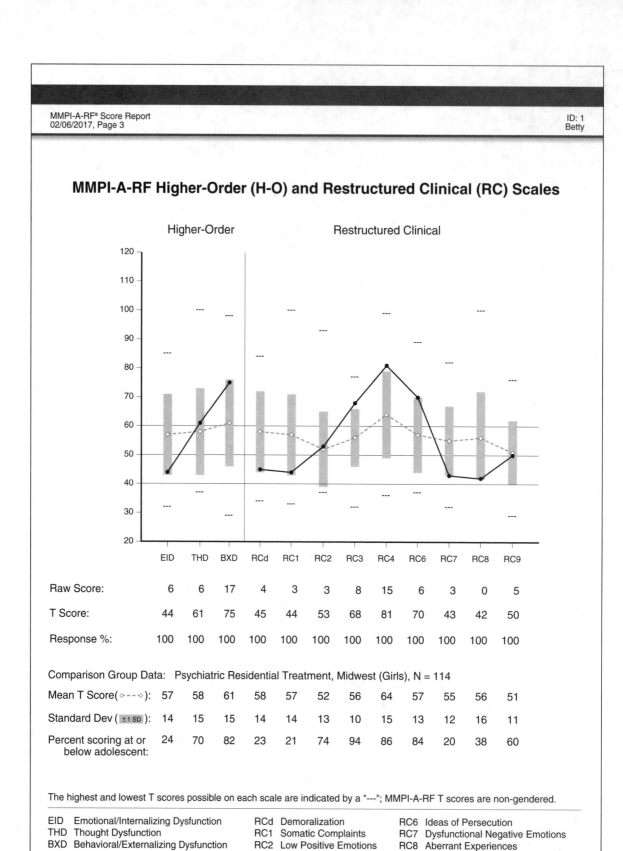

MMPI-A-RF Higher-Order (H-O) and Restructured Clinical (RC) Scales

Higher-Order   Restructured Clinical

	EID	THD	BXD	RCd	RC1	RC2	RC3	RC4	RC6	RC7	RC8	RC9
Raw Score:	6	6	17	4	3	3	8	15	6	3	0	5
T Score:	44	61	75	45	44	53	68	81	70	43	42	50
Response %:	100	100	100	100	100	100	100	100	100	100	100	100

Comparison Group Data: Psychiatric Residential Treatment, Midwest (Girls), N = 114

	EID	THD	BXD	RCd	RC1	RC2	RC3	RC4	RC6	RC7	RC8	RC9
Mean T Score(◇---◇):	57	58	61	58	57	52	56	64	57	55	56	51
Standard Dev (±1 SD):	14	15	15	14	14	13	10	15	13	12	16	11
Percent scoring at or below adolescent:	24	70	82	23	21	74	94	86	84	20	38	60

The highest and lowest T scores possible on each scale are indicated by a "---"; MMPI-A-RF T scores are non-gendered.

EID Emotional/Internalizing Dysfunction	RCd Demoralization
THD Thought Dysfunction	RC1 Somatic Complaints
BXD Behavioral/Externalizing Dysfunction	RC2 Low Positive Emotions
	RC3 Cynicism
	RC4 Antisocial Behavior

RC6 Ideas of Persecution
RC7 Dysfunctional Negative Emotions
RC8 Aberrant Experiences
RC9 Hypomanic Activation

FIGURE 1 Betty's MMPI-A-RF Score Report, continued.

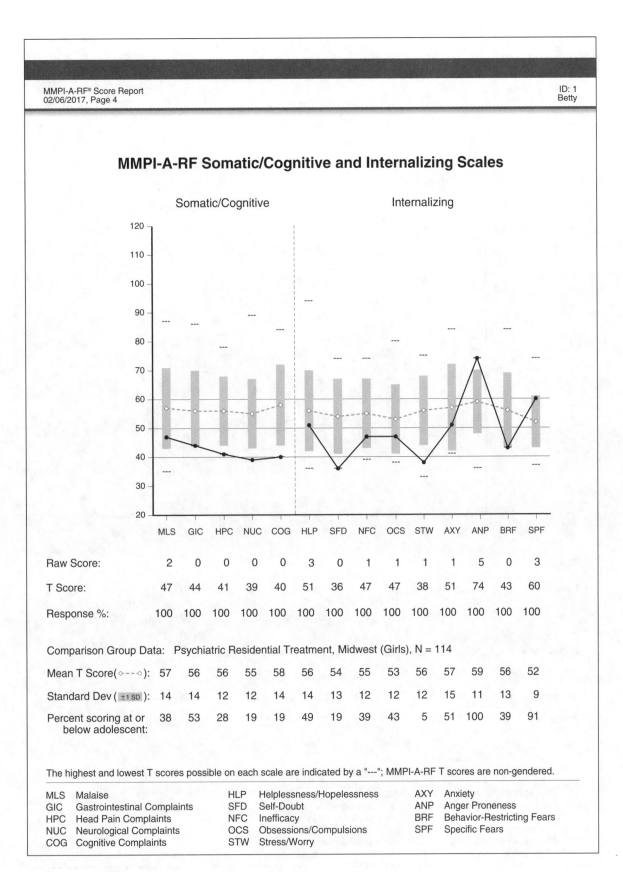

MMPI-A-RF Somatic/Cognitive and Internalizing Scales

	MLS	GIC	HPC	NUC	COG	HLP	SFD	NFC	OCS	STW	AXY	ANP	BRF	SPF
Raw Score:	2	0	0	0	0	3	0	1	1	1	1	5	0	3
T Score:	47	44	41	39	40	51	36	47	47	38	51	74	43	60
Response %:	100	100	100	100	100	100	100	100	100	100	100	100	100	100

Comparison Group Data: Psychiatric Residential Treatment, Midwest (Girls), N = 114

	MLS	GIC	HPC	NUC	COG	HLP	SFD	NFC	OCS	STW	AXY	ANP	BRF	SPF
Mean T Score(◇---◇):	57	56	56	55	58	56	54	55	53	56	57	59	56	52
Standard Dev (±1 SD):	14	14	12	12	14	14	13	12	12	12	15	11	13	9
Percent scoring at or below adolescent:	38	53	28	19	19	49	19	39	43	5	51	100	39	91

The highest and lowest T scores possible on each scale are indicated by a "---"; MMPI-A-RF T scores are non-gendered.

MLS	Malaise	HLP	Helplessness/Hopelessness	AXY	Anxiety
GIC	Gastrointestinal Complaints	SFD	Self-Doubt	ANP	Anger Proneness
HPC	Head Pain Complaints	NFC	Inefficacy	BRF	Behavior-Restricting Fears
NUC	Neurological Complaints	OCS	Obsessions/Compulsions	SPF	Specific Fears
COG	Cognitive Complaints	STW	Stress/Worry		

FIGURE 1 Betty's MMPI-A-RF Score Report, continued.

31

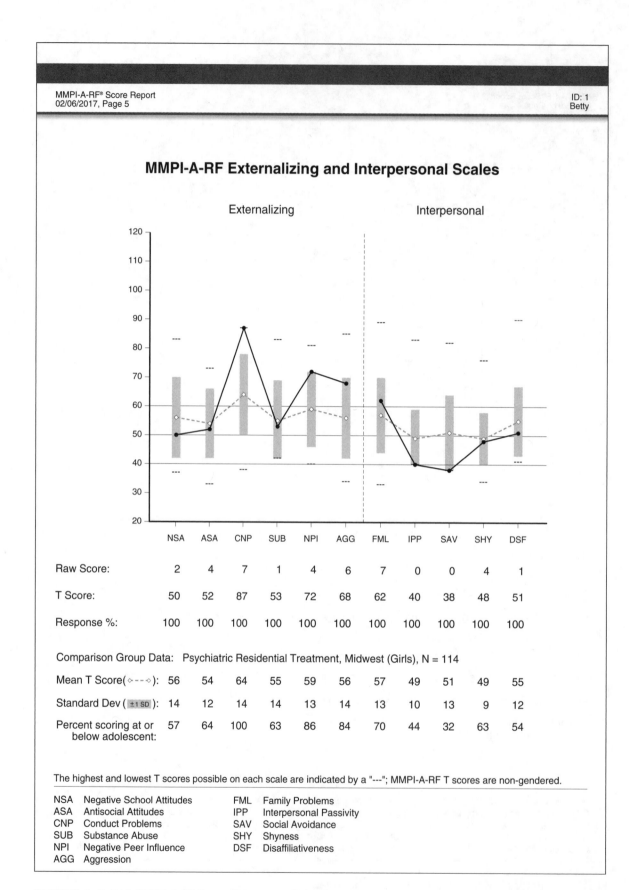

MMPI-A-RF Externalizing and Interpersonal Scales

Externalizing   Interpersonal

	NSA	ASA	CNP	SUB	NPI	AGG	FML	IPP	SAV	SHY	DSF
Raw Score:	2	4	7	1	4	6	7	0	0	4	1
T Score:	50	52	87	53	72	68	62	40	38	48	51
Response %:	100	100	100	100	100	100	100	100	100	100	100

Comparison Group Data: Psychiatric Residential Treatment, Midwest (Girls), N = 114

	NSA	ASA	CNP	SUB	NPI	AGG	FML	IPP	SAV	SHY	DSF
Mean T Score(◇- - -◇):	56	54	64	55	59	56	57	49	51	49	55
Standard Dev (±1 SD):	14	12	14	14	13	14	13	10	13	9	12
Percent scoring at or below adolescent:	57	64	100	63	86	84	70	44	32	63	54

The highest and lowest T scores possible on each scale are indicated by a "---"; MMPI-A-RF T scores are non-gendered.

NSA	Negative School Attitudes	FML	Family Problems
ASA	Antisocial Attitudes	IPP	Interpersonal Passivity
CNP	Conduct Problems	SAV	Social Avoidance
SUB	Substance Abuse	SHY	Shyness
NPI	Negative Peer Influence	DSF	Disaffiliativeness
AGG	Aggression		

FIGURE 1 Betty's MMPI-A-RF Score Report, continued.

32

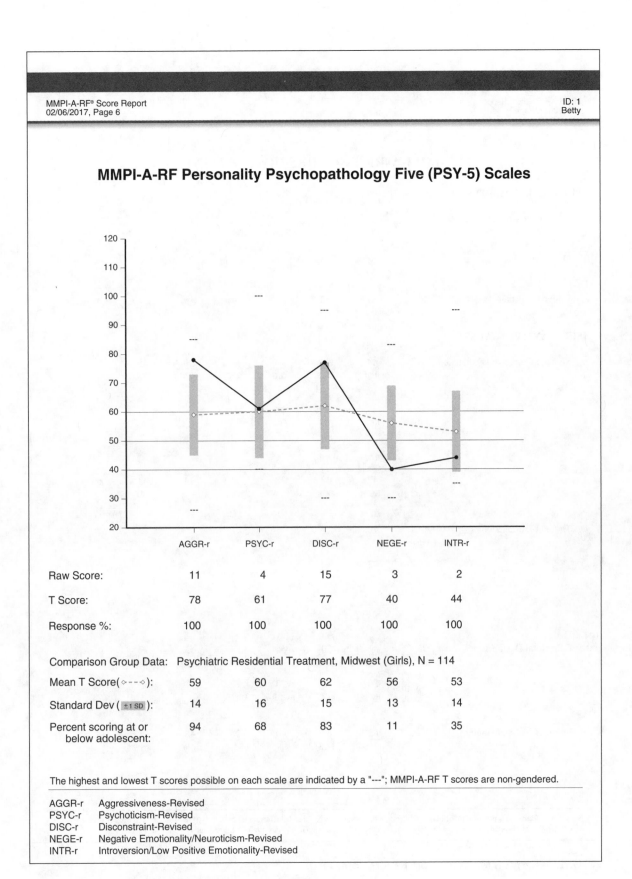

MMPI-A-RF Personality Psychopathology Five (PSY-5) Scales

	AGGR-r	PSYC-r	DISC-r	NEGE-r	INTR-r
Raw Score:	11	4	15	3	2
T Score:	78	61	77	40	44
Response %:	100	100	100	100	100

Comparison Group Data: Psychiatric Residential Treatment, Midwest (Girls), N = 114

	AGGR-r	PSYC-r	DISC-r	NEGE-r	INTR-r
Mean T Score(◇---◇):	59	60	62	56	53
Standard Dev (±1 SD):	14	16	15	13	14
Percent scoring at or below adolescent:	94	68	83	11	35

The highest and lowest T scores possible on each scale are indicated by a "---"; MMPI-A-RF T scores are non-gendered.

AGGR-r	Aggressiveness-Revised
PSYC-r	Psychoticism-Revised
DISC-r	Disconstraint-Revised
NEGE-r	Negative Emotionality/Neuroticism-Revised
INTR-r	Introversion/Low Positive Emotionality-Revised

FIGURE 1 Betty's MMPI-A-RF Score Report, continued.

MMPI-A-RF T SCORES (BY DOMAIN)

PROTOCOL VALIDITY

Content Non-Responsiveness

0	52	59 F	50
CNS	VRIN-r	TRIN-r	CRIN

Over-Reporting

51
F-r

Under-Reporting

61	52
L-r	K-r

SUBSTANTIVE SCALES

Somatic/Cognitive Dysfunction

44	47	44	41	39	40
RC1	MLS	GIC	HPC	NUC	COG

Emotional Dysfunction

44
EID

45	51	36	47
RCd	HLP	SFD	NFC

53	44
RC2	INTR-r

43	47	38	51	74	43	60	40
RC7	OCS	STW	AXY	ANP	BRF	SPF	NEGE-r

Thought Dysfunction

61
THD

70
RC6

42
RC8

61
PSYC-r

Behavioral Dysfunction

75
BXD

81	50	52	87	53	72
RC4	NSA	ASA	CNP	SUB	NPI

50	68	78	77
RC9	AGG	AGGR-r	DISC-r

Interpersonal Functioning

62	68	40	38	48	51
FML	RC3	IPP	SAV	SHY	DSF

Note. This information is provided to facilitate interpretation following the recommended structure for MMPI-A-RF interpretation in Chapter 7 of the *MMPI-A-RF Administration, Scoring, Interpretation, and Technical Manual*, which provides details in the text and an outline in Table 7-1.

FIGURE 1 Betty's MMPI-A-RF Score Report, continued.

Betty's BXD score indicates considerable externalizing, acting-out behavior that very likely results in marked dysfunction and has gotten her into difficulties. Both the RC4 and CNP (Conduct Problems) scales are substantially elevated and indicative of a strong likelihood of conduct-disordered behaviors such as running away from home, theft, and behavioral problems in school as well as substance abuse. She is very likely oppositional and defiant and tends to gravitate toward a negative peer group. Her behavioral problems have likely brought her to the attention of authorities and caused problems in the family. Her elevations on the CNP, DISC-r, ANP, AGG, and AGGR-r indicate that she can become impulsive, angry, and aggressive, has problems with her anger, and is likely to make verbal threats. Given these tendencies as well as the elevation on the FML scale, it is likely that she experiences considerable family conflict. When her scores are analyzed against the comparison group of youth in residential treatment, Betty's elevations on the RC4, CNP, and ANP are greater than one standard deviation above the mean of the girls in the sample, suggesting that even when compared to youth in residential treatment, her acting-out problems are quite substantial. These findings correlate with her history both at home and in residential treatment.

Betty's elevation on THD, RC6, and PSYC-r indicate that she reports significant persecutory ideation and likely engages in aggressive and oppositional behavior as well as fighting and truancy.

It is not surprising that she has substantial interpersonal problems. Her elevations on FML (Family Problems) and RC3 indicate a history of family problems as well as a likely cynical view of relationships. It is likely that she is distrustful of others and thinks that people are primarily motivated by their own self-interest. Although there are not empirical correlates, review of item content given her low scores on the scales of SFD (Self-Doubt), STW (Stress/Worry), SPF (Specific Fears), and SAV (Social Avoidance) may be helpful in understanding how Betty would like to be seen by others.

Betty's MMPI-A-RF results do not indicate any significant emotional dysfunction outside of the previously discussed problems related to anger proneness.

Betty should be considered for diagnoses of externalizing disorders, including conduct and oppositional defiant disorders as well as other disruptive disorders.

Owing to her distrust, cynicism, and disruptive behavior, it is very likely that treatment will be difficult for Betty. Her protocol suggests that she is at significant risk for treatment noncompliance. Targets for treatment include her undercontrolled behavior, anger, and possible phobias, feelings of persecution, and substance abuse. Her family problems must also clearly be a focus of treatment.

Potential assets in treatment include that she produced a valid MMPI-A-RF. This suggests that she can be cooperative, at least enough to engage in the testing and possibly in therapy. She also did not report any negative attitudes toward school or generally antisocial attitudes.

Diagnosis

Betty was diagnosed with Unspecified Trauma and Stressor-Related Disorder as well as an Unspecified Disruptive, Impulse Control, and Conduct Disorder. Although the MMPI-A-RF results did not have clear indications of PTSD, resulting in a diagnosis of an Unspecified Trauma and Stressor-Related Disorder, earlier research with the MMPI-A (Forby et al., 2000) found that there is no single protocol specific to sexually abused youth. Similarly, sexually abused girls experience numerous and differing sequela as they develop (Trickett et al., 2011), as true of Betty.

OUTCOME

Betty was recommended for trauma-specific therapies and continued placement in a residential setting followed by treatment foster care. It was recommended that any psychiatric inpatient stays be brief and focused on stabilization and return to active treatment. A follow-up 12 months later found that she was in treatment foster care and doing well in treatment and in school.

Jim
An Adolescent With Autism

BACKGROUND

Jim is a 17-year-old male who was referred by his outpatient therapist. He has a diagnosis of Autistic Spectrum Disorder, having been originally diagnosed with Asperger's (which has been phased out but was in existence when Jim was originally seen). Owing to threats of violence against his siblings, he is now living with one parent in a separate apartment.

Interview With Youth

During his interview, Jim stated that he was currently living with his father. He described a good relationship with both his mother and his father and said that he is the oldest of his parents' children. When asked to characterize his early childhood, Jim said, "I had a crazy childhood, I used to be hypomanic and depressed but now I am on good medications." He said that he has been attending a specialized school for youth with autism since sixth grade. He is in his senior year and stated that the school "makes me special." He said that he was in public schools until fifth grade, describing them as "Bad—they put me in special classes, and I was picked on by the other kids in school." Jim said he wants to either work with computers or study chemistry. He reported that his best subjects are math and social studies and that his favorite things to do are to go fishing and camping.

Jim denied any significant history of school or behavioral problems, saying that he once had an in-school suspension for cursing out a teacher. He denied any history of substance abuse, relating that he cannot become involved in this "because of my medicines." He said that he does have friends, but when asked to name any male friends, he could not but did say that he had a "girlfriend" whom he met while volunteering at a food pantry with his family. He denied any history of physical, sexual, or emotional abuse. He has not had contact with either the juvenile justice or the child welfare system. He denied fire-setting or animal cruelty. In the first interview, he said that he was working at the school, during the summer, but when seen for the last time, he said that he "quit work because I was tired of it. I was talking back. I got tired of the people."

Asked about mental health treatment, Jim said that his psychiatrist prescribed him medication and that he most recently saw a psychologist in psychotherapy, citing other providers who "didn't work out because my Mom didn't like them." He said that he has been psychiatrically hospitalized "a couple of times" because he had been suicidal but that he no longer has these thoughts "since my medication was increased."

COLLATERAL INFORMATION

Jim's mother and father were interviewed together and then Jim's mother was interviewed separately in a follow-up interview. She also completed a developmental history questionnaire. She stated that her health during pregnancy was good until the midpoint in the last trimester when she was hospitalized for dehydration. She did not use alcohol or illicit drugs while pregnant. She said that the pregnancy was wanted, and that Jim was delivered by natural childbirth after a full-term gestation. Birth weight and delivery were nonremarkable. Jim did not have health problems at birth. However, he did have early feeding problems, requiring being fed every 30 minutes. For the first 3 years of life, he would not sleep at night unless he was with his mother but he gradually was able to separate after that time. He was described as an infant who was "slow to warm up" to others. Developmental milestones were achieved generally nonremarkably. He has always had marked tactile sensitivity and continues with this (for example, not wearing shirts unless the tags are torn out and refusing to wear short sleeve shirts as well as using certain pens or pencils).

Socially, Jim's mother said that Jim "always had issues" and never played "pretend" as a child, nor did he participate in Halloween. Rather, he became absorbed in the "special effects" of the holiday. During kindergarten and first grade, he had no friends but in the second grade, Jim did make one friend, with whom he still has contact. He still makes friends very slowly and will not initiate social interactions such as calling friends or going somewhere with them. He does socialize at school but does much better with adults, remarking that he is "Never happy being a kid."

Jim's mom said his vision and hearing are good as are his gross and fine motor coordination. Transitions and changes in routine are very difficult for him as is independently demonstrating self-care skills. She related that he requires to know the rules of social situations and also needs to follow schedules. He requires a schedule to take his medication and needs supervision, as he will be inconsistent on his own. He does not like to change his clothes and has to be told he needs a shower. He does not have a driver's license and does not travel independently.

Jim attended preschool but had numerous behavioral problems, his mother describing him as a "social misfit." He was hard to manage at home and would not dress for school. He went to a private kindergarten that he "hated and had no friends." He continued with school refusal as well as not getting dressed for school. He attended a charter school in the first and second grades, then public schools through fifth grade. He was described as continuing with behavioral problems, often having considerable difficulty paying attention and as having poor social skills. He struggled with these issues in seventh grade, and was eventually tutored at home, something which was significantly difficult for him, causing him to have to repeat the seventh grade when he entered the special needs school. He has shown improvement and is now in his senior year at this school. He has passed the State Graduation Test.

Jim's mother said that he was first treated for ADHD at the age of 4 with stimulant medication that resulted in him becoming angrier and more irritable rather than any beneficial effects. He was also treated prior to age 8 in occupational therapy for Sensory Integration Disorder. He was then treated for impulsive behavior and anger problems and ADHD and Oppositional Defiant Disorder (ODD) with psychostimulants and an antidepressant (Prozac). His mom reported that Jim has been hospitalized three times with diagnoses of bipolar disorder as well as ADHD/ODD. His current psychiatrist diagnosed him with autism at the age of 11. The mom noted that when Jim received this diagnosis his behavioral problems began to become understandable to Jim's father and himself.

At home, Jim is described as not taking his medications without structure and supervision; he tends to be chronically disorganized and also unaware of the social impact of his behaviors. He does not make friends easily but is able to keep the friends that he does make. He will interrupt others and talk excessively without an awareness of how this impacts them. He tends to often lose his temper and will argue excessively and actively defy adult rules and requests. He tends to annoy others and blame them for his mistakes. He tends to be easily annoyed and will swear. He can be also spiteful and vindictive. He is not physically aggressive but will at times "bully" his siblings. He is easily fatigued and will at times show feelings of worthlessness and excessive guilt. He tends to be irritable and to overeat and shows symptoms of depression such as feelings of hopelessness and has expressed that he wished he were "dead" (although not presently exhibiting suicidal or para-suicidal behaviors). Socially, he shows little interest in others and tends to have excessive emotional reactions to changes in routines and often misses or misunderstands subtle social cues.

Jim's therapist wrote that he was given diagnoses of ADHD, Bipolar Disorder, Anxiety Disorders, and Asperger's Disorder. She noted that most of her work with him was "very sporadic," noting that he was seen very infrequently. She noted that he presented as very anxious, depressed, and that she made an "incredible number of calls to his schools, home, psychiatrist and his physician." The therapist observed that Jim often had difficulty dealing with his brother and sister and that when he was depressed or manic, he would be irritable and easily angered. He was described by his parents as being very oppositional and that they would at times have trouble managing his behavior to the extent that "safety issues needed to be addressed when emotional and behavioral issues intensified." The therapist related that Jim was treated early on with play therapy, then with therapy specific to anger and depression management as well as behavior management and dealing with social situations.

Telephone contact with his psychiatrist confirmed that he had diagnosed Jim with bipolar disorder and autism. Records from his first psychiatric hospitalization indicate that he was admitted at the age of 8 and noted as having "a history of bipolar affective disorder, OCD and ADHD, and was taken to the crisis intervention center by police as a result of violent and aggressive episodes, as well as a threat to kill himself." He was hospitalized for 2 weeks with a diagnosis of Bipolar Disorder II, Obsessive Compulsive Disorder (OCD), and ADHD.

Jim was readmitted to the psychiatric hospital 10 months later and described as being in a "very labile" mood: tearful at one moment and laughing "hysterically the next." He had become increasingly angry and aggressive and threatened to kill his younger brother, with a specific plan of using a knife. He was also noted to have exhibited aggression toward his mother and younger sister as well as cruelty to animals and admitted to hearing voices of people calling his name in a "spooky" tone. Upon admission, he admitted both suicidal and homicidal ideation and was initially quite agitated until he was stabilized on differing medications. The diagnosis remained the same.

His most recent psychiatric hospitalization was 2 years ago and lasted a week. At that time, he reported increasing depression with expressed suicidal thoughts of jumping off a balcony or being hit by a car, which he confided to the school nurse. Upon admission, he also reported auditory hallucinations of hearing his mother calling to him. Again, his medications were adjusted, and he stabilized. He was noted to have considerable challenges with separation from his family after visits. After being stabilized he was discharged. During this admission, he was diagnosed with autism, which was added to his other diagnoses.

Current Behavioral Status

Jim was seen three times by the examiner, his presentation remaining consistent throughout. During his initial interview he appeared to be about his stated age. His hygiene and grooming were adequate, and he wore street clothing that was appropriate to the season. His eye contact throughout the sessions was very poor, a finding often seen in autistic-spectrum youth. He similarly demonstrated deficiencies in social reciprocity in which he would often miss or misinterpret social cues such as pauses in sentence, and nonverbal indications of needing to terminate or modify a subject of conversation.

Jim's attention and cooperation were variable, and he was often distracted by sounds outside the office and objects in the room, and would also make irrelevant comments. His gait and posture were nonremarkable. There were no overt indications of gross or fine motor dysfunction. His speech was not markedly variable in tone, pacing, and volume but had a bookish, "professorish" quality.

There were no overt indications of loosening of associations, flight of ideas, or tangentiality. However, Jim was very literal and concrete in his interpretations of what was said to him. His manner of social interaction was very reserved. His thinking demonstrated somewhat limited ability for verbal abstract reasoning as demonstrated by his ability to identify only basic similarities between related simple objects but not more difficult abstract concepts, and his inability to interpret simple common proverbs in anything more than a concrete recitation.

Jim presented with a stiff and very formal affect to a stated euthymic mood. He denied experiencing, and there were no overt indications of current hallucinations, delusions, or of organized paranoid ideation or other symptoms of serious mental illness.

Jim denied present depression as well as current mood swings or bipolar episodes but related what appeared to be continued episodes of mood instability when he responded to a question about recent mood swings by remarking that he does not have them "as bad as they used to be. Sometimes I have not a mood swing but like a 'buzz' only longer." He stated that his sleep was variable as was his appetite. He denied other symptoms often associated with depression such as loss of interest or pleasure, loss of sexual interest, poor concentration, feelings of hopelessness, or feelings of isolation and hopelessness. Upon specific inquiry, Jim denied any current suicidal or homicidal ideation.

There were no clinical indications of specific phobias, obsessions, or compulsions. Jim was oriented to situation, time, place, and person. His long-term, short-term, and immediate recall functions were intact. His recall of digits from immediate memory was five forward and three reversed, which is fair to adequate. He was able to name three items after distraction of about 5 minutes, suggesting no marked problems with concentration and short-term recall. Cognitive functioning appeared consonant with reports of his functioning in school assessments, noted earlier. His insight and judgment appeared to be much less than typical for his age as ascertained by situational questions and his history.

On the WAIS IV, Jim produced a Verbal Comprehension index of 95, a Perceptual Reasoning score of 100, and a Working Memory index of 92. He showed, relative to the other scores, a weakness in his Processing Speed with a score of 67. His overall, Full-Scale IQ was 89.

Using his mother as the informant, significant impairment was reported in Jim's adaptive functioning with a Vineland II Adaptive Behavior Composite of 61, which is at or below the second percentile compared to same-aged peers. He was moderately low in the domains of communication and in his daily living skills. He was low in the Socialization domain. Clinically significant scores were found in the maladaptive behavior indexes. Clinically significant elevations were found in all of the measures of Maladaptive Behavior.

Jim's mother rated him on the Conners Comprehensive Behavior Rating Scale. The Conners provides standardized comparisons of his behavioral and emotional functioning to a large sample of youth both in a normal sample and a clinical sample. It contains validity scales, content scales, and comparisons to DSM-5 diagnostic criteria. Analysis of the validity scales finds no indications of an overly positive, negative, or inconsistent response style. The Conners content scales were very elevated, indicating more problems than are typically reported in the areas of Emotional Distress, Worrying, Social Problems, Defiant/Aggressive Behaviors, Academic Difficulties, Language Difficulties, Math, Hyperactivity/Impulsivity, Perfectionistic and Compulsive, Violence Potential Indicator, and Physical Symptoms. The DSM-5 Symptom Counts (as noted in the test manual, these scales are insufficient alone for diagnosis but indicate the need for further assessment) were significant for the following scales: ADHD Predominantly Inattentive Presentation, Conduct Disorder, Oppositional Defiant Disorder, Major Depressive Episode, Manic Episode, Separation Anxiety Disorder, Social Phobia, and Autistic Disorder.

His parents separately rated Jim on the Gilliam Asperger's Disorder Rating Scale. This instrument, specific to Asperger's, compares the responder's rating of the adolescent to youth who have a diagnosis of Asperger's. While also insufficient alone for diagnosis, it reflects similarity to a known reference group. In the rating by his mother, Jim's overall Asperger's Disorder Quotient of 118 is at the 89th percentile and falls within the High/Probable range for Asperger's Disorder. Subscale analysis indicated elevations on all the subscales reflecting considerable difficulties in Cognitive Patterns (talking about a single subject excessively, focusing upon a single area with superior knowledge, pedantic speech, memory), Pragmatic Skills (social deficits such as difficulty understanding when others do not like him, changing to a familiar topic when confused without seeking clarification, difficulty in understanding social consequences), Social Interaction (attention to social stimuli, empathy, showing social awareness), and Restricted Patterns of Behavior (insensitivity to needs of others, eccentric behavior, preoccupation with specific subjects or objects that is abnormal in intensity and focus).

Similar ratings were generated by Jim's father with an overall Asperger's Quotient of 105, at the 63rd percentile, which is in the High/Probable range. Marked elevations (above the 75th percentile) were seen in the subscale of Social Interaction, with significant elevations (at or above the 50th percentile) in Cognitive Patterns and Pragmatic Skills but at the 37th percentile (below clinical significance) in the Restricted Patterns of Interest Subscale.

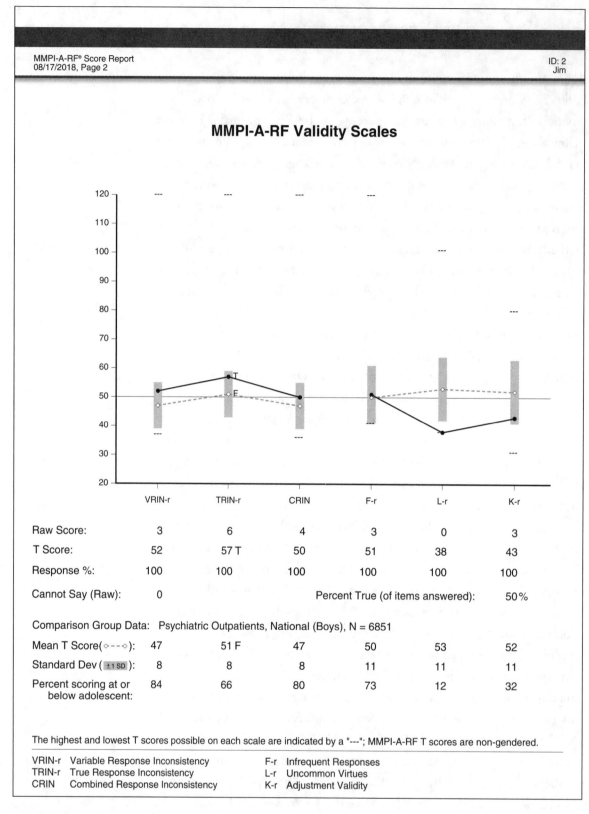

MMPI-A-RF Validity Scales

	VRIN-r	TRIN-r	CRIN	F-r	L-r	K-r
Raw Score:	3	6	4	3	0	3
T Score:	52	57 T	50	51	38	43
Response %:	100	100	100	100	100	100

Cannot Say (Raw): 0   Percent True (of items answered): 50%

Comparison Group Data: Psychiatric Outpatients, National (Boys), N = 6851

	VRIN-r	TRIN-r	CRIN	F-r	L-r	K-r
Mean T Score(◇---◇):	47	51 F	47	50	53	52
Standard Dev (±1 SD):	8	8	8	11	11	11
Percent scoring at or below adolescent:	84	66	80	73	12	32

The highest and lowest T scores possible on each scale are indicated by a "---"; MMPI-A-RF T scores are non-gendered.

VRIN-r Variable Response Inconsistency   F-r Infrequent Responses
TRIN-r True Response Inconsistency   L-r Uncommon Virtues
CRIN   Combined Response Inconsistency   K-r Adjustment Validity

FIGURE 2 Jim's MMPI-A-RF Score Report. Copyright 2016 by the Regents of the University of Minnesota. All rights reserved.

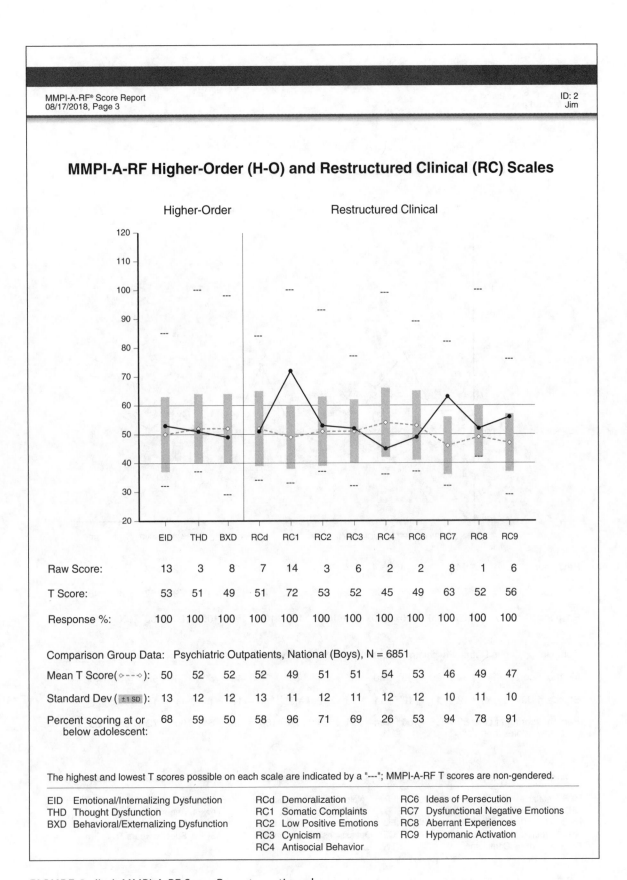

MMPI-A-RF Higher-Order (H-O) and Restructured Clinical (RC) Scales

	EID	THD	BXD	RCd	RC1	RC2	RC3	RC4	RC6	RC7	RC8	RC9
Raw Score:	13	3	8	7	14	3	6	2	2	8	1	6
T Score:	53	51	49	51	72	53	52	45	49	63	52	56
Response %:	100	100	100	100	100	100	100	100	100	100	100	100

Comparison Group Data: Psychiatric Outpatients, National (Boys), N = 6851

	EID	THD	BXD	RCd	RC1	RC2	RC3	RC4	RC6	RC7	RC8	RC9
Mean T Score(◇- - -◇):	50	52	52	52	49	51	51	54	53	46	49	47
Standard Dev (±1 SD):	13	12	12	13	11	12	11	12	12	10	11	10
Percent scoring at or below adolescent:	68	59	50	58	96	71	69	26	53	94	78	91

The highest and lowest T scores possible on each scale are indicated by a "---"; MMPI-A-RF T scores are non-gendered.

EID Emotional/Internalizing Dysfunction	RCd Demoralization	RC6 Ideas of Persecution
THD Thought Dysfunction	RC1 Somatic Complaints	RC7 Dysfunctional Negative Emotions
BXD Behavioral/Externalizing Dysfunction	RC2 Low Positive Emotions	RC8 Aberrant Experiences
	RC3 Cynicism	RC9 Hypomanic Activation
	RC4 Antisocial Behavior	

FIGURE 2 Jim's MMPI-A-RF Score Report, continued.

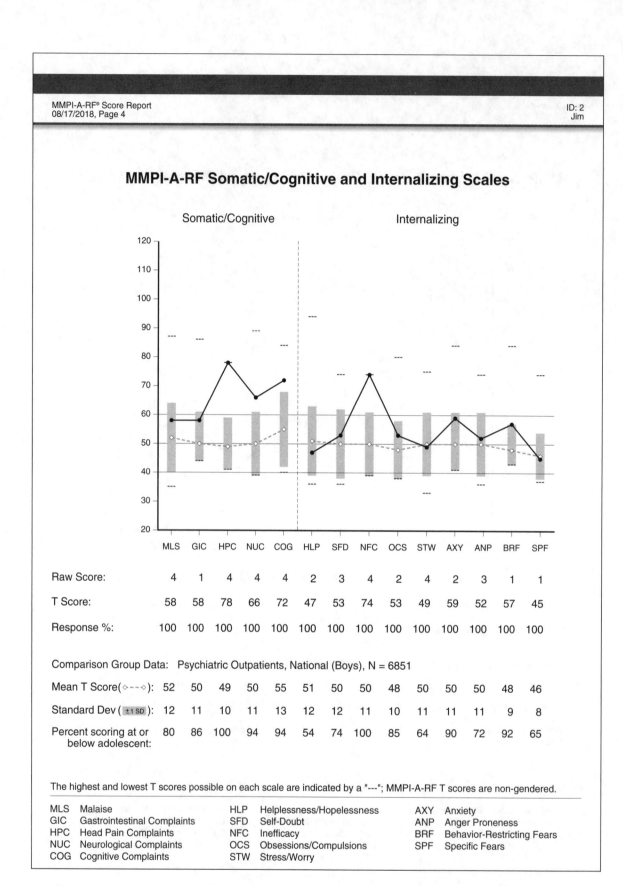

FIGURE 2 Jim's MMPI-A-RF Score Report, continued.

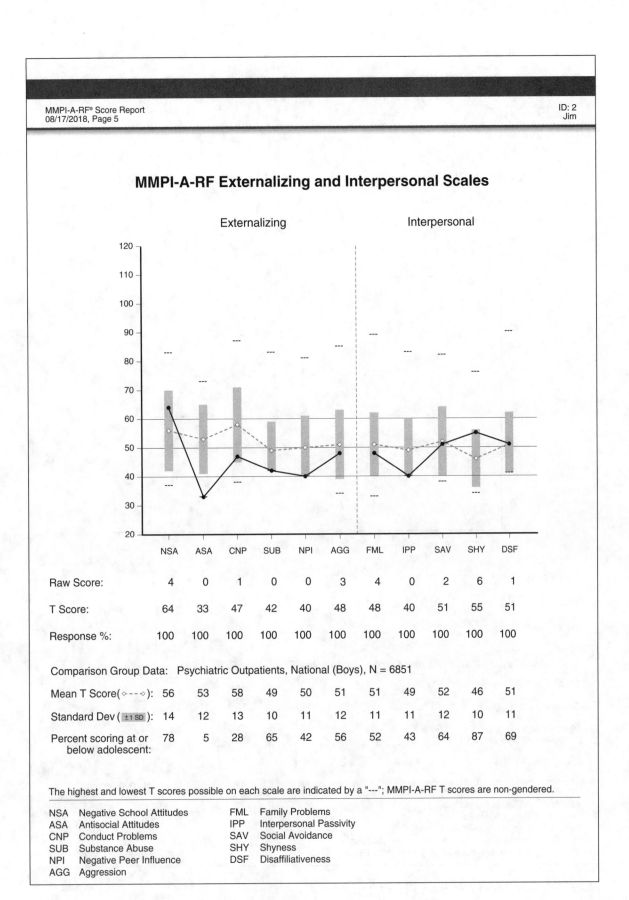

FIGURE 2 Jim's MMPI-A-RF Score Report, continued.

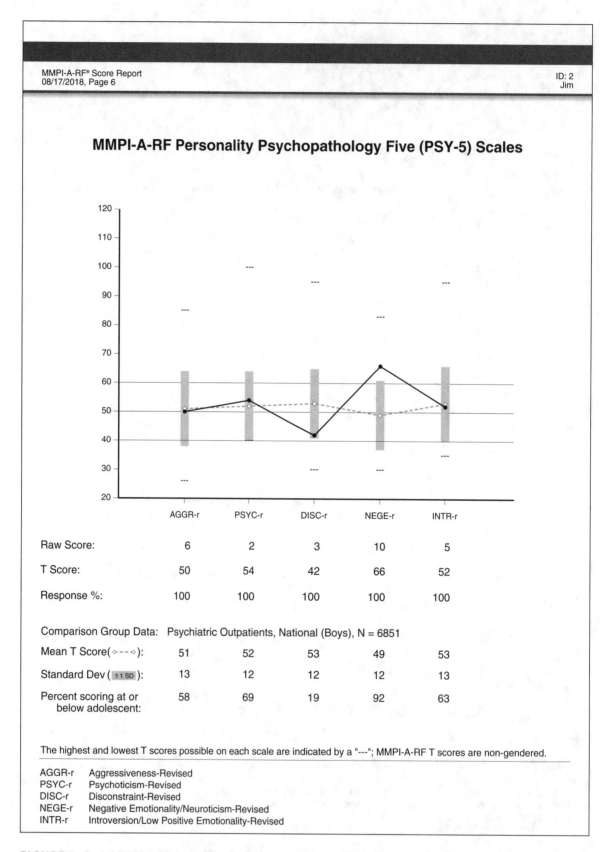

MMPI-A-RF Personality Psychopathology Five (PSY-5) Scales

	AGGR-r	PSYC-r	DISC-r	NEGE-r	INTR-r
Raw Score:	6	2	3	10	5
T Score:	50	54	42	66	52
Response %:	100	100	100	100	100

Comparison Group Data: Psychiatric Outpatients, National (Boys), N = 6851

	AGGR-r	PSYC-r	DISC-r	NEGE-r	INTR-r
Mean T Score(◇---◇):	51	52	53	49	53
Standard Dev (±1 SD):	13	12	12	12	13
Percent scoring at or below adolescent:	58	69	19	92	63

The highest and lowest T scores possible on each scale are indicated by a "---"; MMPI-A-RF T scores are non-gendered.

AGGR-r Aggressiveness-Revised
PSYC-r Psychoticism-Revised
DISC-r Disconstraint-Revised
NEGE-r Negative Emotionality/Neuroticism-Revised
INTR-r Introversion/Low Positive Emotionality-Revised

FIGURE 2 Jim's MMPI-A-RF Score Report, continued.

MMPI-A-RF T SCORES (BY DOMAIN)

PROTOCOL VALIDITY

Content Non-Responsiveness

0	52	57 T	50
CNS	VRIN-r	TRIN-r	CRIN

Over-Reporting

51
F-r

Under-Reporting

38	43
L-r	K-r

SUBSTANTIVE SCALES

Somatic/Cognitive Dysfunction

72	58	58	78	66	72
RC1	MLS	GIC	HPC	NUC	COG

Emotional Dysfunction

53
EID

51	47	53	74
RCd	HLP	SFD	NFC

53	52
RC2	INTR-r

63	53	49	59	52	57	45	66
RC7	OCS	STW	AXY	ANP	BRF	SPF	NEGE-r

Thought Dysfunction

51
THD

49
RC6

52
RC8

54
PSYC-r

Behavioral Dysfunction

49
BXD

45	64	33	47	42	40
RC4	NSA	ASA	CNP	SUB	NPI

56	48	50	42
RC9	AGG	AGGR-r	DISC-r

Interpersonal Functioning

48	52	40	51	55	51
FML	RC3	IPP	SAV	SHY	DSF

Note. This information is provided to facilitate interpretation following the recommended structure for MMPI-A-RF interpretation in Chapter 7 of the *MMPI-A-RF Administration, Scoring, Interpretation, and Technical Manual*, which provides details in the text and an outline in Table 7-1.

FIGURE 2 Jim's MMPI-A-RF Score Report, continued.

MMPI-A-RF

Jim's MMPI-A-RF was valid and interpretable. He appeared to respond relevantly to the item content and there were no indications of either over- or underreporting. His protocol was interpreted using both the normative sample and a comparison group of 6,851 psychiatric outpatient males.

Of immediate concern in Jim's MMPI-A-RF protocol was that he endorsed items related to thoughts of suicide or preoccupation with death. In addition, his protocol had elevated scores on scales RC7 and NEGE, which are correlated with suicidal risk. Analysis of the critical items he endorsed finds that he reported having thoughts of suicide as well as wishing that he were dead. These findings indicate a need for Jim to be assessed for suicide risk and precautions taken if indicated. In the interview, Jim denied thoughts of suicide but acknowledged them when responding to the MMPI-A-RF items and his parents reported that he does express a wish that he was dead. There can be several reasons for the discrepancy between the test findings, the reports of his parents, and what he said in the interview. First, of course, is that adolescents are changeable, and he may have been more open to acknowledging these thoughts on a test than to a person.

Prominent in Jim's protocol are a number of somatic complaints. Analysis of the Substantive scales finds that he reported multiple problems related to head pain as well as vague neurological complaints. Jim is likely to complain of a number of somatic problems.

Jim reported a number of negative emotional experiences including remorse and guilt, and he likely experiences anxiety as well as nightmares, feelings of insecurity, and low self-esteem.

Consistent with his diagnosis of ADHD, Jim reported a diffuse pattern of cognitive complaints and likely experiences problems with attention and concentration as well as slow speech. Additionally, his high score on the NFC (Inefficacy) scale reflects his considerable difficulties in problem-solving and decision-making.

Also, as might be expected given his problems in the schools that he attended previously, Jim's score on the Negative School Attitudes scale was quite elevated, scoring at the 78th percentile when compared to the reference group of 6,851 male psychiatric outpatients. This suggests that school difficulties could include academic problems, poor study habits, and test anxiety, as well as problems with authority in the school and difficulty in motivation. Of note was that Jim reported a much lower than average number of antisocial attitudes.

Jim did not affirm items indicating thought dysfunction or significant interpersonal problems. Because records indicate that Jim has had psychotic symptoms in the past, and he has clearly struggled interpersonally, the absence of elevations on these scales indicates either limited insight or unwillingness to acknowledge these difficulties. It is possible that although Jim continues to experience significant challenges, he is making progress in the specialized school for youth with autism and has made gains in these areas of dysfunction, something that is reported by his parents, which is an asset for continued treatment.

MMPI-A-RF scores indicated the advisability of a medical evaluation to determine the extent to which genuine physical problems contributed to Jim's somatic preoccupation. The MMPI-A-RF suggested diagnostic considerations of Emotional Internalizing Disorders (Somatic Symptom and Related Disorders if physical origins for the complaints can be ruled out as well as anxiety-related disorders). Behavioral-Externalizing Disorders to be considered were ADHD and related neurodevelopmental disorders.

Assets that could be of value in his treatment are that he does not appear to have poor ties with reality and could rationally connect with his therapist. The lack of elevation on interpersonal problems measures would indicate that Jim does not perceive relationships as primarily problematic and might engage in a therapeutic relationship.

Diagnosis

With consideration of the other clinical data, Jim was given a diagnosis of Autistic Spectrum Disorder, Unspecified Mood or Bipolar Disorder and Attention Deficit Hyperactivity Disorder, Combined, as well as a rule out of a Somatic Symptom Disorder.

OUTCOME

Intensive home-based services specific to youth living with autism were implemented as well as referral to a mentoring program. His other services were continued. Given the MMPI-A-RF findings, a treatment team meeting was held to discuss how to improve Jim's experience of school and his motivation. It was also suggested that the MMPI-A-RF identified areas in which he has made progress and that treatment efforts had made a difference. A follow-up 6 months later found significant improvement in his anger management skills and that he and his father had returned home.

Mary

A Female With a Family History of Schizophrenia and Bipolar Disorder

BACKGROUND

Mary, a 16-year-old female, was referred for a psychological consultation by her residential treatment center. She had been placed there because her parents found her with marijuana in her car. When they confronted her, she ran away and was found while attempting to hang herself. She was first psychiatrically hospitalized and then transitioned to a secure residential center.

Interview With Youth

In a clinical interview, Mary described her childhood as "not good," saying that her father was a physically and emotionally abusive alcoholic who committed suicide when she was 10 years old. She stated that her mother has remarried but is in the process of divorce. Mary said that the death of her father was "traumatic . . . it changed my life . . . we had to move to a new town." Mary also said that her mother became more involved with her stepfather and "pushed me out of the picture." She indicated that her mother "told me that she is going to give me up when I turned 16 but emotionally, she gave me up when I was 10." She said that the conflicts with her mother resulted in Mary moving in with her aunt but that her mother took away her Social Security money when she did that. To the best of her knowledge, she has had no major developmental or health problems as a child.

Mary reported that she has a 21-year-old stepbrother and a 22-year-old stepsister and that she has a poor relationship with each. She said that she has had one serious boyfriend but was not involved with anyone prior to her placement.

Mary indicated that she is currently in the 11th grade but should be in the 12th. She stated that she has never been in special education and has earned A's and B's. She said that her mother removed her from high school and placed her in an online program after she was caught with drugs, adding that she had a suspension at the end of the ninth grade for bringing drugs to her high school.

Mary stated that she first drank alcohol at the age of 8 but does not generally like it and last drank about a year and a half ago. She acknowledged drinking to intoxication at least twice. She said that she started smoking marijuana at the age of 10, describing it as her "drug of choice" and saying that she began smoking on a daily basis "a year or so ago." She tried LSD and mushrooms within the last year. She did not believe she has a substance abuse problem.

Mary reported that her father physically and emotionally abused her. She said that she was sexually molested in the past but would not report any details, saying that after the abuse was reported, she has refused to talk about it with "countless counselors." She denied any history of fire-setting or animal cruelty. Mary said that she appeared before the juvenile court for a status offense (unruly child) and then on the instant charges. She has never been in a detention facility.

Mary said that she has been in counseling "so many times" since the age of 8, thinking that she has seen at least six therapists. She said that she was seeing a therapist when hospitalized, telling me that she does not believe that services have helped her, including being hospitalized and a prior residential stay at this facility. She reported a lengthy history of cutting herself and said that she has done so since the age of 12. She acknowledges a lengthy history of mental illness in her family, saying that her mother has schizophrenia and her father was an alcoholic and had "undiagnosed bipolar disorder."

Mary denied any significant medical problems. She said that she had never been medically hospitalized (other than for a tonsillectomy and adenoidectomy) and denied any history of head trauma, loss of consciousness, and any other neurological involvement, but said that she suffers from chronic migraines. At the time of the examination, she was prescribed Effexor, an antidepressant.

COLLATERAL INFORMATION

The intake summary at the residential center described Mary as a "very bright and talented young woman" but with a history of substance abuse, a mood disorder, and self-harming behavior that is also reflected in her family history. Her father was an alcoholic who was violent with Mary. Her father committed suicide when she was 10. It indicated further that her mother has schizophrenia as well as PTSD and a history of substance abuse. There is also a history of a family uncle who committed suicide when Mary was 5 and her maternal grandfather has a history of substance abuse. The maternal grandmother has also recently been diagnosed with Alzheimer's disease. It also noted that Mary, her aunt, grandmother, and great-grandmother (who also has Alzheimer's) live together. The relationship between Mary and her mother is strained but Mary and her aunt are close.

The residential treatment center records indicated Mary had a history of marijuana use and reported being physically, sexually, and emotionally abused. She noted that she had been twice suspended from school. The first time was for threatening to kill a peer after she made disparaging comments about her deceased father and the second was for fighting with a female peer. This resulted in a 2-month residential placement. The discharge diagnosis was Major Depression with Psychotic Features; however, a review of her records finds no reporting of Mary experiencing any psychotic symptoms.

Mary's therapist's records were reviewed. An intake summary noted that there was a strong family history of both mental illness and substance abuse as well as a history of trauma and family conflict. A diagnosis of Major Depressive Disorder Severe with Psychotic Features, Posttraumatic Stress Disorder, and a rule out of a Cannabis-Related Disorder was advanced, and a guarded prognosis was reported.

Current Behavioral Status

Mary was appropriately dressed and groomed in clothing that was neat and clean. Her hygiene and grooming were adequate.

There were no overt indications of loosening of associations, flight of ideas, or tangentiality. Mary's psychomotor activity was nonremarkable. Her speech was normal in tone, pacing, and volume. Her attention span was characterized by at least a moderate degree of distraction (meaning that she had to be refocused to task periodically but was able to return to what she was doing). Her manner of social interaction was outwardly friendly and polite but tended to be primarily superficially cooperative and somewhat disengaged. She did, however, complete all of the tasks requested of her.

Mary presented with an appropriate and expressive affect to a stated "depressed" mood. When asked to rate her subjective level of distress (SUDS), she described her present degree of emotional upset as being an 8/9 out of a possible 10, ascribing her emotional discomfort to "being here and the fact that I'm almost 17 and this is holding me back."

Mary reported that when she goes to sleep, she sometimes hears a whisper of her name (suggestive of hypnogogic phenomena) and also said that once when caught by her mother smoking marijuana she noticed a "waving" sensation to the floors and walls (suggestive of a potential toxic response). During her interview there were no overt indications of hallucinations, delusions, or paranoia. She gave no behavioral evidence of visual, gustatory, olfactory, or tactile hallucinations. As such, there were no observable indications of the types of perceptual abnormalities typically and genuinely associated with psychosis.

Mary denied and gave no evidence of specific delusional thinking. She demonstrated no systematic paranoid delusions or grandiosity. Accordingly, there appears to be no overt clinical or behavioral evidence in the content of thought as would be typically seen with seriously mentally ill adolescents.

Mary reported a number of symptoms typically associated with depression such as poor sleep, difficulty in concentration, and increased irritability. She denied others such as limited appetite, hopelessness, loss of interest or pleasure, loss of sexual interest. Also, upon specific inquiry, she denied active suicidal ideation, intent, or plan. She related that she continues, however, to have periodic, "random" thoughts of self-harm, but denied any intent of acting on them. She also denied homicidal ideation.

When asked to describe any history of mood swings, Mary stated that throughout her life, she has experienced rapidly changing moods and complained of episodic past racing thoughts (symptoms associated with mood disorders). She denied any history of manic periods but acknowledged impulsive and reckless behaviors.

Mary spontaneously reported that she suffers from multiple phobias including heights, darkness, and germs. She denied any intrusive obsessive thinking or compulsive behavior but said that she has periodic ego-dystonic thoughts of sexual intercourse and hurting others. When I asked her about "flashbacks" and other symptoms associated with trauma exposure, she endorsed having flashbacks of being sexually molested and the death of her father. She reported that she still suffers from nightmares.

Mary was alert and responsive to her environment and there were no problems observed with her attention. She was oriented to time, place, person, and situation. Her fund of general information suggested average to above-average intellectual functioning.

Mary's concentration was adequate as evidenced by her attention and focus in the conversation with the examiner. Her immediate recall was adequate as demonstrated by her ability to recall five digits forward and three in reverse order. Concentration was also demonstrated to be adequate by her ability to perform simple mental calculations. Her short-term recall was adequate as demonstrated by her ability to recall three items from memory after a 10-minute distraction. She also showed adequate capacity for verbal abstract reasoning as demonstrated in her ability to state conceptual similarities between related objects and concepts, including more complex abstractions. This was also demonstrated in her ability to interpret commonly used proverbs. Her insight and judgment did appear to be limited as determined by both her history and response to situational questions.

On the K-BIT 2, Mary obtained a Vocabulary score of 112, a Nonverbal score of 106, and her overall Composite IQ standard score was 111.

Mary was also given the Slosson Oral Reading Test. Her score indicated that she reads at the 12th grade level, which is above her current grade placement.

MMPI-A-RF

Mary's MMPI-A-RF protocol was valid and interpretable. There were no indications of nonresponsiveness to item content nor of under- or overreporting of problems. Her protocol was compared to 114 girls in a Midwest residential treatment center. In general, her protocol was very similar to the comparison group, but she reported a significantly greater (more than one standard deviation) level of malaise.

Mary's protocol indicated that she responded in the keyed direction to a test item related to thoughts about killing herself. Her elevations on RCd and SFD are correlated with risk for suicide. Given both her history of suicidal behavior as well as her family history, the MMPI-A-RF indicates continued, significant concern about her engaging in self-harming behavior, including suicide attempts. Mary should be evaluated for a risk of self-harm and appropriate precautions taken if needed.

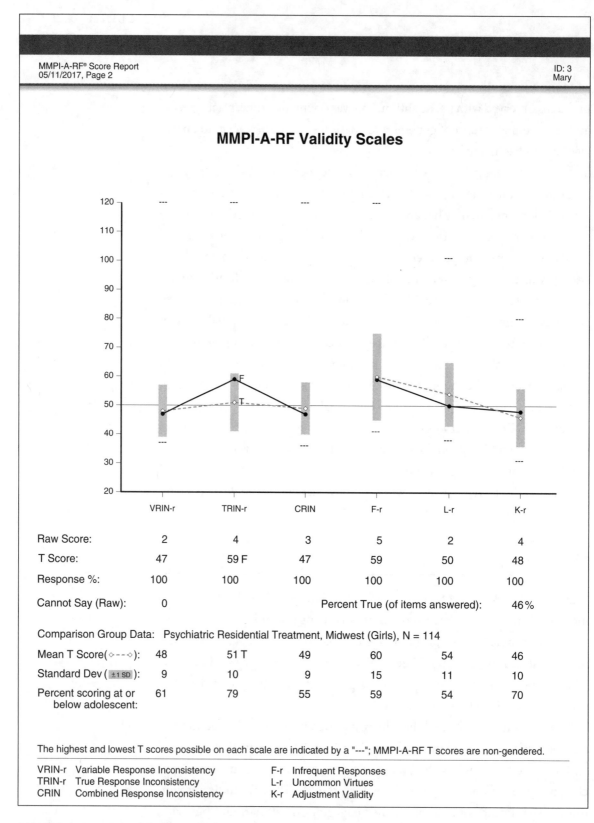

MMPI-A-RF Validity Scales

	VRIN-r	TRIN-r	CRIN	F-r	L-r	K-r
Raw Score:	2	4	3	5	2	4
T Score:	47	59 F	47	59	50	48
Response %:	100	100	100	100	100	100

Cannot Say (Raw):   0   Percent True (of items answered):   46%

Comparison Group Data: Psychiatric Residential Treatment, Midwest (Girls), N = 114

	VRIN-r	TRIN-r	CRIN	F-r	L-r	K-r
Mean T Score(◇---◇):	48	51 T	49	60	54	46
Standard Dev (±1 SD):	9	10	9	15	11	10
Percent scoring at or below adolescent:	61	79	55	59	54	70

The highest and lowest T scores possible on each scale are indicated by a "---"; MMPI-A-RF T scores are non-gendered.

VRIN-r	Variable Response Inconsistency	F-r	Infrequent Responses
TRIN-r	True Response Inconsistency	L-r	Uncommon Virtues
CRIN	Combined Response Inconsistency	K-r	Adjustment Validity

FIGURE 3 Mary's MMPI-A-RF Score Report. Copyright 2016 by the Regents of the University of Minnesota. All rights reserved.

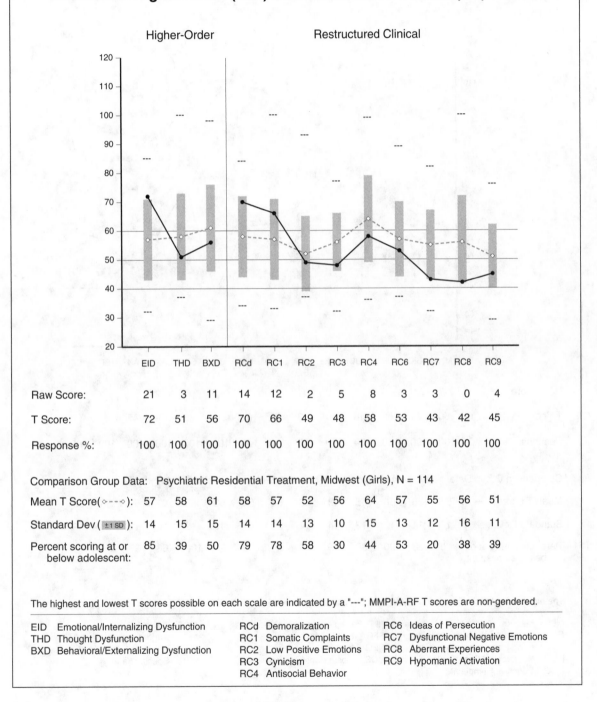

MMPI-A-RF Higher-Order (H-O) and Restructured Clinical (RC) Scales

Higher-Order   Restructured Clinical

	EID	THD	BXD	RCd	RC1	RC2	RC3	RC4	RC6	RC7	RC8	RC9
Raw Score:	21	3	11	14	12	2	5	8	3	3	0	4
T Score:	72	51	56	70	66	49	48	58	53	43	42	45
Response %:	100	100	100	100	100	100	100	100	100	100	100	100

Comparison Group Data: Psychiatric Residential Treatment, Midwest (Girls), N = 114

	EID	THD	BXD	RCd	RC1	RC2	RC3	RC4	RC6	RC7	RC8	RC9
Mean T Score(◇--◇):	57	58	61	58	57	52	56	64	57	55	56	51
Standard Dev (±1 SD):	14	15	15	14	14	13	10	15	13	12	16	11
Percent scoring at or below adolescent:	85	39	50	79	78	58	30	44	53	20	38	39

The highest and lowest T scores possible on each scale are indicated by a "---"; MMPI-A-RF T scores are non-gendered.

EID	Emotional/Internalizing Dysfunction	RCd Demoralization	RC6 Ideas of Persecution
THD	Thought Dysfunction	RC1 Somatic Complaints	RC7 Dysfunctional Negative Emotions
BXD	Behavioral/Externalizing Dysfunction	RC2 Low Positive Emotions	RC8 Aberrant Experiences
		RC3 Cynicism	RC9 Hypomanic Activation
		RC4 Antisocial Behavior	

FIGURE 3 Mary's MMPI-A-RF Score Report, continued.

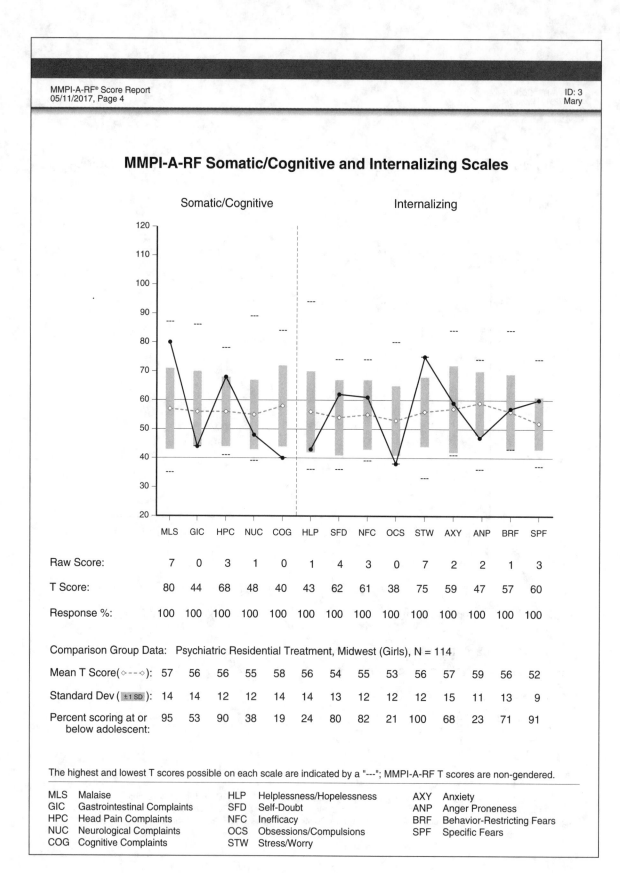

MMPI-A-RF Somatic/Cognitive and Internalizing Scales

	MLS	GIC	HPC	NUC	COG	HLP	SFD	NFC	OCS	STW	AXY	ANP	BRF	SPF
Raw Score:	7	0	3	1	0	1	4	3	0	7	2	2	1	3
T Score:	80	44	68	48	40	43	62	61	38	75	59	47	57	60
Response %:	100	100	100	100	100	100	100	100	100	100	100	100	100	100

Comparison Group Data: Psychiatric Residential Treatment, Midwest (Girls), N = 114

	MLS	GIC	HPC	NUC	COG	HLP	SFD	NFC	OCS	STW	AXY	ANP	BRF	SPF
Mean T Score(◇---◇):	57	56	56	55	58	56	54	55	53	56	57	59	56	52
Standard Dev (±1 SD):	14	14	12	12	14	14	13	12	12	12	15	11	13	9
Percent scoring at or below adolescent:	95	53	90	38	19	24	80	82	21	100	68	23	71	91

The highest and lowest T scores possible on each scale are indicated by a "---"; MMPI-A-RF T scores are non-gendered.

MLS	Malaise	HLP	Helplessness/Hopelessness	AXY	Anxiety
GIC	Gastrointestinal Complaints	SFD	Self-Doubt	ANP	Anger Proneness
HPC	Head Pain Complaints	NFC	Inefficacy	BRF	Behavior-Restricting Fears
NUC	Neurological Complaints	OCS	Obsessions/Compulsions	SPF	Specific Fears
COG	Cognitive Complaints	STW	Stress/Worry		

FIGURE 3 Mary's MMPI-A-RF Score Report, continued.

60

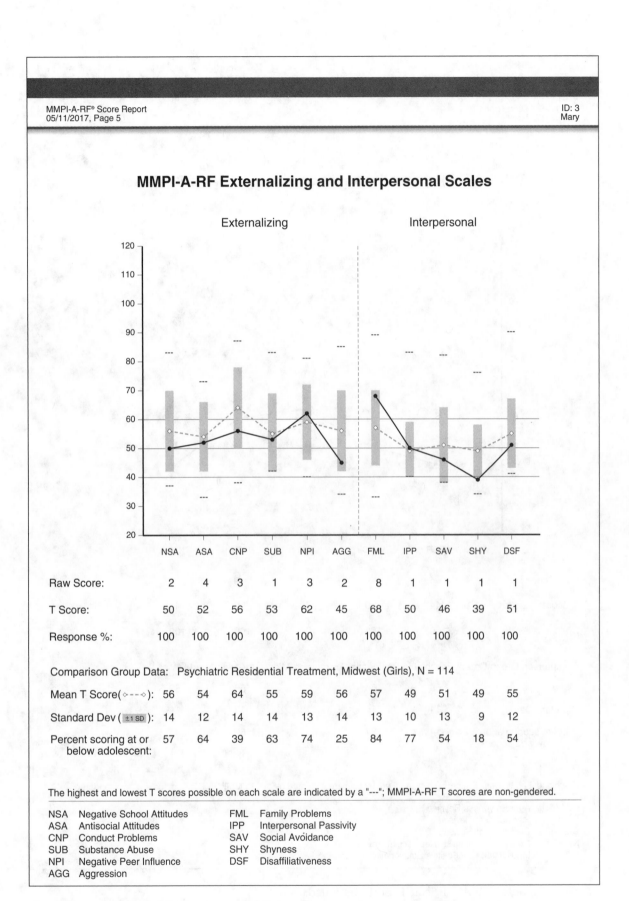

MMPI-A-RF Externalizing and Interpersonal Scales

Externalizing   Interpersonal

	NSA	ASA	CNP	SUB	NPI	AGG	FML	IPP	SAV	SHY	DSF
Raw Score:	2	4	3	1	3	2	8	1	1	1	1
T Score:	50	52	56	53	62	45	68	50	46	39	51
Response %:	100	100	100	100	100	100	100	100	100	100	100

Comparison Group Data: Psychiatric Residential Treatment, Midwest (Girls), N = 114

Mean T Score(◇---◇):	56	54	64	55	59	56	57	49	51	49	55
Standard Dev (±1 SD):	14	12	14	14	13	14	13	10	13	9	12
Percent scoring at or below adolescent:	57	64	39	63	74	25	84	77	54	18	54

The highest and lowest T scores possible on each scale are indicated by a "---"; MMPI-A-RF T scores are non-gendered.

NSA	Negative School Attitudes	FML	Family Problems
ASA	Antisocial Attitudes	IPP	Interpersonal Passivity
CNP	Conduct Problems	SAV	Social Avoidance
SUB	Substance Abuse	SHY	Shyness
NPI	Negative Peer Influence	DSF	Disaffiliativeness
AGG	Aggression		

FIGURE 3 Mary's MMPI-A-RF Score Report, continued.

61

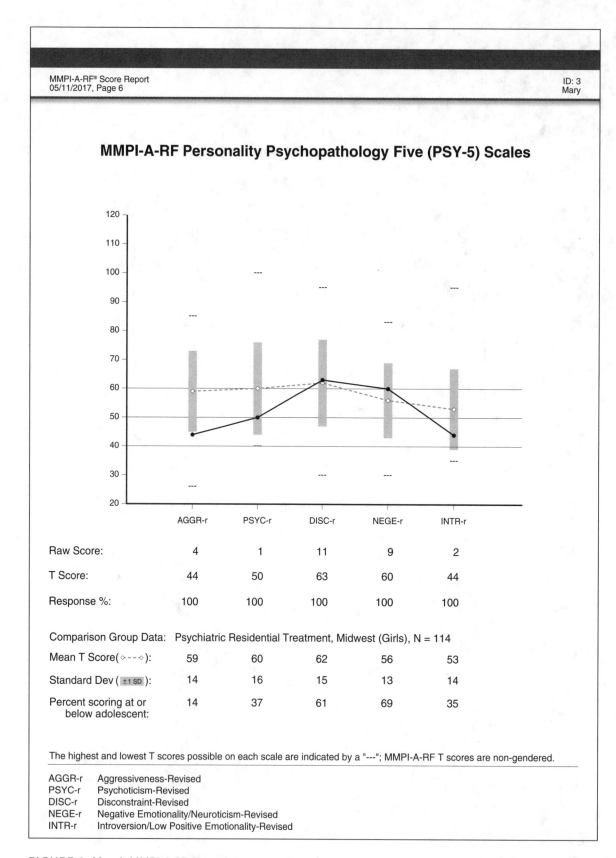

MMPI-A-RF Personality Psychopathology Five (PSY-5) Scales

	AGGR-r	PSYC-r	DISC-r	NEGE-r	INTR-r
Raw Score:	4	1	11	9	2
T Score:	44	50	63	60	44
Response %:	100	100	100	100	100

Comparison Group Data: Psychiatric Residential Treatment, Midwest (Girls), N = 114

	AGGR-r	PSYC-r	DISC-r	NEGE-r	INTR-r
Mean T Score(◇---◇):	59	60	62	56	53
Standard Dev (±1 SD):	14	16	15	13	14
Percent scoring at or below adolescent:	14	37	61	69	35

The highest and lowest T scores possible on each scale are indicated by a "---"; MMPI-A-RF T scores are non-gendered.

AGGR-r	Aggressiveness-Revised
PSYC-r	Psychoticism-Revised
DISC-r	Disconstraint-Revised
NEGE-r	Negative Emotionality/Neuroticism-Revised
INTR-r	Introversion/Low Positive Emotionality-Revised

FIGURE 3 Mary's MMPI-A-RF Score Report, continued.

MMPI-A-RF T SCORES (BY DOMAIN)

PROTOCOL VALIDITY

Content Non-Responsiveness

0	47	59 F	47
CNS	VRIN-r	TRIN-r	CRIN

Over-Reporting

59
F-r

Under-Reporting

50	48
L-r	K-r

SUBSTANTIVE SCALES

Somatic/Cognitive Dysfunction

66	80	44	68	48	40
RC1	MLS	GIC	HPC	NUC	COG

Emotional Dysfunction

72		70	43	62	61		
EID		RCd	HLP	SFD	NFC		

49	44
RC2	INTR-r

43	38	75	59	47	57	60	60
RC7	OCS	STW	AXY	ANP	BRF	SPF	NEGE-r

Thought Dysfunction

51		53
THD		RC6

42
RC8

50
PSYC-r

Behavioral Dysfunction

56		58	50	52	56	53	62
BXD		RC4	NSA	ASA	CNP	SUB	NPI

45	45	44	63
RC9	AGG	AGGR-r	DISC-r

Interpersonal Functioning

68	48	50	46	39	51
FML	RC3	IPP	SAV	SHY	DSF

Note. This information is provided to facilitate interpretation following the recommended structure for MMPI-A-RF interpretation in Chapter 7 of the *MMPI-A-RF Administration, Scoring, Interpretation, and Technical Manual*, which provides details in the text and an outline in Table 7-1.

FIGURE 3 Mary's MMPI-A-RF Score Report, continued.

Mary is experiencing considerable emotional distress as reported by the elevation on scale EID, which is slightly above one standard deviation from the mean of the comparison group. Review of the Restructured Clinical scales finds elevations on RCd, indicating that she reports feeling sad and dissatisfied with her current life circumstances and that she is likely to feel sad and anxious and that life is a strain and to experience problems with attention and concentration and to complain of low energy and fatigue. In addition to the elevated RCd, Mary generated elevated scores on the Specific Problems scales of SFD (Self-Doubt), NFC (Inefficiency), STW (Stress/Worry), SPF (Specific Fears), and on the PSY-5 NEGE-r scale. She reports feeling overwhelmed and likely has poor self-esteem. Mary likely feels very inferior to others, tends to be self-defeating, passive, introverted, and thinks very poorly of herself. Mary also has trouble making decisions, likely procrastinates, and has very limited coping skills. Mary also reported an above-average level of stress and worry and is likely anxious. She also reports multiple fears and phobias.

Scores on the Somatic/Cognitive scales MLS (Malaise) and HPC (Head Pain Complaints) in conjunction with RC1 indicate that Mary reported a number of somatic complaints that include head pain. Overall, she is likely to have multiple somatic complaints as well as a general sense of malaise, poor physical health, weakness, and fatigue. In addition, it is likely that Mary complains of poor sleep.

Although BXD (Behavioral Dysfunction) was not elevated, Specific Problems scale NPI (Negative Peer Influence) as well as the PSY-5 DISC-r scale were elevated. This indicates that Mary is prone to affiliate with a negative peer group. She likely demonstrates oppositional and defiant behavior that can result in rule breaking, as well as legal charges such as running away, substance abuse, and school truancy and can be impulsive.

Within the area of Interpersonal Functioning, the FML (Family Problems) scale is elevated. Mary's family life is likely very conflictual, and she does not perceive her family to be a source of emotional support. She likely engages in lying as well as having problems with authority figures.

Mary had no significant elevations on Substantive scales associated with thought dysfunction. This finding is similar to what she reported in the clinical interview and what was also observed. However, she does have a substantial family history of mental illness and should be monitored for emergence of symptoms in that overt psychotic symptoms are less common in youth her age.

Mary's MMPI-A-RF protocol suggests that consideration be given to a possible somatic symptom disorder (if physical findings are negative), internalizing disorders, depression-related disorders as well as stress-related disorders and specific phobias. In addition, some type of Behavioral-Externalizing Disorder such as Conduct Disorder should be considered.

Mary should have a medical examination to rule out any genuine physical problems that might contribute to her somatic focus. She also should be further evaluated for substance abuse problems. As noted in the interview, Mary was quite reticent to discuss details of the possible abuse in her life, other than to say that she had disclosed it to other mental health professionals. These findings could suggest that the trauma she experienced continues to have a significant impact on her life since it remains reflected in the testing.

Challenges to treatment include probable difficulty accepting a psychological explanation of her physical symptoms. Because of her passivity and malaise, she may be difficult to engage in treatment.

Potential treatment assets include that Mary presently does not appear to have a poor tie with reality and could engage rationally in treatment. In addition, limited elevations were found in the scales associated with behavioral dysfunction. Mary does not appear to have antisocial attitudes or tendencies that would actively interfere with treatment progress. Given her history of trauma as well as the MMPI-A-RF data, it is imperative that any treatment approach with Mary be trauma-informed.

Diagnosis

Mary was given diagnoses of Major Depressive Disorder, Posttraumatic Stress Disorder, and Cannabis Use Disorder.

OUTCOME

Mary was recommended for intensive individual and group therapy using a specific treatment model for persons with active or a history of self-harming behaviors. She was also recommended for anger management groups, social skills groups, and further substance abuse assessment. A trauma-informed care approach was recommended for every modality. It was also recommended that her residential stay be as short as possible and that when she was discharged, she would be seen in intensive home-based services.

Robert

A Male With Anxiety, Attention Deficit Hyperactivity Disorder, and Obsessive-Compulsive Symptoms

BACKGROUND

Robert is an 18-year-old male referred by his pediatrician for a psychological consultation. He had complaints of severe anxiety as well as a diagnosis of Attention-Deficit Hyperactivity Disorder, Combined. He was prescribed Adderall, a psychostimulant.

COLLATERAL INFORMATION

Robert's parents are divorced, and he lives with his mother. His father has not been involved in Robert's life for about 6 years and, according to Robert's mother, is an alcoholic. Robert's mother's pregnancy was complicated by gestational diabetes and hypotension. She reported that Robert achieved developmental milestones normally but did have problems with startling, which continue. He was an easy temperament infant who socialized well. He did have expressive speech delay and was placed in speech therapy in preschool but had no speech impediments after kindergarten.

Robert was diagnosed with ADHD at the age of 7 and has been treated with medications since that time. He has an IEP in school for his ADHD, qualifying under "Other Health Impaired." Robert has a sister, 1 year older, who has always excelled in school both socially and academically. According to his parents, Robert has always tried to match his sister's achievement but has never been successful. As an illustration, Robert's older sister now attends a prestigious university out of state. Robert, however, works at a convenience store and is taking one course at a local community college. He lives at home and does not have a driver's license and remains dependent either on his parents or ridesharing for transportation.

Robert has never had any behavioral problem; however, he can be impulsive and socially intrusive with peers, often blurting out questions and then quickly apologizing. At home, he can be argumentative and somewhat oppositional. In the past, he has had some compulsive behaviors such as counting the cars that would drive by the house. He also ruminates about social difficulties.

Current Behavioral Status

Robert was appropriately dressed and groomed for his interview. His hygiene was adequate. There were no overt indications of loosening of associations, flight of ideas, or tangentiality. His psychomotor activity was nonremarkable. His speech was normal in tone, pacing, and volume. His attention span was characterized by frequent distraction, but he could be easily redirected. His manner of social interaction was friendly and polite but had a very dependent and immature manner. To illustrate, when asked to describe his feelings, he would do so but then would quickly ask if he had done so correctly.

Robert presented with an appropriate and expressive affect and a stated generally anxious mood. He rated his subjective level of emotional distress as a 7 out of a possible 10, citing his anxiety over school.

There were no overt indications of hallucinations, delusions, or paranoia. Robert denied current depression as well as any disturbances in his sleep, health, or appetite. He denied suicidal or homicidal ideation, intent, plans, or access to means. He was future oriented. He did not appear hopeless and had social supports in his friends at band and school. He presented with anxiety as well as complaints of obsessive thinking.

Robert's recall functions were clinically intact. He was oriented to time, place, person, and situation. Insight and judgment were seemingly very immature for his age.

Robert's mother completed the Conners Comprehensive Behavior Rating Scales—a norm-referenced assessment of emotional and behavioral problems in youth. The findings indicated the presence of severe anxiety symptoms. The ratings suggested potential diagnoses of Attention Deficit Hyperactivity Disorder, Combined Type and Generalized Anxiety Disorder.

MMPI-A-RF Validity Scales

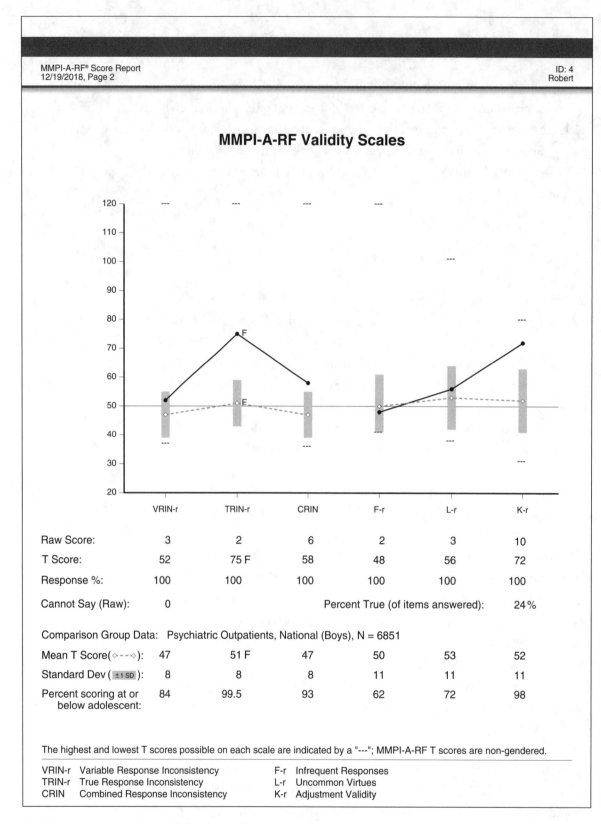

	VRIN-r	TRIN-r	CRIN	F-r	L-r	K-r
Raw Score:	3	2	6	2	3	10
T Score:	52	75 F	58	48	56	72
Response %:	100	100	100	100	100	100

Cannot Say (Raw): 0   Percent True (of items answered): 24%

Comparison Group Data: Psychiatric Outpatients, National (Boys), N = 6851

	VRIN-r	TRIN-r	CRIN	F-r	L-r	K-r
Mean T Score(◇- - -◇):	47	51 F	47	50	53	52
Standard Dev (±1 SD):	8	8	8	11	11	11
Percent scoring at or below adolescent:	84	99.5	93	62	72	98

The highest and lowest T scores possible on each scale are indicated by a "---"; MMPI-A-RF T scores are non-gendered.

VRIN-r	Variable Response Inconsistency	F-r	Infrequent Responses
TRIN-r	True Response Inconsistency	L-r	Uncommon Virtues
CRIN	Combined Response Inconsistency	K-r	Adjustment Validity

FIGURE 4 Robert's MMPI-A-RF Score Report. Copyright 2016 by the Regents of the University of Minnesota. All rights reserved.

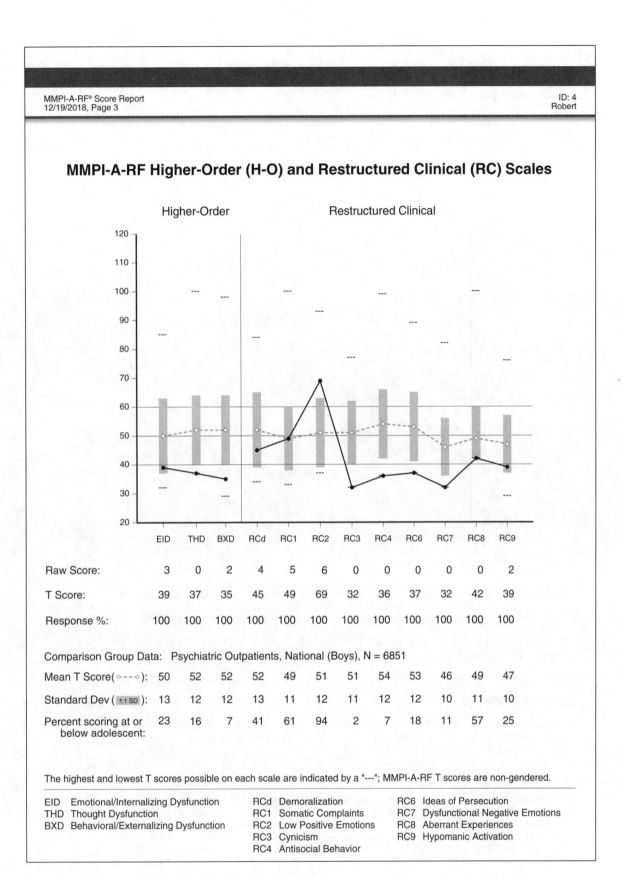

MMPI-A-RF Higher-Order (H-O) and Restructured Clinical (RC) Scales

	EID	THD	BXD	RCd	RC1	RC2	RC3	RC4	RC6	RC7	RC8	RC9
Raw Score:	3	0	2	4	5	6	0	0	0	0	0	2
T Score:	39	37	35	45	49	69	32	36	37	32	42	39
Response %:	100	100	100	100	100	100	100	100	100	100	100	100

Comparison Group Data: Psychiatric Outpatients, National (Boys), N = 6851

	EID	THD	BXD	RCd	RC1	RC2	RC3	RC4	RC6	RC7	RC8	RC9
Mean T Score(◇---◇):	50	52	52	52	49	51	51	54	53	46	49	47
Standard Dev (±1 SD):	13	12	12	13	11	12	11	12	12	10	11	10
Percent scoring at or below adolescent:	23	16	7	41	61	94	2	7	18	11	57	25

The highest and lowest T scores possible on each scale are indicated by a "---"; MMPI-A-RF T scores are non-gendered.

EID	Emotional/Internalizing Dysfunction	RCd	Demoralization
THD	Thought Dysfunction	RC1	Somatic Complaints
BXD	Behavioral/Externalizing Dysfunction	RC2	Low Positive Emotions
		RC3	Cynicism
		RC4	Antisocial Behavior

RC6	Ideas of Persecution
RC7	Dysfunctional Negative Emotions
RC8	Aberrant Experiences
RC9	Hypomanic Activation

FIGURE 4   Robert's MMPI-A-RF Score Report, continued.

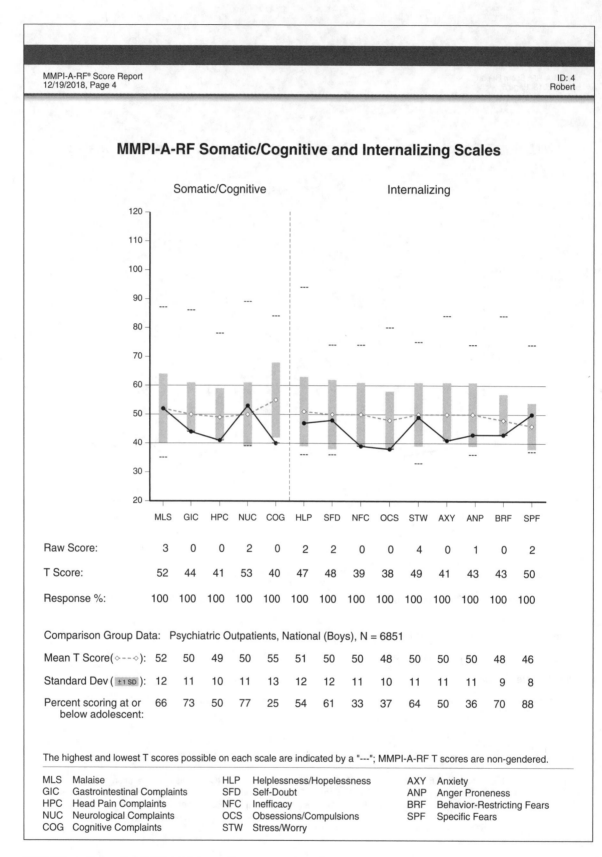

FIGURE 4 Robert's MMPI-A-RF Score Report, continued.

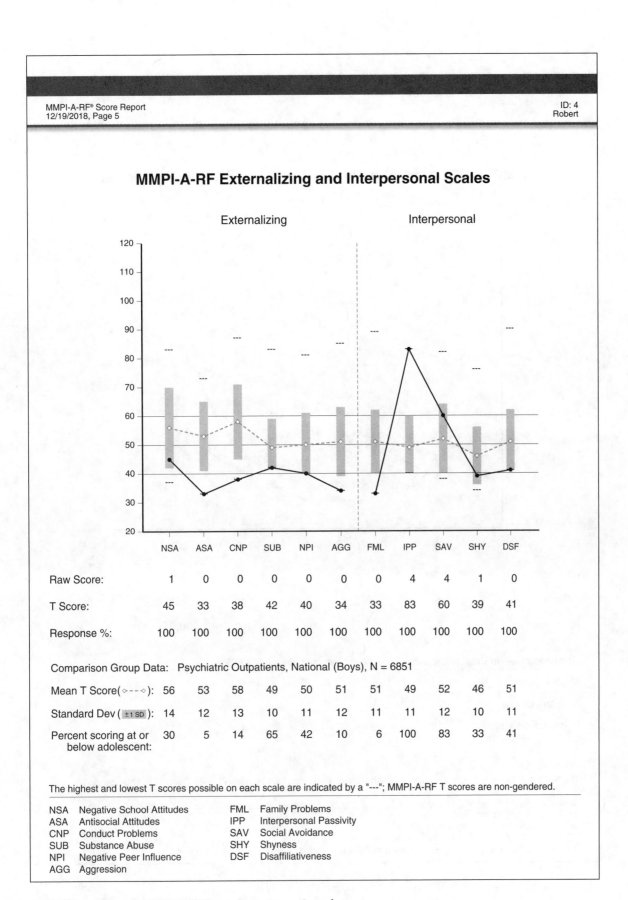

MMPI-A-RF Externalizing and Interpersonal Scales

	NSA	ASA	CNP	SUB	NPI	AGG	FML	IPP	SAV	SHY	DSF
Raw Score:	1	0	0	0	0	0	0	4	4	1	0
T Score:	45	33	38	42	40	34	33	83	60	39	41
Response %:	100	100	100	100	100	100	100	100	100	100	100

Comparison Group Data: Psychiatric Outpatients, National (Boys), N = 6851

	NSA	ASA	CNP	SUB	NPI	AGG	FML	IPP	SAV	SHY	DSF
Mean T Score(◇- - -◇):	56	53	58	49	50	51	51	49	52	46	51
Standard Dev (±1 SD):	14	12	13	10	11	12	11	11	12	10	11
Percent scoring at or below adolescent:	30	5	14	65	42	10	6	100	83	33	41

The highest and lowest T scores possible on each scale are indicated by a "---"; MMPI-A-RF T scores are non-gendered.

NSA	Negative School Attitudes		FML	Family Problems
ASA	Antisocial Attitudes		IPP	Interpersonal Passivity
CNP	Conduct Problems		SAV	Social Avoidance
SUB	Substance Abuse		SHY	Shyness
NPI	Negative Peer Influence		DSF	Disaffiliativeness
AGG	Aggression			

FIGURE 4 Robert's MMPI-A-RF Score Report, continued.

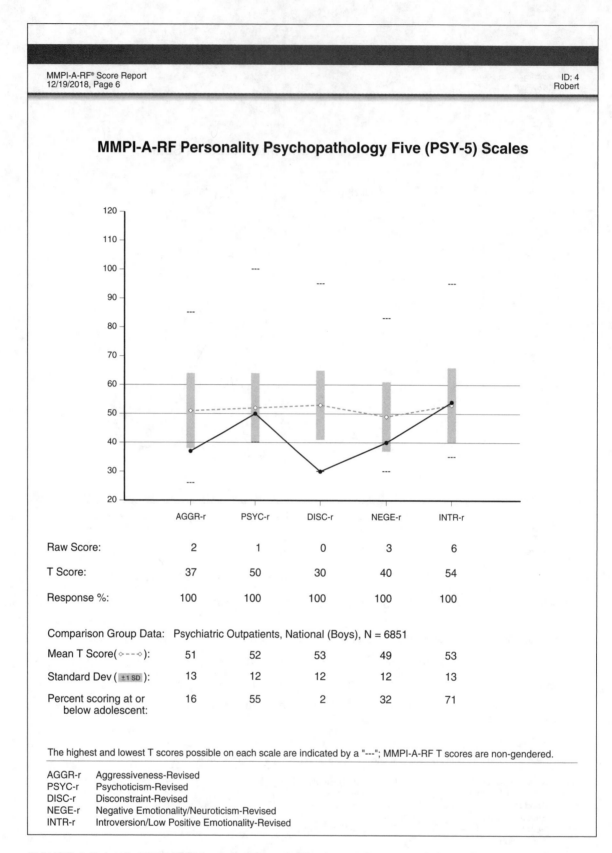

MMPI-A-RF Personality Psychopathology Five (PSY-5) Scales

	AGGR-r	PSYC-r	DISC-r	NEGE-r	INTR-r
Raw Score:	2	1	0	3	6
T Score:	37	50	30	40	54
Response %:	100	100	100	100	100

Comparison Group Data: Psychiatric Outpatients, National (Boys), N = 6851

	AGGR-r	PSYC-r	DISC-r	NEGE-r	INTR-r
Mean T Score(◇---◇):	51	52	53	49	53
Standard Dev (±1 SD):	13	12	12	12	13
Percent scoring at or below adolescent:	16	55	2	32	71

The highest and lowest T scores possible on each scale are indicated by a "---"; MMPI-A-RF T scores are non-gendered.

AGGR-r	Aggressiveness-Revised
PSYC-r	Psychoticism-Revised
DISC-r	Disconstraint-Revised
NEGE-r	Negative Emotionality/Neuroticism-Revised
INTR-r	Introversion/Low Positive Emotionality-Revised

FIGURE 4   Robert's MMPI-A-RF Score Report, continued.

MMPI-A-RF T SCORES (BY DOMAIN)

PROTOCOL VALIDITY

Content Non-Responsiveness

0	52	75 F	58
CNS	VRIN-r	TRIN-r	CRIN

Over-Reporting

48
F-r

Under-Reporting

56	72
L-r	K-r

SUBSTANTIVE SCALES

Somatic/Cognitive Dysfunction

49	52	44	41	53	40
RC1	MLS	GIC	HPC	NUC	COG

Emotional Dysfunction

39							
EID							

45	47	48	39
RCd	HLP	SFD	NFC

69	54
RC2	INTR-r

32	38	49	41	43	43	50	40
RC7	OCS	STW	AXY	ANP	BRF	SPF	NEGE-r

Thought Dysfunction

37
THD

37
RC6

42
RC8

50
PSYC-r

Behavioral Dysfunction

35
BXD

36	45	33	38	42	40
RC4	NSA	ASA	CNP	SUB	NPI

39	34	37	30
RC9	AGG	AGGR-r	DISC-r

Interpersonal Functioning

33	32	83	60	39	41
FML	RC3	IPP	SAV	SHY	DSF

Note. This information is provided to facilitate interpretation following the recommended structure for MMPI-A-RF interpretation in Chapter 7 of the *MMPI-A-RF Administration, Scoring, Interpretation, and Technical Manual*, which provides details in the text and an outline in Table 7-1.

FIGURE 4 Robert's MMPI-A-RF Score Report, continued.

MMPI-A-RF

Robert was given the MMPI-A-RF. Because he is 18, he could have been administered the MMPI-2-RF or the MMPI-A-RF. The MMPI-A-RF was chosen because Robert continues to be primarily supported by his family and has not yet functioned independently. Robert's MMPI-A-RF protocol was valid and interpretable. The comparison group used was composed of 6,851 psychiatric outpatient boys.

Robert's MMPI-A-RF, with an elevation on COG, indicated a diffuse pattern of cognitive complaints with attention problems, difficulties with concentration, and slowed speech. These findings are very consistent with his presentation in the interview as well as his history.

His protocol contained elevations on Specific Problems scales STW (Stress and Worry), AXY (Anxiety), ANP (Anger Proneness), and SPF (Specific Fears). This indicates that Robert reported feeling anxious and as having many specific fears. He also reported an above-average level of stress and worry and likely has problems with sleeplessness. He also reports a high level of anger problems including being impatient and irritable. He may make verbal threats. Robert also reported multiple fears and phobias.

Robert also generated an elevation on NFC, indicating that he is likely indecisive and ineffective in coping with difficulties. He is also likely very passive and tends to procrastinate.

There were no indications of Thought Dysfunction, Behavioral Dysfunction, or Internalizing Dysfunction in Robert's MMPI-A-RF results.

Diagnostic considerations indicated by Robert's MMPI-A-RF results include ADHD and related neurodevelopment disorders, anxiety-related disorders, disruptive impulse-control disorders, and specific phobias.

Assets to assist in treatment suggested by the MMPI-A-RF were that he does not appear to have significant problems with thought dysfunction. Although he has trouble with his anger, he does not appear to have indications of antisocial behavioral tendencies or severe disconstraint. He is not disinterested in people nor is he cynical about them, which can be helpful in establishing a therapeutic relationship.

Diagnosis

Robert was given the diagnoses of Attention Deficit Hyperactivity Disorder, Combined Type, as well as Unspecified Anxiety Disorder.

OUTCOME

Robert was seen for 15 sessions in cognitive behavioral therapy and also in social skills and anger management groups. Given the anxiety identified on the MMPI-A-RF, he was prescribed an SSRI. He terminated successfully and was seen for one follow-up session about 90 days later and reported that he continued to do well.

Sally

A Youth With Opioid Use Disorder

BACKGROUND

Sally is a 15-year-old female referred by her outpatient therapist for diagnostic assessment and treatment recommendations. She lives with her parents and has a history of testing positive for opioids on random drug screens.

Interview With Youth

Sally reported that she lives "on and off with my parents," indicating that her parents have periodically separated and currently do not live together. Asked why she thought that she was being seen by the examiner, Sally said, "They say I have problems—I got involved with Drug Court and I am court ordered not to hang out with my ex-boyfriend."

Sally indicated that she is the youngest of three children born to her parents, whom she said are no longer living together but are not yet divorced. She said she "just found out that my father had an affair" and she is angry with him, reporting a history of conflict. She described herself as a "Daddy's girl" and described an otherwise positive relationship with her father. She also described a positive relationship with her older brother, who is now serving in the United States Air Force.

Sally said that she moved to a new city about a year ago and she does not like having to move. She indicated that she has made friends in "all groups" and acknowledged that she tends to associate with youth who have behavioral and substance abuse problems but said that she is trying to change her peer groups to more positive youth. Sally reported that she enjoys playing softball, X-Box, and computers.

Sally is now in the ninth grade. She indicated that she does not like school and described her peers as "judgmental—too much drama." Sally said she was expelled from her last school after she assaulted a female peer. She indicated that while her grades are generally very poor, she is not in special education and attributes her poor performance to behavioral problems. Sally said that she has frequently been suspended for conduct problems such as skipping classes, smoking marijuana, smoking cigarettes, and being disruptive. She related that her career goal is to join the Navy and later pursue cosmetology (indicating that her grades are too poor for her to enter into a career academy while still in high school).

Sally denied present substance abuse, stating that the court is too closely monitoring her. She acknowledged a history of cannabis use beginning in the fifth grade, which progressed to daily use until the eighth grade. She began drinking alcohol in the sixth grade but said that she did not drink often, preferring marijuana. She also acknowledged abuse of heroin, cocaine, and LSD and prescription pills, saying that she preferred using prescription pain pills or heroin. She stated that she has been in various substance abuse treatment programs but indicated that she did not think she needs more treatment because she has "heard it all before."

Sally alleged that a neighbor sexually molested her when she was 10. She reported that she disclosed this to a counselor, but the abuse allegations were never substantiated.

Sally denied any history of child welfare involvement or out-of-home placement in residential treatment. She also denied any history of fire-setting or animal cruelty.

Sally said that her first juvenile court involvement was at the age of 14 for misdemeanor theft and she was placed in community service though the court did not accept her community service as being satisfactory. She said that she has subsequently had charges for assault and truancy as well as multiple probation violations for positive drug tests, skipping school and curfew, indicating that she "can't count" the number of times that she has been held in detention.

Sally said that she first entered outpatient treatment in the fifth grade. She has just started with a new therapist but said, "I want to stop counseling because it is pointless—I already know everything—I'm mentally stable."

Sally reported that she has had three inpatient treatment episodes. In the fifth grade, she was admitted for self-injurious behaviors, in the eighth grade for an "accidental overdose—but part of me wanted to do it," and in the ninth grade for an "accidental overdose of pills," indicating that she was hospitalized for that and has also been seen in the crisis unit at the local hospital. She said that she thinks that the cutting behavior was the result of her abuse and that she stopped "2 years ago." She is unaware of any family history of mental illness.

Sally denied any significant medical problems. She said that she is not currently taking any medication but has in the past been prescribed Adderall, Zoloft, Geodon, Cymbalta, and Prozac. She said that she has never been medically hospitalized and denied any history of head trauma, loss of consciousness, and any other neurological involvement.

COLLATERAL INFORMATION

Sally's parents reported that she "moves back and forth" between their residences. Sally's mother said that her pregnancy and delivery with Sally was nonremarkable. She was 20 when she gave birth to Sally. Gestation was full term, and the pregnancy was planned. Sally was a healthy infant who achieved developmental milestones normally. She attended kindergarten and elementary school in another school district and did generally well. However, she had considerable separation anxiety. There were no behavioral problems.

When she entered middle school, Sally began to have frequent behavioral problems and was initially bullied but later bullied other youth. It was at that time that she disclosed the alleged sexual abuse. Sally has not had an IEP. In the sixth and eighth grades, she "barely passed" and made generally "minimal" effort in school with behavior that is described as "defiant, not listening and some fighting." She was expelled, as noted earlier, for fighting. Initially, when she entered high school she did better; however, she has subsequently associated with negative peers and has continued to have suspensions for skipping class and smoking.

Sally's parents reported that she was involved with juvenile court for theft, truancy, and assaulting a student while on probation. She has been in juvenile detention about three or four times and has had numerous probation violations. She is involved in drug court and uses "pot and pills." They said, "she knows the system and how to play it." Sally is now in an intensive outpatient program and is doing better but they believe that she still "needs to be on the right medications" for her anxiety and depression.

In her first psychiatric hospitalization, Sally was admitted following a suicide attempt involving overdosing on pills. Upon admission, she had reported that she was planning on taking more pills and would cut her wrists if that didn't kill her. She also reported that she recently disclosed ongoing sexual abuse by her cousin to her outpatient therapist and that there was an ongoing investigation. The discharge diagnosis was Major Depression, Recurrent, Severe, Without Psychotic Features and Posttraumatic Stress Disorder. The discharge medications were Seroquel and Cymbalta.

Her next inpatient stay was for suicidal ideation and an overdose on Prozac and Adderall. It noted that she alluded to constant arguments with her mother and that she felt unwanted by her. It was also reported that she had been previously in outpatient mental health and substance abuse counseling and had been abusing marijuana and prescription pain medicines. It was noted that she had a history of sexual abuse and a family history that was positive for substance abuse. She was diagnosed with ADHD and Major Depressive Disorder as well as antisocial personality traits.

Sally's current treatment records indicate that she was admitted to an intensive outpatient program. Admission diagnoses were Hallucinogen Abuse, Sedative Hypnotic or Anxiolytic Abuse, Cannabis Dependence, Alcohol Dependence, and Opioid Dependence.

Her current therapist told the examiner that she has seen Sally in various settings and now sees her in therapy at a private clinic. Her therapist said that a focus of therapy remains Sally's poor choices—such as sexual acting out. Although the diagnosis currently is Oppositional Defiant Disorder, her clinical impression is that the issues are much deeper than that and are related to Sally's abuse victimization and a lack of responsiveness by her family when she reported being sexually abused.

Current Behavioral Status

Sally was appropriately dressed and groomed in clothing that was neat, clean, and appropriately arranged. Her hygiene and grooming were adequate.

There were no overt indications of loosening of associations, flight of ideas, or tangentiality. Sally's psychomotor activity was nonremarkable. Her speech was normal in tone, pacing, and volume. Her attention span was characterized by at least a moderate degree of distraction. Her manner of social interaction was outwardly friendly, polite, and cooperative but tended to be primarily superficially cooperative and manipulative and markedly interpersonally dramatic.

Sally presented with an appropriate and expressive affect and stated "good" mood. When asked to rate her subjective level of distress (SUDS) she described her present degree of emotional upset as being a 7/8 out of a possible 10, ascribing her emotional discomfort to "drug court and probation."

There were no overt indications of hallucinations, delusions, or paranoia (symptoms of serious mental illness or loss of contact with reality). Sally gave no behavioral evidence of visual, gustatory, olfactory, or tactile hallucinations. She gave no behavioral evidence of hearing or responding to hallucinations during any of the examinations.

Sally denied and gave no evidence of specific delusional thinking (ideas of thought broadcasting/thought insertion). She gave no evidence of systematic paranoid delusions or grandiosity—other than to say that she believes that she is being followed. Accordingly, there appears to be no overt clinical or behavioral evidence in the content of her thought as would be typically seen with seriously mentally ill adolescents.

Sally denied symptoms typically associated with depression such as limited appetite, hopelessness, loss of interest or pleasure, loss of sexual interest, but did complain of poor sleep, loss of sexual desire, difficulty in concentration, and increased irritability, which are often symptoms associated with depression. Also, upon specific inquiry, she denied active suicidal ideation, intent, or plan. She also denied homicidal ideation.

When asked to describe any history of mood swings, Sally stated that throughout her life, she has experienced rapidly changing moods and she complained of past racing thoughts. Asked to describe this, she said, "I used to have them—I blacked out a lot. I went crazy. I would cuss out teachers and beat up people." She said that the last time she had such a "blackout" was in the eighth grade. Asked about her mood swings, Sally said that she will quickly become angry but then added, "I can control it better now."

Sally reported normative phobias of snakes and spiders but denied any intrusive obsessive thinking or compulsive behavior. When asked about "flashbacks" and other symptoms associated with trauma exposure, she endorsed having flashbacks in the past, saying, "I used to have them, but they stopped when my stepsister left," telling me that she had a number of conflicts with her stepsister and that these would serve as a trigger for flashbacks of the earlier abuse she had suffered. She reported that she still experiences nightmares.

Sally was alert and responsive to her environment and there were no problems observed with her attention or concentration. She was oriented to time, place, person, and situation. Her fund of general information suggested average to below average intellectual functioning.

Sally's concentration was adequate as evidenced by her attention and focus in the conversation with the examiner. Her immediate recall was adequate as demonstrated by her ability to recall five digits forward and three in reverse order. Concentration was also demonstrated to be adequate by her ability to perform simple mental calculations. Her short-term recall was adequate as demonstrated by her ability to recall three items from memory after a 10-minute distraction. She also showed limited capacity for verbal abstract reasoning as demonstrated in her ability to state conceptual similarities between related objects and concepts but was somewhat concrete in that she had difficulty with more complex abstractions. She demonstrated an ability to interpret commonly used proverbs. Her insight and judgment did appear to be limited as determined by both her history and response to situational questions.

On the K-BIT 2, Sally earned a Vocabulary score of 82. She earned a Nonverbal standard score of 91. Her overall Composite IQ standard score was 89.

Sally was also given the Slosson Oral Reading Test. Her score indicated that she reads at the 7.3 grade level, which is below her current grade placement.

MMPI-A-RF

Sally's MMPI-A-RF protocol was compared to a reference group of 4,848 psychiatric outpatient girls. Her Validity scale scores indicate that she responded relevantly and consistently to the test items and there is no indication of overreporting. Her score of 60 on K-r indicated possible underreporting, as it is uncommon in psychiatric outpatients. Sally presented herself as being well adjusted. Because Sally in fact has had several significant problems, this finding indicates that any absence of elevations on the Substantive scales should be interpreted with caution as they may underestimate the actual level of Sally's problems.

Sally's protocol did not reflect problems in the Somatic/Cognitive, Emotional and Thought Dysfunction domains. However, because of the potential of underreporting, problems in these areas cannot be ruled out, especially given her clinical history.

As might be expected with Sally's history of acting out and substance abuse, she was found to have a significant elevation on one of the Specific Problems

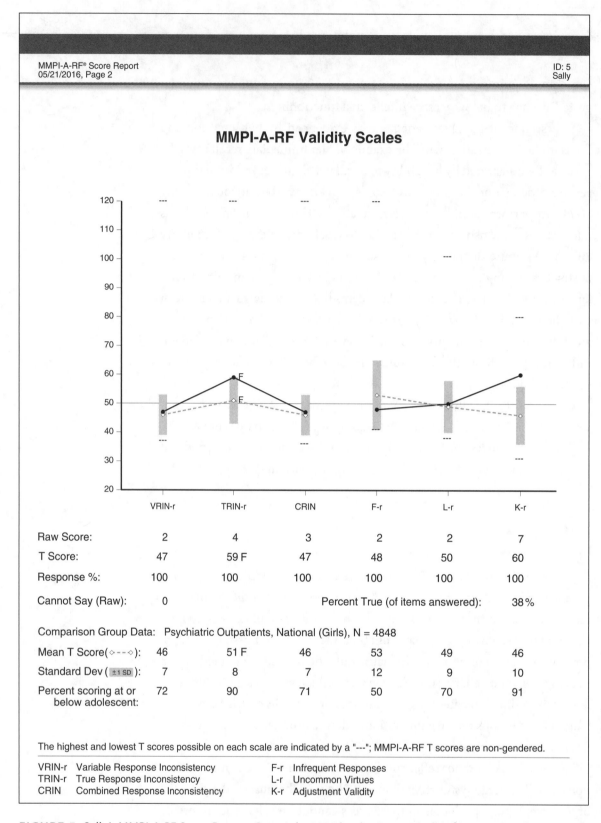

MMPI-A-RF Validity Scales

	VRIN-r	TRIN-r	CRIN	F-r	L-r	K-r
Raw Score:	2	4	3	2	2	7
T Score:	47	59 F	47	48	50	60
Response %:	100	100	100	100	100	100

Cannot Say (Raw): 0   Percent True (of items answered): 38%

Comparison Group Data: Psychiatric Outpatients, National (Girls), N = 4848

	VRIN-r	TRIN-r	CRIN	F-r	L-r	K-r
Mean T Score(◇---◇):	46	51 F	46	53	49	46
Standard Dev (±1 SD):	7	8	7	12	9	10
Percent scoring at or below adolescent:	72	90	71	50	70	91

The highest and lowest T scores possible on each scale are indicated by a "---"; MMPI-A-RF T scores are non-gendered.

VRIN-r	Variable Response Inconsistency	F-r	Infrequent Responses
TRIN-r	True Response Inconsistency	L-r	Uncommon Virtues
CRIN	Combined Response Inconsistency	K-r	Adjustment Validity

FIGURE 5 Sally's MMPI-A-RF Score Report. Copyright 2016 by the Regents of the University of Minnesota. All rights reserved.

MMPI-A-RF Higher-Order (H-O) and Restructured Clinical (RC) Scales

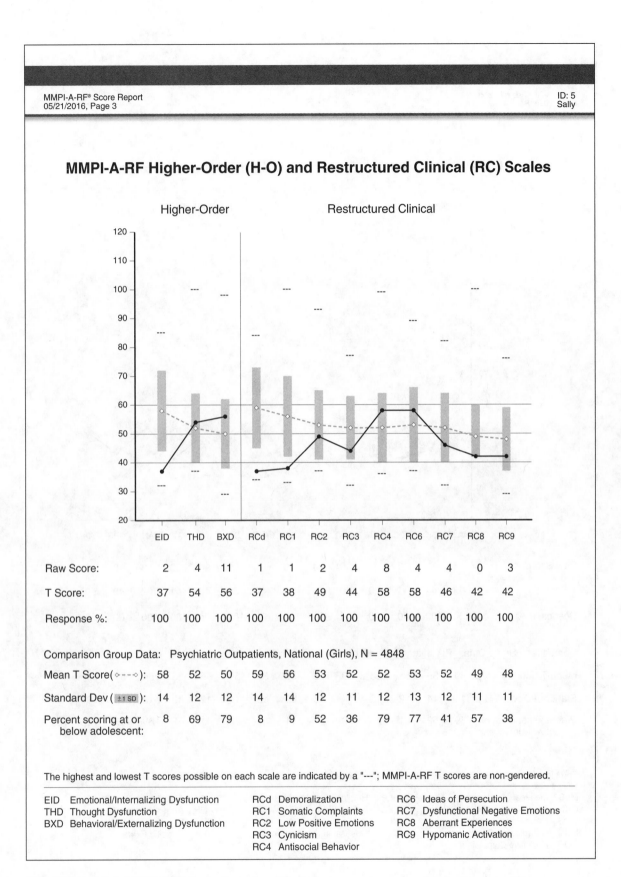

	EID	THD	BXD	RCd	RC1	RC2	RC3	RC4	RC6	RC7	RC8	RC9
Raw Score:	2	4	11	1	1	2	4	8	4	4	0	3
T Score:	37	54	56	37	38	49	44	58	58	46	42	42
Response %:	100	100	100	100	100	100	100	100	100	100	100	100

Comparison Group Data: Psychiatric Outpatients, National (Girls), N = 4848

	EID	THD	BXD	RCd	RC1	RC2	RC3	RC4	RC6	RC7	RC8	RC9
Mean T Score(◇- - -◇):	58	52	50	59	56	53	52	52	53	52	49	48
Standard Dev (±1 SD):	14	12	12	14	14	12	11	12	13	12	11	11
Percent scoring at or below adolescent:	8	69	79	8	9	52	36	79	77	41	57	38

The highest and lowest T scores possible on each scale are indicated by a "---"; MMPI-A-RF T scores are non-gendered.

EID Emotional/Internalizing Dysfunction	RCd Demoralization	RC6 Ideas of Persecution
THD Thought Dysfunction	RC1 Somatic Complaints	RC7 Dysfunctional Negative Emotions
BXD Behavioral/Externalizing Dysfunction	RC2 Low Positive Emotions	RC8 Aberrant Experiences
	RC3 Cynicism	RC9 Hypomanic Activation
	RC4 Antisocial Behavior	

FIGURE 5 Sally's MMPI-A-RF Score Report, continued.

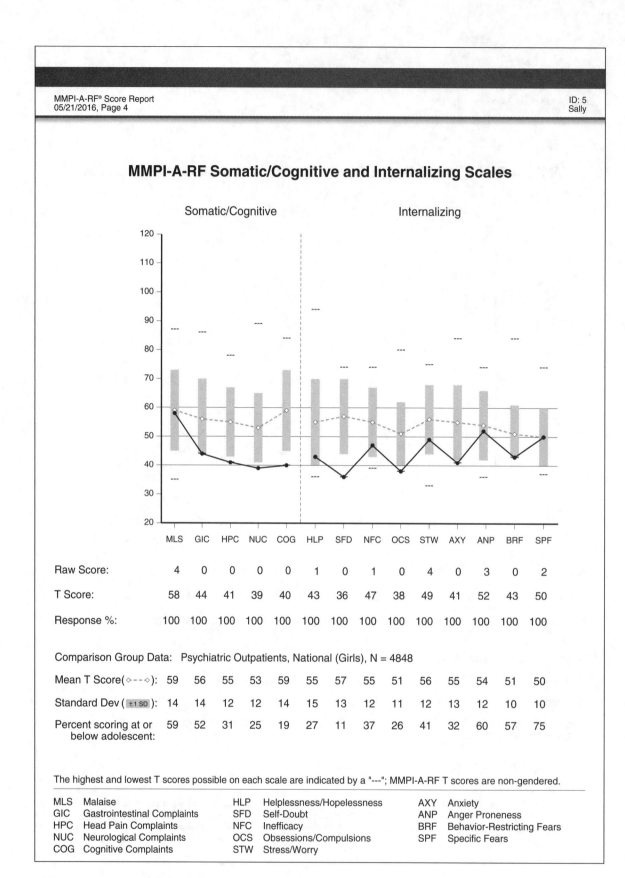

MMPI-A-RF Somatic/Cognitive and Internalizing Scales

Somatic/Cognitive   Internalizing

	MLS	GIC	HPC	NUC	COG	HLP	SFD	NFC	OCS	STW	AXY	ANP	BRF	SPF
Raw Score:	4	0	0	0	0	1	0	1	0	4	0	3	0	2
T Score:	58	44	41	39	40	43	36	47	38	49	41	52	43	50
Response %:	100	100	100	100	100	100	100	100	100	100	100	100	100	100

Comparison Group Data: Psychiatric Outpatients, National (Girls), N = 4848

	MLS	GIC	HPC	NUC	COG	HLP	SFD	NFC	OCS	STW	AXY	ANP	BRF	SPF
Mean T Score(◇--◇):	59	56	55	53	59	55	57	55	51	56	55	54	51	50
Standard Dev (±1 SD):	14	14	12	12	14	15	13	12	11	12	13	12	10	10
Percent scoring at or below adolescent:	59	52	31	25	19	27	11	37	26	41	32	60	57	75

The highest and lowest T scores possible on each scale are indicated by a "---"; MMPI-A-RF T scores are non-gendered.

MLS	Malaise	HLP	Helplessness/Hopelessness	AXY	Anxiety
GIC	Gastrointestinal Complaints	SFD	Self-Doubt	ANP	Anger Proneness
HPC	Head Pain Complaints	NFC	Inefficacy	BRF	Behavior-Restricting Fears
NUC	Neurological Complaints	OCS	Obsessions/Compulsions	SPF	Specific Fears
COG	Cognitive Complaints	STW	Stress/Worry		

FIGURE 5 Sally's MMPI-A-RF Score Report, continued.

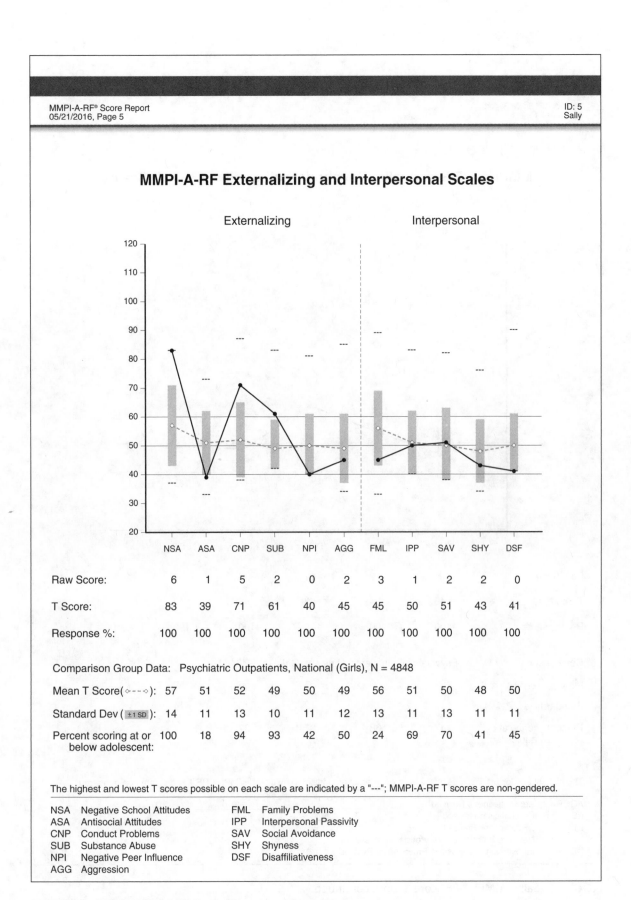

MMPI-A-RF Externalizing and Interpersonal Scales

Externalizing Interpersonal

	NSA	ASA	CNP	SUB	NPI	AGG	FML	IPP	SAV	SHY	DSF
Raw Score:	6	1	5	2	0	2	3	1	2	2	0
T Score:	83	39	71	61	40	45	45	50	51	43	41
Response %:	100	100	100	100	100	100	100	100	100	100	100

Comparison Group Data: Psychiatric Outpatients, National (Girls), N = 4848

	NSA	ASA	CNP	SUB	NPI	AGG	FML	IPP	SAV	SHY	DSF
Mean T Score(◇---◇):	57	51	52	49	50	49	56	51	50	48	50
Standard Dev (±1 SD):	14	11	13	10	11	12	13	11	13	11	11
Percent scoring at or below adolescent:	100	18	94	93	42	50	24	69	70	41	45

The highest and lowest T scores possible on each scale are indicated by a "---"; MMPI-A-RF T scores are non-gendered.

NSA	Negative School Attitudes	FML	Family Problems
ASA	Antisocial Attitudes	IPP	Interpersonal Passivity
CNP	Conduct Problems	SAV	Social Avoidance
SUB	Substance Abuse	SHY	Shyness
NPI	Negative Peer Influence	DSF	Disaffiliativeness
AGG	Aggression		

FIGURE 5 Sally's MMPI-A-RF Score Report, continued.

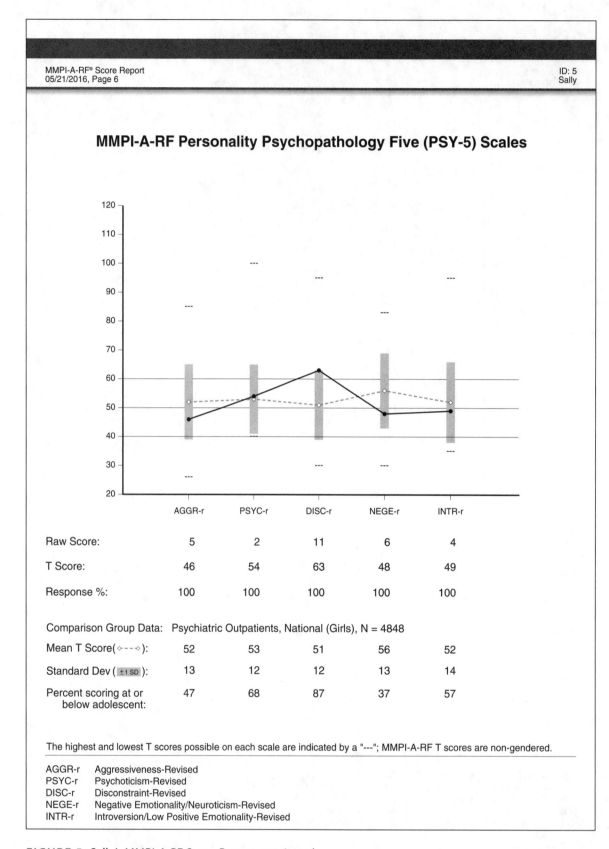

MMPI-A-RF Personality Psychopathology Five (PSY-5) Scales

	AGGR-r	PSYC-r	DISC-r	NEGE-r	INTR-r
Raw Score:	5	2	11	6	4
T Score:	46	54	63	48	49
Response %:	100	100	100	100	100

Comparison Group Data: Psychiatric Outpatients, National (Girls), N = 4848

	AGGR-r	PSYC-r	DISC-r	NEGE-r	INTR-r
Mean T Score(◇- - -◇):	52	53	51	56	52
Standard Dev (±1 SD):	13	12	12	13	14
Percent scoring at or below adolescent:	47	68	87	37	57

The highest and lowest T scores possible on each scale are indicated by a "---"; MMPI-A-RF T scores are non-gendered.

AGGR-r	Aggressiveness-Revised
PSYC-r	Psychoticism-Revised
DISC-r	Disconstraint-Revised
NEGE-r	Negative Emotionality/Neuroticism-Revised
INTR-r	Introversion/Low Positive Emotionality-Revised

FIGURE 5 Sally's MMPI-A-RF Score Report, continued.

MMPI-A-RF T SCORES (BY DOMAIN)

PROTOCOL VALIDITY

Content Non-Responsiveness

0	47	59 F	47
CNS	VRIN-r	TRIN-r	CRIN

Over-Reporting

48
F-r

Under-Reporting

50	60
L-r	K-r

SUBSTANTIVE SCALES

Somatic/Cognitive Dysfunction

38	58	44	41	39	40
RC1	MLS	GIC	HPC	NUC	COG

Emotional Dysfunction

37
EID

37	43	36	47
RCd	HLP	SFD	NFC

49	49
RC2	INTR-r

46	38	49	41	52	43	50	48
RC7	OCS	STW	AXY	ANP	BRF	SPF	NEGE-r

Thought Dysfunction

54
THD

58
RC6

42
RC8

54
PSYC-r

Behavioral Dysfunction

56
BXD

58	83	39	71	61	40
RC4	NSA	ASA	CNP	SUB	NPI

42	45	46	63
RC9	AGG	AGGR-r	DISC-r

Interpersonal Functioning

45	44	50	51	43	41
FML	RC3	IPP	SAV	SHY	DSF

Note. This information is provided to facilitate interpretation following the recommended structure for MMPI-A-RF interpretation in Chapter 7 of the *MMPI-A-RF Administration, Scoring, Interpretation, and Technical Manual*, which provides details in the text and an outline in Table 7-1.

FIGURE 5 Sally's MMPI-A-RF Score Report, continued.

scales that comprise the behavioral dysfunction domain (CNP). She reported a very negative attitude toward school and is likely to have a history of poor academic achievement, behavioral problems in school, and conflicts with authority figures. She may also experience test anxiety, have poor study habits, and be difficult to motivate. Sally likely would prefer to associate with her friends rather than attend school and most probably views school as being boring and a waste of her time.

In addition, as indicated by elevations on CNP (Conduct Problems) and DISC-r (Disconstraint) Sally reports multiple conduct problems that likely include physical aggression, theft, truancy, oppositional and defiant behavior, and running away from home, findings that are well-documented in her history. Her behavioral problems have likely brought her to the attention of authorities such as court and school disciplinary staff. Finally, her elevation on SUB reflects Sally's history of polysubstance abuse and is similar to that of youth who have had residential treatment for substance abuse. Sally also likely tends to associate with a negative peer group.

The MMPI-A-RF results point to possible diagnoses of Conduct Disorder and a Substance Abuse Disorder for further consideration. However, in light of the underreporting discussed earlier, other diagnoses cannot be ruled out.

Critical in Sally's treatment will be the need to address the potential underreporting that may manifest as defensiveness and denial in therapy. In light of her history of having been abused, Sally's underreporting may have roots in her trauma victimization. While the MMPI-A-RF cannot rule in or rule out abuse, especially given the underreporting, it can still be of treatment planning value. Youth who have been abused may act out behaviorally and may, understandably, be guarded and defensive. The combination of her underreporting, acting out, and trauma victimization suggests that any treatment approach be trauma informed.

Sally's tendency to act out and her substance abuse should be addressed in treatment. Because of her underreporting and her statements to the examiner that she does not see mental health counseling as helpful, it is suggested that initial treatment be problem focused and give her specific tools and techniques as well as problem-solving skills. Owing both to her oppositional features as well as her underreporting and history of trauma, it is quite possible that an insight-oriented approach will not be successful and may actually result in her either leaving treatment early or only superficially cooperating until she is no longer mandated to attend.

Diagnosis

Sally was given the diagnoses of Unspecified Disruptive, Conduct and Impulse Control Behavior Disorder; Unspecified Anxiety Disorder-Rule Out Post-traumatic Stress Disorder (unconfirmed allegations of abuse); Alcohol Use Disorder, Severe; Cannabis Use Disorder, Severe; and Opioid Use Disorder Severe.

OUTCOME

It was recommended that Sally continue in outpatient therapy and also be referred back to an intensive outpatient program. Residential treatment was recommended if she tested positive for drugs. Family therapy, using intensive home-based models such as Multisystemic Therapy (Borduin et al., 1990), was recommended as well as a referral to a mentoring program. It was also recommended that all treatment follow a trauma-informed model. Given her reluctance to engage in more mental health counseling, it was recommended that her individual therapist focus upon practical skills and problem-solving. Sally completed the intensive outpatient program and follow-up with home-based services. She has had episodes of relapse into substance abuse but has been able to stabilize and has not required additional residential treatment.

Sam

A Youth With Attention Deficit Hyperactivity Disorder and Depression

BACKGROUND

Sam is a 17-year-old high school junior who was referred by his pediatrician for consultation about his diagnosis and treatment needs.

COLLATERAL INFORMATION

Sam is the youngest of five sons and lives with his parents. His mother reported that her pregnancy and delivery with Sam were nonremarkable and that he achieved developmental milestones normally. He does not have a significant medical history and there is no history of head trauma, seizure, or other neurological problems. He has been treated in the past for ADHD.

Sam had surgery to correct hearing deficits as a child. He was described by his mother as being somewhat slower in gross motor skills, and that he has always been "very, very shy." He showed separation anxiety through the fourth grade and had considerable problems separating from his parents at bedtime until he was about 7 years old. There is a family history of depression as well as attention deficit and learning difficulties with mathematics. Sam gets along very well with his siblings and his parents. There has been no history of any behavioral problems either at home or in school.

Sam has not received special educational services while in school. He has struggled with self-esteem as well as deciding whether to play baseball, eventually deciding not to this year, which he believes was the right choice for him.

Current Behavioral Status

Sam was appropriately dressed and groomed. His hygiene was adequate. There were no overt indications of loosening of associations, flight of ideas, or tangentiality. His psychomotor activity was nonremarkable. His speech was normal in tone, pacing, and volume. His attention span was adequate. His manner of social interaction was friendly, polite, and cooperative.

Sam presented with an appropriate and expressive affect to a reported neutral mood. There were no overt indications of hallucinations, delusions, or paranoia. He denied current depression as well as any disturbances in his sleep, health, or appetite. He did acknowledge a history of poor self-esteem as well as struggling making decisions and staying focused. He also acknowledged overeating when he feels depressed. Sam denied suicidal or homicidal ideation. He was future oriented. He did not appear hopeless and had social support. He did not present with symptoms of anxiety, phobias, obsessions, or compulsions. His recall functions were clinically intact. He was oriented to time, place, person, and situation. Insight and judgment were adequate for his age.

On the WAIS IV, Sam was found to have a Verbal Comprehension Index of 107. His Working Memory Index was 111. His Processing Speed Index was 97. Overall, his Full-Scale IQ score was 110. The WIAT III scores were all in the average range with no significant learning problems identified.

Sam's mother and five of his teachers rated him on the Devereaux Scales of Mental Disorders. Significant findings were seen in each rating on scales measuring Attention, Depression, and Anxiety.

MMPI-A-RF

Sam's MMPI-A-RF was valid. He responded appropriately to the item content. There were no indications of either over- or underreporting. His scores on the MMPI-A-RF measures of inconsistent responding were considerably below average, an uncommon finding for youth tested in psychiatric treatment settings, and noteworthy because of his history of ADHD diagnosis. The comparison group used was 6,851 outpatient boys.

Of greatest concern in Sam's protocol were scores associated with risk for suicidal ideation or behavior. Sam's elevations on HLP (Helplessness/Hopelessness), SFD (Self-Doubt), and NEGE-r (Negative Emotionality)

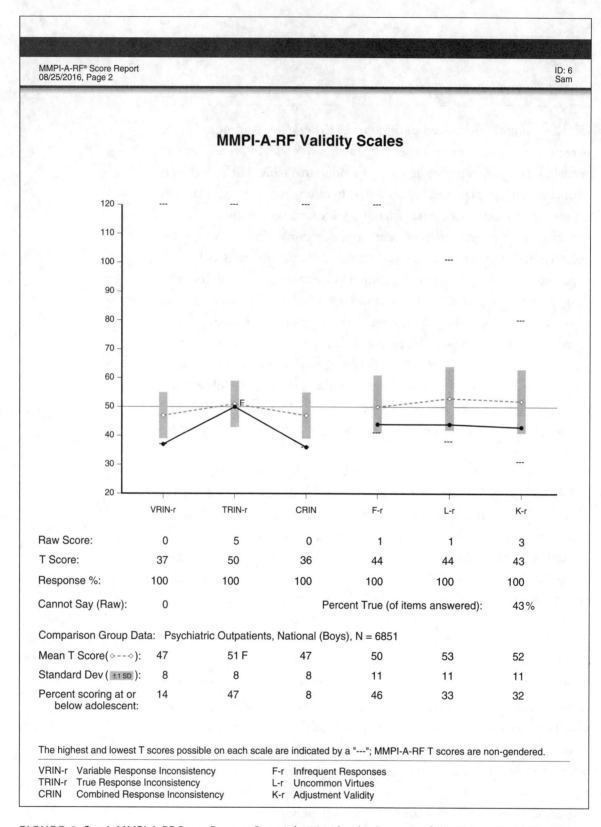

MMPI-A-RF Validity Scales

	VRIN-r	TRIN-r	CRIN	F-r	L-r	K-r
Raw Score:	0	5	0	1	1	3
T Score:	37	50	36	44	44	43
Response %:	100	100	100	100	100	100

Cannot Say (Raw): 0   Percent True (of items answered): 43%

Comparison Group Data: Psychiatric Outpatients, National (Boys), N = 6851

	VRIN-r	TRIN-r	CRIN	F-r	L-r	K-r
Mean T Score(◇---◇):	47	51 F	47	50	53	52
Standard Dev (±1 SD):	8	8	8	11	11	11
Percent scoring at or below adolescent:	14	47	8	46	33	32

The highest and lowest T scores possible on each scale are indicated by a "---"; MMPI-A-RF T scores are non-gendered.

VRIN-r	Variable Response Inconsistency	F-r	Infrequent Responses
TRIN-r	True Response Inconsistency	L-r	Uncommon Virtues
CRIN	Combined Response Inconsistency	K-r	Adjustment Validity

FIGURE 6 Sam's MMPI-A-RF Score Report.

MMPI-A-RF Higher-Order (H-O) and Restructured Clinical (RC) Scales

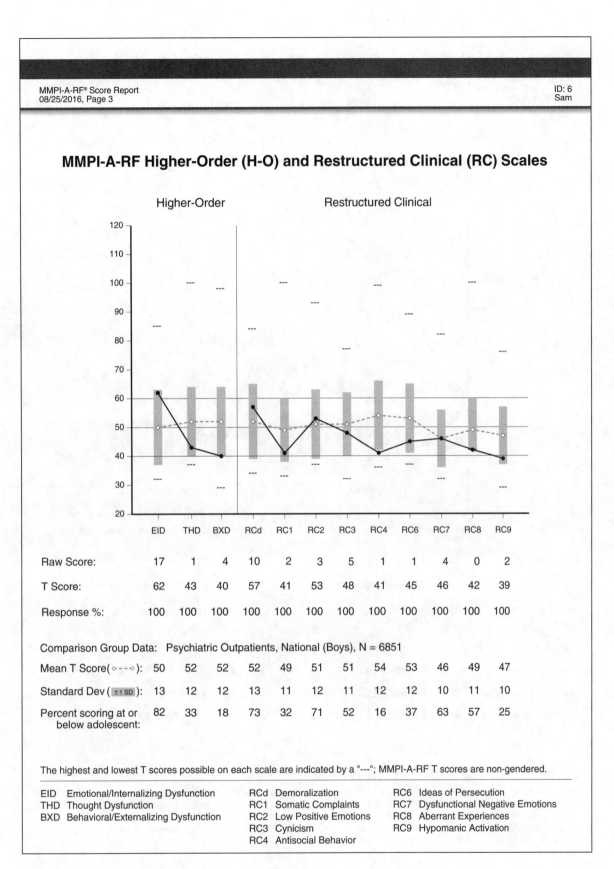

	EID	THD	BXD	RCd	RC1	RC2	RC3	RC4	RC6	RC7	RC8	RC9
Raw Score:	17	1	4	10	2	3	5	1	1	4	0	2
T Score:	62	43	40	57	41	53	48	41	45	46	42	39
Response %:	100	100	100	100	100	100	100	100	100	100	100	100

Comparison Group Data: Psychiatric Outpatients, National (Boys), N = 6851

	EID	THD	BXD	RCd	RC1	RC2	RC3	RC4	RC6	RC7	RC8	RC9
Mean T Score(◇--◇):	50	52	52	52	49	51	51	54	53	46	49	47
Standard Dev (±1 SD):	13	12	12	13	11	12	11	12	12	10	11	10
Percent scoring at or below adolescent:	82	33	18	73	32	71	52	16	37	63	57	25

The highest and lowest T scores possible on each scale are indicated by a "---"; MMPI-A-RF T scores are non-gendered.

EID	Emotional/Internalizing Dysfunction	RCd	Demoralization
THD	Thought Dysfunction	RC1	Somatic Complaints
BXD	Behavioral/Externalizing Dysfunction	RC2	Low Positive Emotions
		RC3	Cynicism
		RC4	Antisocial Behavior

RC6	Ideas of Persecution
RC7	Dysfunctional Negative Emotions
RC8	Aberrant Experiences
RC9	Hypomanic Activation

FIGURE 6 Sam's MMPI-A-RF Score Report, continued.

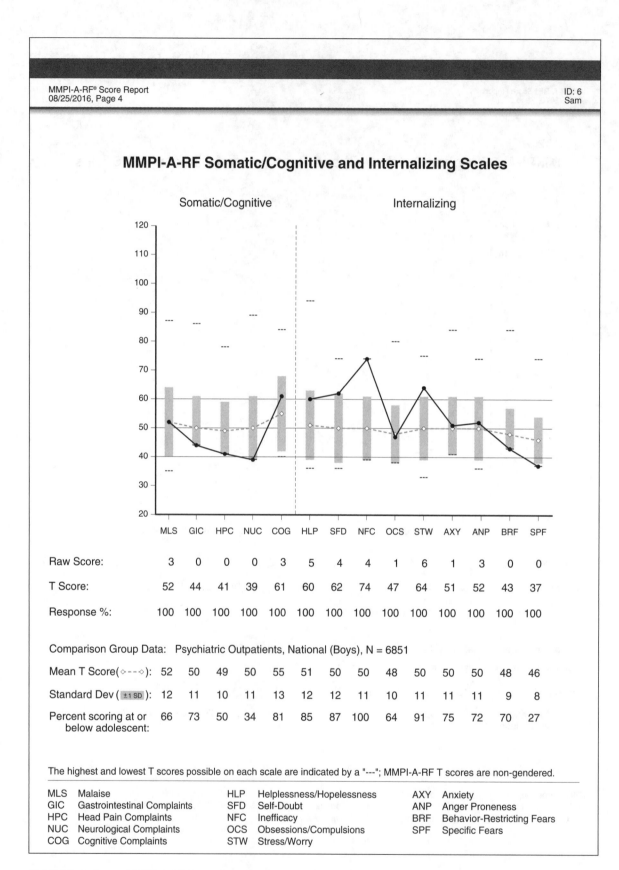

MMPI-A-RF Somatic/Cognitive and Internalizing Scales

	MLS	GIC	HPC	NUC	COG	HLP	SFD	NFC	OCS	STW	AXY	ANP	BRF	SPF
Raw Score:	3	0	0	0	3	5	4	4	1	6	1	3	0	0
T Score:	52	44	41	39	61	60	62	74	47	64	51	52	43	37
Response %:	100	100	100	100	100	100	100	100	100	100	100	100	100	100

Comparison Group Data: Psychiatric Outpatients, National (Boys), N = 6851

Mean T Score(◇--◇):	52	50	49	50	55	51	50	50	48	50	50	50	48	46
Standard Dev (±1 SD):	12	11	10	11	13	12	12	11	10	11	11	11	9	8
Percent scoring at or below adolescent:	66	73	50	34	81	85	87	100	64	91	75	72	70	27

The highest and lowest T scores possible on each scale are indicated by a "---"; MMPI-A-RF T scores are non-gendered.

MLS	Malaise	HLP	Helplessness/Hopelessness
GIC	Gastrointestinal Complaints	SFD	Self-Doubt
HPC	Head Pain Complaints	NFC	Inefficacy
NUC	Neurological Complaints	OCS	Obsessions/Compulsions
COG	Cognitive Complaints	STW	Stress/Worry

AXY	Anxiety
ANP	Anger Proneness
BRF	Behavior-Restricting Fears
SPF	Specific Fears

FIGURE 6   Sam's MMPI-A-RF Score Report, continued.

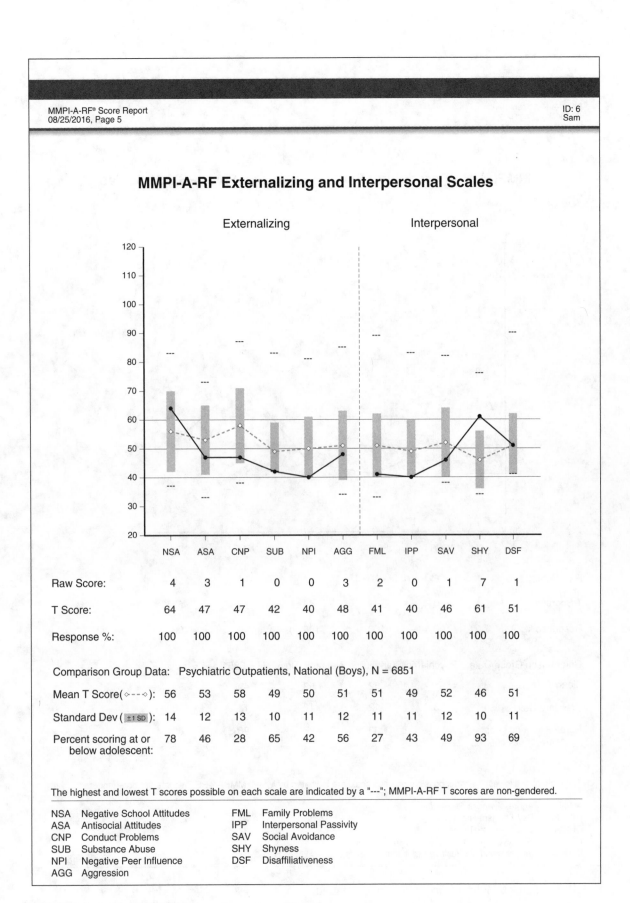

MMPI-A-RF Externalizing and Interpersonal Scales

	NSA	ASA	CNP	SUB	NPI	AGG	FML	IPP	SAV	SHY	DSF
Raw Score:	4	3	1	0	0	3	2	0	1	7	1
T Score:	64	47	47	42	40	48	41	40	46	61	51
Response %:	100	100	100	100	100	100	100	100	100	100	100

Comparison Group Data: Psychiatric Outpatients, National (Boys), N = 6851

	NSA	ASA	CNP	SUB	NPI	AGG	FML	IPP	SAV	SHY	DSF
Mean T Score(◇---◇):	56	53	58	49	50	51	51	49	52	46	51
Standard Dev (±1 SD):	14	12	13	10	11	12	11	11	12	10	11
Percent scoring at or below adolescent:	78	46	28	65	42	56	27	43	49	93	69

The highest and lowest T scores possible on each scale are indicated by a "---"; MMPI-A-RF T scores are non-gendered.

NSA Negative School Attitudes
ASA Antisocial Attitudes
CNP Conduct Problems
SUB Substance Abuse
NPI Negative Peer Influence
AGG Aggression

FML Family Problems
IPP Interpersonal Passivity
SAV Social Avoidance
SHY Shyness
DSF Disaffiliativeness

FIGURE 6 Sam's MMPI-A-RF Score Report, continued.

95

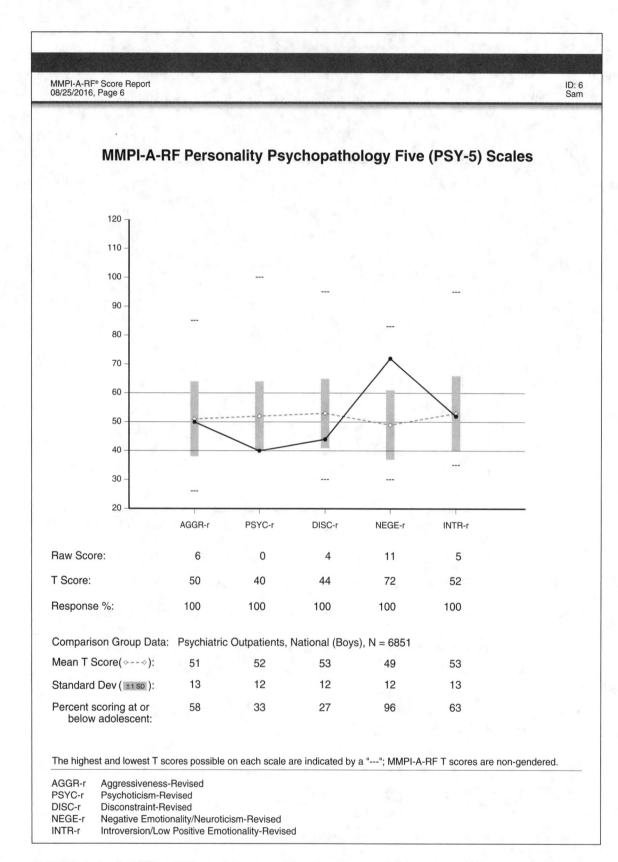

MMPI-A-RF Personality Psychopathology Five (PSY-5) Scales

	AGGR-r	PSYC-r	DISC-r	NEGE-r	INTR-r
Raw Score:	6	0	4	11	5
T Score:	50	40	44	72	52
Response %:	100	100	100	100	100

Comparison Group Data: Psychiatric Outpatients, National (Boys), N = 6851

	AGGR-r	PSYC-r	DISC-r	NEGE-r	INTR-r
Mean T Score(◇---◇):	51	52	53	49	53
Standard Dev (±1 SD):	13	12	12	12	13
Percent scoring at or below adolescent:	58	33	27	96	63

The highest and lowest T scores possible on each scale are indicated by a "---"; MMPI-A-RF T scores are non-gendered.

AGGR-r   Aggressiveness-Revised
PSYC-r   Psychoticism-Revised
DISC-r   Disconstraint-Revised
NEGE-r   Negative Emotionality/Neuroticism-Revised
INTR-r   Introversion/Low Positive Emotionality-Revised

FIGURE 6 Sam's MMPI-A-RF Score Report, continued.

MMPI-A-RF T SCORES (BY DOMAIN)

PROTOCOL VALIDITY

Content Non-Responsiveness

0	37	50	36
CNS	VRIN-r	TRIN-r	CRIN

Over-Reporting

44
F-r

Under-Reporting

44	43
L-r	K-r

SUBSTANTIVE SCALES

Somatic/Cognitive Dysfunction

41	52	44	41	39	61
RC1	MLS	GIC	HPC	NUC	COG

Emotional Dysfunction

62		57	60	62	74			
EID		RCd	HLP	SFD	NFC			
		53	52					
		RC2	INTR-r					
		46	47	64	51	52	43	37	72
		RC7	OCS	STW	AXY	ANP	BRF	SPF	NEGE-r

Thought Dysfunction

43		45
THD		RC6
		42
		RC8
		40
		PSYC-r

Behavioral Dysfunction

40		41	64	47	47	42	40
BXD		RC4	NSA	ASA	CNP	SUB	NPI
		39	48	50	44		
		RC9	AGG	AGGR-r	DISC-r		

Interpersonal Functioning

41	48	40	46	61	51
FML	RC3	IPP	SAV	SHY	DSF

Note. This information is provided to facilitate interpretation following the recommended structure for MMPI-A-RF interpretation in Chapter 7 of the *MMPI-A-RF Administration, Scoring, Interpretation, and Technical Manual*, which provides details in the text and an outline in Table 7-1.

FIGURE 6 Sam's MMPI-A-RF Score Report, continued.

are correlated with suicide risk. As was the case in his interview when he denied thoughts of suicide, Sam did not respond in the keyed direction to items that had direct suicidal content. This, however, does not negate Sam's risk of suicidal behavior and underscores the need for careful assessment and observation.

Sam's MMPI-A-RF protocol indicated significant emotional dysfunction. His elevated scores on EID and NEGE-r and the Specific Problems scales HLP, SFD, and NFC (Inefficacy) indicate that Sam feels he is ineffective in coping with difficulties and that he likely procrastinates. Sam also reported feelings of self-doubt, uselessness, and poor self-esteem. Sam likely feels inferior to others. He is often depressed and sad. Often, his behaviors are self-defeating. He likely degrades himself and is passive. Overall, Sam likely feels hopeless and helpless, that he is a failure, and that life has treated him unfairly. Sam believes that he truly cannot be helped, has very low-self-esteem, and often gives up easily. Sam is at risk for self-harming behaviors such as self-mutilation. When these factors are considered along with the low score on RC9, he appears to be depressed, with below-average levels of activation and environmental engagement. Additionally, the elevation on STW indicates an above-average degree of stress, worry, and anxiety and potential problems with sleep and concentration.

Sam's protocol also had an elevation on COG (Cognitive Complaints). He reported a diffuse pattern of cognitive problems and likely continues to experience attention problems, difficulties with concentration, and slow speech. Sam also reports an above-average level of stress and worry. He is likely often anxious and complained of poor sleep.

While the MMPI-A-RF cannot diagnose disorders such as ADHD, this case illustrates how it may be helpful in these assessments. Sam was already diagnosed and was in treatment for ADHD, yet he continued to report problems and symptoms associated with this disorder. In addition, Sam reported a considerable level of depression. Depression can also cause problems in attention, concentration, and memory. The MMPI-A-RF suggested that Sam's treatment should be two-pronged in direction. His depression should be addressed in treatment and is at a level often seen in youth who require antidepressant medication. In addition, if Sam is not compliant with his ADHD medication, his treatment regimen may not be as effective.

A possible treatment asset identified on the MMPI-A-RF was the lack of elevation on the FML (Family Problems) scale. Sam and his parents both describe a positive and supportive relationship. The engagement and encouragement of his parents can be a very important treatment asset in Sam's case.

Diagnosis

Sam was diagnosed with Attention Deficit Hyperactivity Disorder, Unspecified Depressive Disorder, and Unspecified Anxiety Disorder.

OUTCOME

His physician reviewed the findings and Sam was placed on an SSRI antidepressant medication. Sam received cognitive behavioral therapy along with interventions focused upon his strengths. He was also placed in a social skills group as well as a peer support group for youth with ADHD. Sam was also seen in family counseling and his parents were informed about specific ways to encourage him to complete his work and ways to intervene when he fell behind. He graduated from high school and went on successfully to college.

Sarah

A Sexually Victimized Youth

BACKGROUND

Sarah is a 17-year-old female who was referred by a county children's services agency for assessment and treatment recommendations. A case had been opened after she had stolen a cellphone and was caught sending sexually inappropriate material to a young adult male. The electronic material contained sexually themed texts, nude pictures of herself and the male, and plans for the male to come to her house after her parents had gone to sleep. Prior to this incident, she had returned home from a residential treatment center where she had been placed for about a year after acting out in a similar manner. The referral material also indicated that an adult male had sexually abused her when she was 13. The perpetrator, a family friend, was convicted and sent to prison. At the time of the assessment, Sarah remained in her mother's house.

Interview With Youth

Sarah reported that her parents did not marry because her mother became pregnant in high school. Her mother married her stepfather about 4 years ago. She related a history of conflict with her mother dating back to the age of 5, noting that at that age, she once ran away "because of some sweaters she made me wear." Sarah described a very changeable and often turbulent relationship with her mother but said that she believes her mother "tries to take care of me." She reported seeing her birth father about once a month and has a generally good relationship with him. Sarah said that she and her stepfather are often in conflict, noting that she was worried that he would be angry with her when she came home from this appointment because she had taken her brother's laptop to school without permission.

Sarah reported that she has a half-sister by her father and a half-brother by her mother. She said she has had one serious dating relationship, in the seventh grade. She indicated she has no close girlfriends, saying "Girls are annoying."

Sarah is in the 12th grade and wants to have a career as a nurse. She said that she has never been in special education but acknowledged that she has had in-school suspensions for disciplinary infractions. Sarah has worked at a local grocery store.

Sarah denied present substance abuse, stating that the court monitors her. She reported that she has never used alcohol, but she began smoking marijuana at the age of 13 and would smoke on a daily basis. She denied abuse of any other illicit drugs or abuse of prescription drugs.

Sarah stated that at the age of 13, she was sexually abused by an adult family friend and that he was incarcerated as a result of his abuse. She indicated that she has never been physically abused. She has never been involved with the juvenile court.

Sarah said that she has had three different therapists and did not like the first two, indicating that she was resistant and typically would not participate. She has just started seeing a new therapist and said that she likes him. Sarah reported that she was in a residential placement for about 11 months and stated she "hated it—they were too strict—I got myself kicked out." Although she has never been psychiatrically hospitalized, she was in the partial hospitalization program at a local facility. Sarah reported that she has been diagnosed with "OCD, ODD, ADD. Maybe Borderline and Depression and Anxiety." She is prescribed psychiatric medication but could not recall its name.

Sarah indicated that "a long time ago" she thought of suicide but has never attempted it. She reported that she used to cut herself on the arms and legs but has not done so for about a year.

Sarah denied any significant medical problems. She said that as a young child she had a tonsillectomy. She indicated that she has never been medically hospitalized and denied any history of head trauma, loss of consciousness, and any other neurological involvement.

COLLATERAL INFORMATION

Sarah's mother, who also completed a developmental history questionnaire, reported that her pregnancy and delivery with Sarah were nonremarkable and that she was 16 when she became pregnant. She received regular medical care. Labor was 18 hours, but Sarah was a healthy baby with an "easy" temperament who obtained developmental milestones normally. However, at age 8 months, Sarah stopped sleeping through the night and became quite difficult. During her toddlerhood, she was headstrong, quite active, and her mother described this period as "a tough year." She noted Sarah had some peculiarities such as not wanting to wear long sleeves and refusing to brush her hair. During this time, Sarah's birth father was in and out of her life. Sarah and her mother lived with her mother's parents until Sarah was 3 years old. Sarah's mother indicated that Sarah's behavioral problems significantly worsened around that age and that she went to parenting classes and read as much as she could but nothing she did seemed to help. When Sarah was in the fourth grade, her teacher suggested that she be evaluated and as a result, Sarah was diagnosed with ADHD Predominantly Inattentive Type and put on medication. She did not improve and remained quite defiant. Eventually, she was placed in residential treatment but was terminated from the program. Her mother reported that she and her husband obtained a second mortgage on their house to pay for Sarah's treatment. Since she returned, Sarah has been involved in home-based therapy as well as Dialectical Behavior Therapy (Landes & Linehan, 2015).

Sarah disclosed to her residential treatment therapist that was sexually abused by another uncle in addition to the abuse that had been earlier identified. Sarah's mother indicated that she was informed that while Sarah was in placement, she reportedly gave more disclosures of the second alleged abuse. However, no charges were ever filed against this family member.

Presently, Sarah continues to have behavioral problems. She has been involved in "sexting" and has taken a small amount of money from her mother. Sarah is reported to continue to cut herself and has met up with a boy she did not know for a sexual encounter.

Sarah's mother said that she has not observed her to have rapid mood swings, manic periods, bizarre behavior, or responding to nonobservable stimuli. In addition to this information, she conveyed on the developmental history form that Sarah is not suspected to be involved in significant substance abuse. Sarah does not have an IEP but is disruptive, her grades have shown a significant decline, and she seems no longer invested in school.

Sarah recently began treatment at a local mental health agency. Her current medications are Fluvoxamine, Methylphenidate, Clonidine, and Abilify.

At the age of 14, Sarah was assessed in a research study addressing the use of an atypical antipsychotic for the treatment of ADHD. She was administered the K-SADS, a measure of psychiatric disorders. Sarah was seen as qualifying for diagnoses of ADHD and Oppositional Defiant Disorder. Using the K-BIT 2, she was found to have a Verbal score of 109 (average), a Nonverbal score of 114 (average), and an IQ Composite of 114 (average). Sarah was classified as a "responder" to treatment, and it was recommended that she continue with Concerta and Risperdal.

A treatment summary by her first therapist reported diagnoses of ADHD and ODD. It was noted that Sarah was seen for four sessions, but treatment was discontinued before its goals were met. Her next therapist reported that she was seen for about 6 months due to severe behavioral problems, mood swings, and oppositional defiant behaviors. She was diagnosed with ADHD and ODD.

Sarah was referred to a partial hospitalization program and attended four sessions but was discharged after her mother called and indicated that since beginning the group program her behavior had worsened, and she was lying, stealing, and cutting. The discharge diagnosis was Depressive Disorder, Not Otherwise Specified.

The discharge materials from the therapeutic boarding school indicated that Sarah was discharged from that facility "due to lack of cooperation and willingness to follow through on outlined expectations." No diagnosis was provided in the discharge summary.

Current Behavioral Status

Sarah was appropriately dressed and groomed in clothing that was neat, clean, and appropriately arranged. Her hygiene was adequate.

There were no overt indications of loosening of associations, flight of ideas, or tangentiality. Sarah's psychomotor activity was nonremarkable (that is to say, she was not hyperactive or agitated nor was she lethargic or nonresponsive). Her speech was normal in tone, pacing, and volume. Her attention span was characterized by at least a moderate degree of distraction (meaning that she had to be refocused to task periodically but was able to return to what she was doing). Her manner of social interaction was outwardly friendly, polite, and cooperative but tended to be primarily superficially cooperative and somewhat interpersonally dramatic.

Sarah presented with an appropriate and expressive affect to an observed neutral mood. When asked to rate her subjective level of distress (SUDS) she described her present degree of emotional upset as being a 5/8 out of a possible 10, saying that "I'm irrational all over the place. I think I'm Bipolar. I have rapid mood swings where I am laughing and crying for no reason."

Sarah denied, and there were no overt indications of hallucinations, delusions, or paranoia. She gave no behavioral evidence of visual, gustatory, olfactory, or tactile hallucinations. She gave no behavioral evidence of hearing or responding to hallucinations during any of the examinations.

Sarah denied and gave no evidence of specific delusional thinking. She gave no evidence of systematic paranoid delusions or grandiosity. Accordingly, there appear to be no overt clinical or behavioral symptoms that would be typically seen with seriously mentally ill adolescents.

Sarah denied most symptoms typically associated with depression such as limited appetite, hopelessness, loss of interest or pleasure, loss of sexual interest, but did complain of poor sleep ("It's poor—my mind races"), and increased irritability, which are often symptoms associated with depression. Also, upon specific inquiry, she denied active suicidal ideation, intent, or plan as well as homicidal ideation.

When asked to describe any history of mood swings, Sarah stated that throughout her life, she has experienced rapidly changing moods and complained of past racing thoughts. She denied other symptoms often associated with Bipolar Disorder such as marked hyperactivity and grandiosity but acknowledged that she can be reckless and show poor impulse control (but described these in a manner not always associated with mood changes).

Sarah reported normative fears ("the dark") and did not appear to be phobic. She complained of chronic anxiety and that she will often pick at her skin. Sarah also described herself as "OCD—I'm always counting in my head and tapping—I have rituals." When asked about "flashbacks" and other symptoms associated with trauma exposure, she reported having flashbacks and nightmares of her abuse.

Sarah was alert and responsive to her environment and there were no problems observed with her level of alertness. She was oriented to time, place, person, and situation. Her fund of general information suggested intact abilities as ascertained by her answers to questions of common knowledge.

Sarah's concentration was adequate as evidenced by her attention and focus in the conversation with the examiner. Her immediate recall was adequate as demonstrated by her ability to recall five digits forward and three in reverse order. Concentration was also demonstrated to be adequate by her ability to perform simple mental calculations. Her short-term recall was adequate as demonstrated by her ability to recall three items from memory after a 10-minute distraction. She showed capacity as well for verbal abstract reasoning as demonstrated in her ability to state conceptual similarities between related objects and concepts including more complex abstractions. This was also demonstrated in her ability to interpret commonly used proverbs. Her insight and judgment did appear to be limited as determined by both her history and her responses to situational questions.

On the K-BIT 2, Sarah achieved a Vocabulary Standard score of 101. She earned a Nonverbal standard score of 101. Her overall Composite IQ standard score was 102.

Sarah was also given the Slosson Oral Reading Test. Her score indicated that she reads at the 12th grade level.

Sarah's mother completed the Conners Comprehensive Behavior Rating Scale, an empirically based rating scale of emotional and behavioral problems in youth. The CBRS-P contains validity scales and analysis found that there was not an overly positive response set nor were there indications of a negative response style. The inconsistency response scale, however, indicated inconsistent responding that may have impacted the validity of the test findings.

With that caution noted, the ratings by Sarah's mother indicated that Sarah has significant problems in the areas of emotional distress, social problems, defiant and aggressive behaviors, and risk for physical aggression.

The results were similar to those of youth who have been diagnosed with ADHD Predominantly Inattentive Type, Oppositional Defiant Disorder, Conduct Disorder, Major Depression, and Manic Episodes.

Sarah also completed the Trauma Symptom Checklist for Children (Briere, 1996). The TSCC measures posttraumatic stress and related psychological symptomatology in children ages 8–16 years who have experienced traumatic events, such as physical or sexual abuse, major loss, or natural disasters, or who have been a witness to violence. The TSCC manual contains norms for use with 17-year-olds and is appropriate for use with youth of her age as they are essentially similar with the need for a downward adjustment of one scale (Anger).

The TSCC includes two validity scales (Underresponse and Hyper-response), six clinical scales (Anxiety, Depression, Anger, Posttraumatic Stress, Dissociation, and Sexual Concerns), and eight critical items.

The TSCC was valid and interpretable. Sarah's profile had clinically significant elevations in the scales of Anxiety, Depression, and Sexual Distress.

Sarah endorsed a number of items associated with experiencing generalized anxiety and worry as well as specific fears. Such elevations often reflect the presence of an anxiety disorder or the anxious hyperarousal associated with posttraumatic stress disorder, or both. High scorers may have posttraumatic fears associated with previous victimization or having witnessed violence against others. Some youth with this elevation may project their anxiety into unrealistic fears of events that have not yet occurred.

She also endorsed many items associated with depression including feelings of sadness, unhappiness, and loneliness. She may have episodes of tearfulness and of guilt. High scores may reflect a depressive episode or a more long-term dysthymia. Such youth often try to avoid others and may see themselves as unworthy or bad and may describe feelings of self-hatred and can be associated with youth who are suicidal and/or self-injurious.

Additionally, her elevation on the Sexual Concerns scales indicated both sexual distress and sexual preoccupation. Youth with similar elevations may have had a history of being prematurely sexualized or sexually traumatized. As well, her item endorsement suggests considerable distress and conflicts associated with sex.

Overall, her profile is similar to youth who are diagnosed with trauma-related anxiety disorders, including Posttraumatic Stress Disorder as well as Acute Stress Reaction or an Adjustment Disorder.

MMPI-A-RF

Sarah's protocol was not indicative of either under- or overreporting of problems, though there was evidence of a moderate level of fixed True responding. This level of inconsistent responding does not invalidate the protocol. It does suggest that the scores on the Validity and Substantive scales should be interpreted with some caution. In the context of both Sarah's history of trauma and her prior diagnoses, it is suggested that critical items endorsed in the true direction should be explored to gain a better understanding of how she thinks and feels.

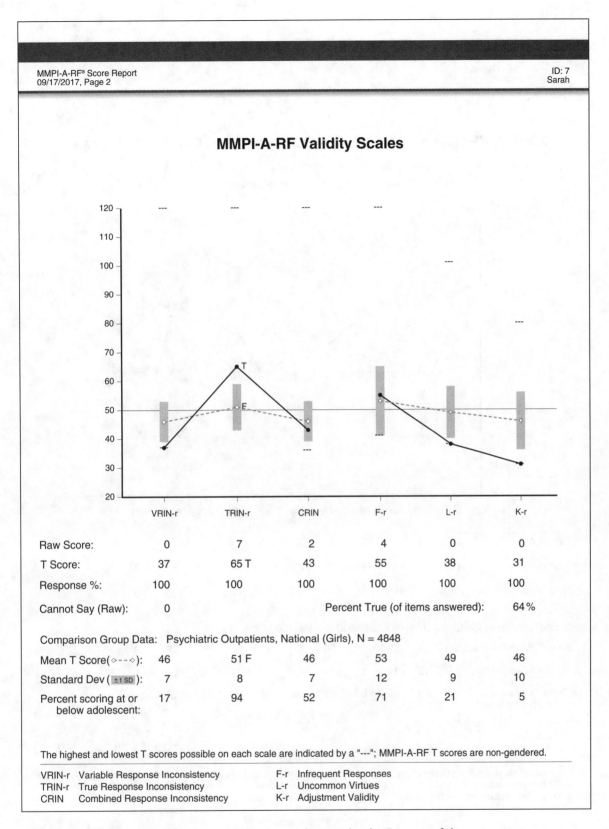

MMPI-A-RF Validity Scales

	VRIN-r	TRIN-r	CRIN	F-r	L-r	K-r
Raw Score:	0	7	2	4	0	0
T Score:	37	65 T	43	55	38	31
Response %:	100	100	100	100	100	100

Cannot Say (Raw): 0 Percent True (of items answered): 64%

Comparison Group Data: Psychiatric Outpatients, National (Girls), N = 4848

	VRIN-r	TRIN-r	CRIN	F-r	L-r	K-r
Mean T Score(◇- - -◇):	46	51 F	46	53	49	46
Standard Dev (±1 SD):	7	8	7	12	9	10
Percent scoring at or below adolescent:	17	94	52	71	21	5

The highest and lowest T scores possible on each scale are indicated by a "---"; MMPI-A-RF T scores are non-gendered.

VRIN-r	Variable Response Inconsistency		F-r	Infrequent Responses
TRIN-r	True Response Inconsistency		L-r	Uncommon Virtues
CRIN	Combined Response Inconsistency		K-r	Adjustment Validity

FIGURE 7 Sarah's MMPI-A-RF Score Report. Copyright 2016 by the Regents of the University of Minnesota. All rights reserved.

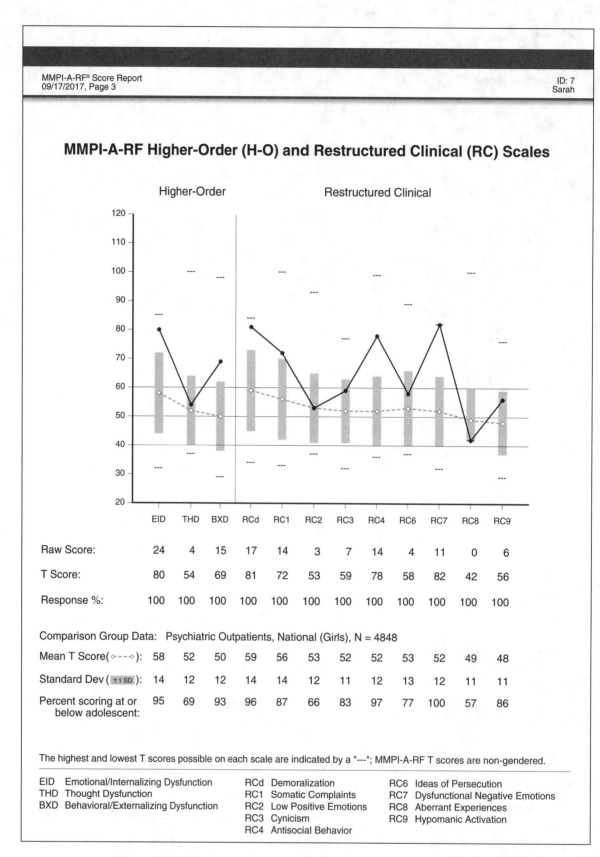

MMPI-A-RF Higher-Order (H-O) and Restructured Clinical (RC) Scales

	EID	THD	BXD	RCd	RC1	RC2	RC3	RC4	RC6	RC7	RC8	RC9
Raw Score:	24	4	15	17	14	3	7	14	4	11	0	6
T Score:	80	54	69	81	72	53	59	78	58	82	42	56
Response %:	100	100	100	100	100	100	100	100	100	100	100	100

Comparison Group Data: Psychiatric Outpatients, National (Girls), N = 4848

Mean T Score(◇---◇):	58	52	50	59	56	53	52	52	53	52	49	48
Standard Dev (±1 SD):	14	12	12	14	14	12	11	12	13	12	11	11
Percent scoring at or below adolescent:	95	69	93	96	87	66	83	97	77	100	57	86

The highest and lowest T scores possible on each scale are indicated by a "---"; MMPI-A-RF T scores are non-gendered.

EID Emotional/Internalizing Dysfunction
THD Thought Dysfunction
BXD Behavioral/Externalizing Dysfunction

RCd Demoralization
RC1 Somatic Complaints
RC2 Low Positive Emotions
RC3 Cynicism
RC4 Antisocial Behavior

RC6 Ideas of Persecution
RC7 Dysfunctional Negative Emotions
RC8 Aberrant Experiences
RC9 Hypomanic Activation

FIGURE 7 Sarah's MMPI-A-RF Score Report, continued.

108

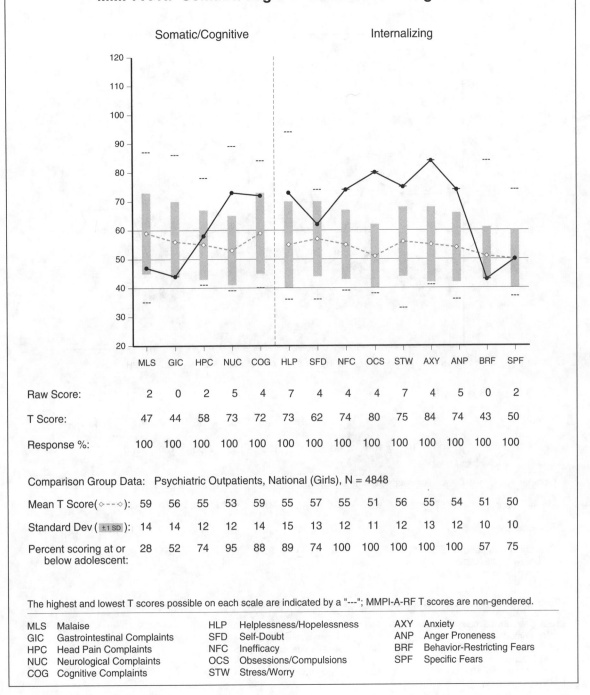

MMPI-A-RF Somatic/Cognitive and Internalizing Scales

	MLS	GIC	HPC	NUC	COG	HLP	SFD	NFC	OCS	STW	AXY	ANP	BRF	SPF
Raw Score:	2	0	2	5	4	7	4	4	4	7	4	5	0	2
T Score:	47	44	58	73	72	73	62	74	80	75	84	74	43	50
Response %:	100	100	100	100	100	100	100	100	100	100	100	100	100	100

Comparison Group Data: Psychiatric Outpatients, National (Girls), N = 4848

Mean T Score(◇---◇):	59	56	55	53	59	55	57	55	51	56	55	54	51	50
Standard Dev (±1 SD):	14	14	12	12	14	15	13	12	11	12	13	12	10	10
Percent scoring at or below adolescent:	28	52	74	95	88	89	74	100	100	100	100	100	57	75

The highest and lowest T scores possible on each scale are indicated by a "---"; MMPI-A-RF T scores are non-gendered.

MLS	Malaise	HLP	Helplessness/Hopelessness	AXY	Anxiety
GIC	Gastrointestinal Complaints	SFD	Self-Doubt	ANP	Anger Proneness
HPC	Head Pain Complaints	NFC	Inefficacy	BRF	Behavior-Restricting Fears
NUC	Neurological Complaints	OCS	Obsessions/Compulsions	SPF	Specific Fears
COG	Cognitive Complaints	STW	Stress/Worry		

FIGURE 7 Sarah's MMPI-A-RF Score Report, continued.

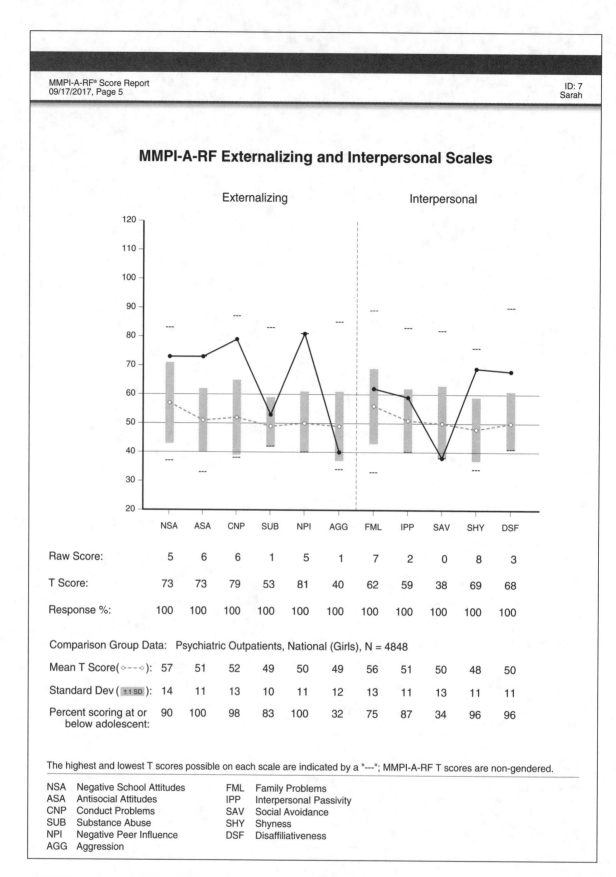

MMPI-A-RF Externalizing and Interpersonal Scales

Externalizing   Interpersonal

	NSA	ASA	CNP	SUB	NPI	AGG	FML	IPP	SAV	SHY	DSF
Raw Score:	5	6	6	1	5	1	7	2	0	8	3
T Score:	73	73	79	53	81	40	62	59	38	69	68
Response %:	100	100	100	100	100	100	100	100	100	100	100

Comparison Group Data: Psychiatric Outpatients, National (Girls), N = 4848

	NSA	ASA	CNP	SUB	NPI	AGG	FML	IPP	SAV	SHY	DSF
Mean T Score(◇- - -◇):	57	51	52	49	50	49	56	51	50	48	50
Standard Dev (±1 SD):	14	11	13	10	11	12	13	11	13	11	11
Percent scoring at or below adolescent:	90	100	98	83	100	32	75	87	34	96	96

The highest and lowest T scores possible on each scale are indicated by a "---"; MMPI-A-RF T scores are non-gendered.

NSA	Negative School Attitudes		FML	Family Problems
ASA	Antisocial Attitudes		IPP	Interpersonal Passivity
CNP	Conduct Problems		SAV	Social Avoidance
SUB	Substance Abuse		SHY	Shyness
NPI	Negative Peer Influence		DSF	Disaffiliativeness
AGG	Aggression			

FIGURE 7 Sarah's MMPI-A-RF Score Report, continued.

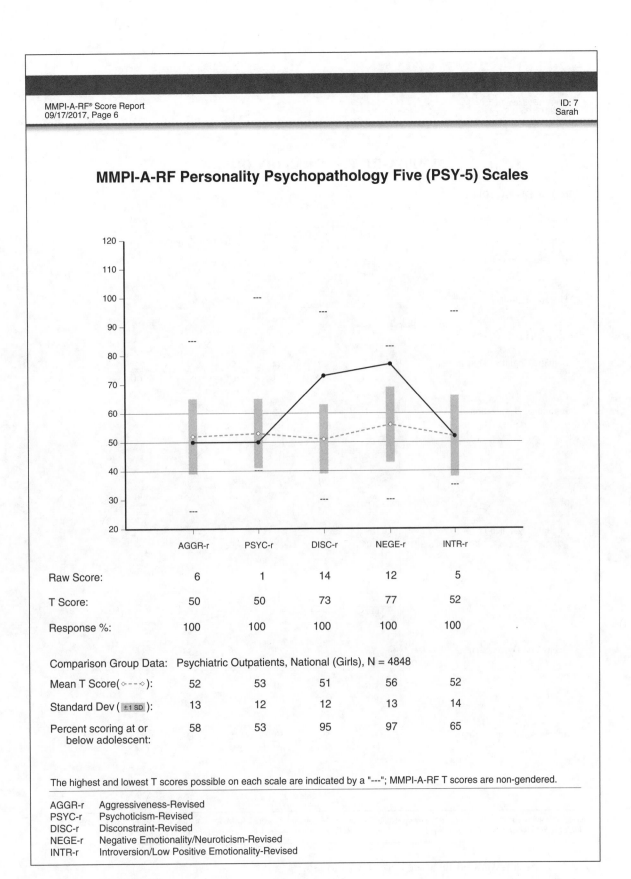

MMPI-A-RF Personality Psychopathology Five (PSY-5) Scales

	AGGR-r	PSYC-r	DISC-r	NEGE-r	INTR-r
Raw Score:	6	1	14	12	5
T Score:	50	50	73	77	52
Response %:	100	100	100	100	100

Comparison Group Data: Psychiatric Outpatients, National (Girls), N = 4848

	AGGR-r	PSYC-r	DISC-r	NEGE-r	INTR-r
Mean T Score(◇--◇):	52	53	51	56	52
Standard Dev (±1 SD):	13	12	12	13	14
Percent scoring at or below adolescent:	58	53	95	97	65

The highest and lowest T scores possible on each scale are indicated by a "---"; MMPI-A-RF T scores are non-gendered.

AGGR-r   Aggressiveness-Revised
PSYC-r   Psychoticism-Revised
DISC-r   Disconstraint-Revised
NEGE-r   Negative Emotionality/Neuroticism-Revised
INTR-r   Introversion/Low Positive Emotionality-Revised

FIGURE 7   Sarah's MMPI-A-RF Score Report, continued.

MMPI-A-RF T SCORES (BY DOMAIN)

PROTOCOL VALIDITY

Content Non-Responsiveness	0	37	65 T	43
	CNS	VRIN-r	TRIN-r	CRIN

Over-Reporting	55
	F-r

Under-Reporting	38	31
	L-r	K-r

SUBSTANTIVE SCALES

Somatic/Cognitive Dysfunction	72	47	44	58	73	72
	RC1	MLS	GIC	HPC	NUC	COG

Emotional Dysfunction 80
                       EID

81	73	62	74
RCd	HLP	SFD	NFC

53	52
RC2	INTR-r

82	80	75	84	74	43	50	77
RC7	OCS	STW	AXY	ANP	BRF	SPF	NEGE-r

Thought Dysfunction 54
                     THD

58
RC6

42
RC8

50
PSYC-r

Behavioral Dysfunction 69
                        BXD

78	73	73	79	53	81
RC4	NSA	ASA	CNP	SUB	NPI

56	40	50	73
RC9	AGG	AGGR-r	DISC-r

Interpersonal Functioning	62	59	59	38	69	68
	FML	RC3	IPP	SAV	SHY	DSF

Note. This information is provided to facilitate interpretation following the recommended structure for MMPI-A-RF interpretation in Chapter 7 of the *MMPI-A-RF Administration, Scoring, Interpretation, and Technical Manual,* which provides details in the text and an outline in Table 7-1.

FIGURE 7 Sarah's MMPI-A-RF Score Report, continued.

Sarah responded affirmatively to MMPI-A-RF items with content related directly to suicidal thoughts or preoccupation with death. Her elevations on RCd, HLP (Helplessness/Hopelessness), SFD (Self-Doubts), NEGE-r, coupled with her elevation on DISC-r also raise concerns about risk for self-harm, which should be actively monitored.

Sarah's elevation on EID (Emotional/Internalizing Dysfunction) indicates considerable emotional distress that likely rises to the level of a perceived crisis. Her score falls one standard deviation above the mean for the reference group of 4,848 girls in psychiatric outpatient treatment. She describes an above-average level of negative emotional experiences that include feeling very irritable, and feelings of remorse and apprehension. She most likely feels intense and pervasive anxiety with symptoms such as feelings of dread, nightmares, and frequent fears. Sarah also reports a very high level of obsessive thoughts and compulsive behaviors to a degree that she probably is compulsive and has problems with her thinking as result. Sarah reports, in addition, a considerable degree of stress and worry and that she has trouble sleeping. Sarah acknowledges a history of problems with her anger and irritability. This may be seen in her feeling very impatient with others. Her anger problems may rise to a level of making threats.

Sarah describes herself as feeling very depressed. She likely feels isolated from others and tends to feel overwhelmed by life and that she is not able to cope with difficulties and stresses that she experiences. Sarah has difficulty making decisions and most probably procrastinates. She acknowledges feelings of hopelessness, that she is a failure, and that life has given her a raw deal. Sarah feels that she cannot be helped and tends to give up easily. Sarah feels inferior to others, dislikes herself, and is nonassertive. These are characteristics associated with the risk of self-harming behavior including self-mutilation as well as the previously noted risk of suicide.

Sarah reports several somatic complaints that include vague neurological symptoms as well as difficulties thinking and concentrating.

Sarah acknowledges a history of significant acting-out behaviors that have resulted in considerable difficulties in her life. She reports a higher-than-average level of behaviors associated with externalizing disorders and rule-breaking behavior. Sarah reports several problems due to her tendency to associate with negative peers. Her responses acknowledge difficulties with authorities, substance abuse, aggression, truancy, lying and oppositional behavior, and legal contacts. Sarah describes several antisocial attitudes. Her family problems are characterized by conflict and discord.

Sarah's protocol is very similar to youth who have serious psychological and behavioral problems. It is also consistent with earlier diagnoses reported in her clinical history. In addition to the immediate need for an assessment of risk for self-harm, the MMPI-A-RF data indicated a need for continued and intensive treatment. Because she reports several somatic and cognitive problems, she should be referred for additional medical and neuropsychological assessment. Sarah may reject any psychological attributions for her physical symptoms, however.

Sarah's problems are behavioral, academic, and involve substance abuse. Because she has difficulties in many areas, including family functioning, it is imperative that Sarah's psychological treatment not take place in isolation. Her therapist should coordinate with other providers to avoid duplication of services or conflicts in approach.

A possible treatment asset that can be identified is that Sarah's THD and associated substantive scales are not elevated. She is in contact with reality and can understand and apply what she might learn in therapy.

Diagnosis

Sarah was diagnosed with Posttraumatic Stress Disorder, Unspecified Depressive Disorder, and emerging features of Borderline Personality Disorder.

OUTCOME

It was recommended that Sarah continue in Dialectical Behavioral Therapy and that all services be trauma informed. She was also recommended for anger management interventions. It was strongly recommended that her therapist not directly participate in any decisions concerning future sanctions by authorities to help to reduce the potential of "splitting" or other manipulative behaviors. Family intervention was suggested using the Functional Family Therapy model (Sexton & Alexander, 2000) for home-based services. In light of her expressed interests, it was recommended that Sarah be referred to creative art therapy as well as animal-assisted therapy. It was also suggested that a mentoring program would be useful as would strength-based volunteer activities to increase her self-esteem.

Steve

A Male With a History of Noncompliance With Diabetes Medication

BACKGROUND

Steve is a 17-year-old male who was referred by his endocrinologist for chronic noncompliance with insulin and dietary treatment for Type 1 Diabetes that was diagnosed at age 8. Steve is the youngest of five children born to his parents. According to a developmental history and a narrative supplied by his mother, her pregnancy and delivery were nonremarkable. He was described as always being oppositional and defiant. During preschool and elementary school, he had extreme separation anxiety and began treatment at age 8. He was seen in psychotherapy and unsuccessfully tried on an SSRI (Zoloft). He has also been prescribed Focalin and Concerta for ADHD. Developmental milestones were nonremarkable. There is no history of abuse or neglect. He has never been psychiatrically hospitalized. His mother indicated that the father has had substance abuse problems and she is concerned about that for Steve. He is in his senior year at a career center.

Current Behavioral Status

Steve was appropriately dressed and groomed. His hygiene was adequate. There were no overt indications of loosening of associations, flight of ideas, or tangentiality. His psychomotor activity was nonremarkable. His speech was normal in tone, pacing, and volume. His attention span was adequate. His manner of social interaction was friendly, polite, and cooperative. He was somewhat socially reserved.

Steve presented with an appropriate and expressive affect to a reported recently depressed mood. There were no overt indications of hallucinations, delusions, or paranoia. He denied any disturbances in his health or appetite beyond coping with his diabetes and saying that he has been sleeping too much recently but not to a problematic level. He denied suicidal or homicidal ideation upon specific inquiry. He was future oriented. He did not appear hopeless and had social supports. He did not present with symptoms of anxiety, phobias, obsessions, or compulsions. His recall functions were clinically intact. He was oriented to time, place, person, and situation. Insight and judgment were fair to adequate for his age.

MMPI-A-RF

Steve's MMPI-A-RF was compared to a reference group of 96 male youth in a medical setting. Although there were no indications of under- or over-reporting of problems, Steve responded in an inconsistent manner owing to fixed True responding. This level of inconsistency did not invalidate the test results but indicated that the Validity and Substantive scales should be interpreted with some caution.

Steve responded affirmatively to items specific to content involving suicidal thoughts and his elevated scores on RCd, HLP (Helplessness/Hopelessness), SFD (Self-Doubt), and NEGE-r are correlated with suicide risk in adolescents. Risk for self-harm should therefore be closely monitored.

Steve's responses indicate considerable emotional distress. He reports feeling sad, depressed, and dissatisfied with his life. Steve also reports poor self-esteem, that he feels useless, and that he often doubts himself. He likely feels inferior to others, tends to be very negative in how he thinks about himself, and is passive and nonassertive. Steve also likely feels that he is a failure, that he has gotten a raw deal in life, and he feels hopeless about things changing and believes he cannot be helped. In addition to risk of suicide, his responses indicated that Steve is at risk for self-mutilation.

Steve's protocol is also notable for somatic and cognitive dysfunction owing to his reports of poor health, weakness, and/or fatigue, as evidenced by elevations on MLS (Malaise) and COG (Cognitive Problems). He presents with multiple somatic complaints and complains of sleeplessness, low energy, and fatigue.

As indicated on NSA (Negative School Attitudes), Steve acknowledges negative attitudes toward school. He does not like school and likely has academic problems and test anxiety. He is likely difficult to motivate

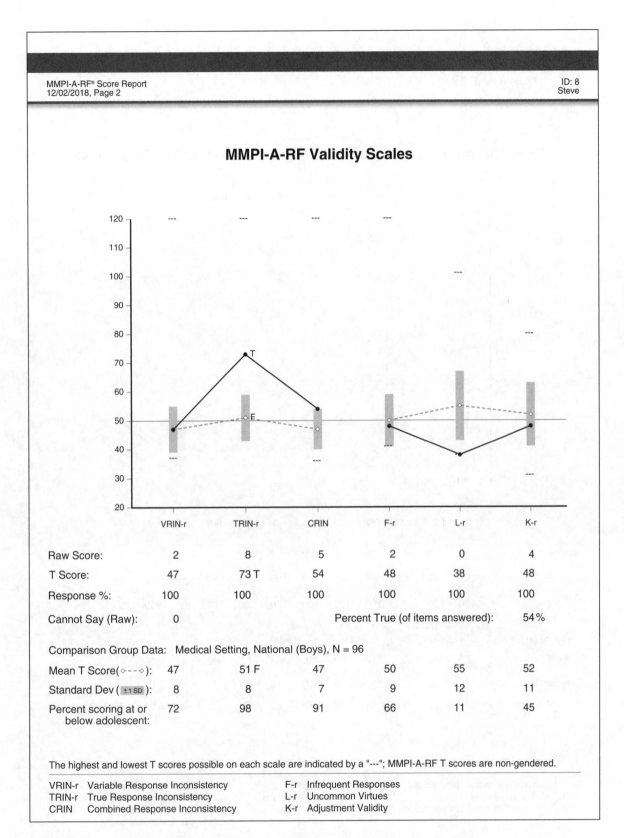

MMPI-A-RF Validity Scales

	VRIN-r	TRIN-r	CRIN	F-r	L-r	K-r
Raw Score:	2	8	5	2	0	4
T Score:	47	73 T	54	48	38	48
Response %:	100	100	100	100	100	100

Cannot Say (Raw): 0   Percent True (of items answered): 54%

Comparison Group Data: Medical Setting, National (Boys), N = 96

	VRIN-r	TRIN-r	CRIN	F-r	L-r	K-r
Mean T Score(◇---◇):	47	51 F	47	50	55	52
Standard Dev (±1 SD):	8	8	7	9	12	11
Percent scoring at or below adolescent:	72	98	91	66	11	45

The highest and lowest T scores possible on each scale are indicated by a "---"; MMPI-A-RF T scores are non-gendered.

VRIN-r	Variable Response Inconsistency	F-r	Infrequent Responses
TRIN-r	True Response Inconsistency	L-r	Uncommon Virtues
CRIN	Combined Response Inconsistency	K-r	Adjustment Validity

FIGURE 8 Steve's MMPI-A-RF Score Report. Copyright 2016 by the Regents of the University of Minnesota. All rights reserved.

117

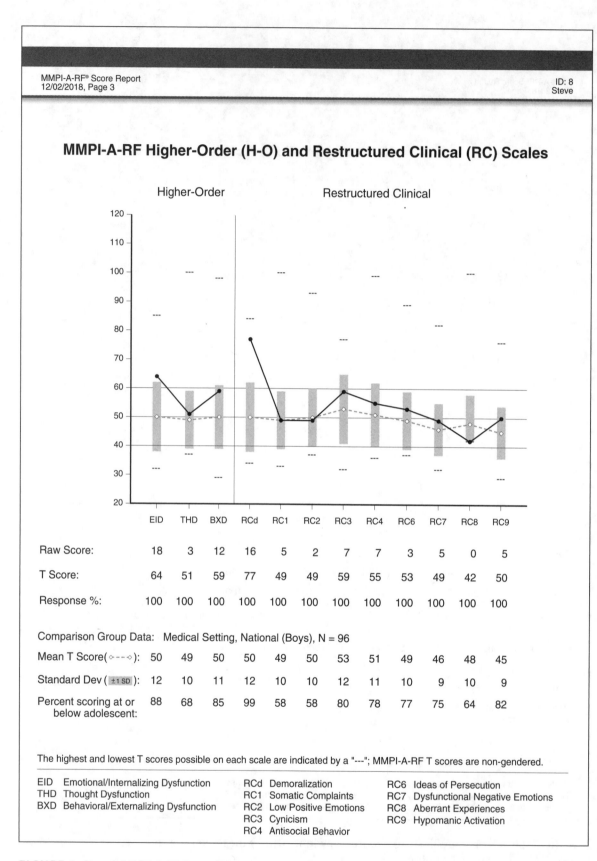

MMPI-A-RF Higher-Order (H-O) and Restructured Clinical (RC) Scales

Higher-Order | Restructured Clinical

	EID	THD	BXD	RCd	RC1	RC2	RC3	RC4	RC6	RC7	RC8	RC9
Raw Score:	18	3	12	16	5	2	7	7	3	5	0	5
T Score:	64	51	59	77	49	49	59	55	53	49	42	50
Response %:	100	100	100	100	100	100	100	100	100	100	100	100

Comparison Group Data: Medical Setting, National (Boys), N = 96

	EID	THD	BXD	RCd	RC1	RC2	RC3	RC4	RC6	RC7	RC8	RC9
Mean T Score(◇---◇):	50	49	50	50	49	50	53	51	49	46	48	45
Standard Dev (±1 SD):	12	10	11	12	10	10	12	11	10	9	10	9
Percent scoring at or below adolescent:	88	68	85	99	58	58	80	78	77	75	64	82

The highest and lowest T scores possible on each scale are indicated by a "---"; MMPI-A-RF T scores are non-gendered.

EID Emotional/Internalizing Dysfunction	RCd Demoralization	RC6 Ideas of Persecution
THD Thought Dysfunction	RC1 Somatic Complaints	RC7 Dysfunctional Negative Emotions
BXD Behavioral/Externalizing Dysfunction	RC2 Low Positive Emotions	RC8 Aberrant Experiences
	RC3 Cynicism	RC9 Hypomanic Activation
	RC4 Antisocial Behavior	

FIGURE 8 Steve's MMPI-A-RF Score Report, continued.

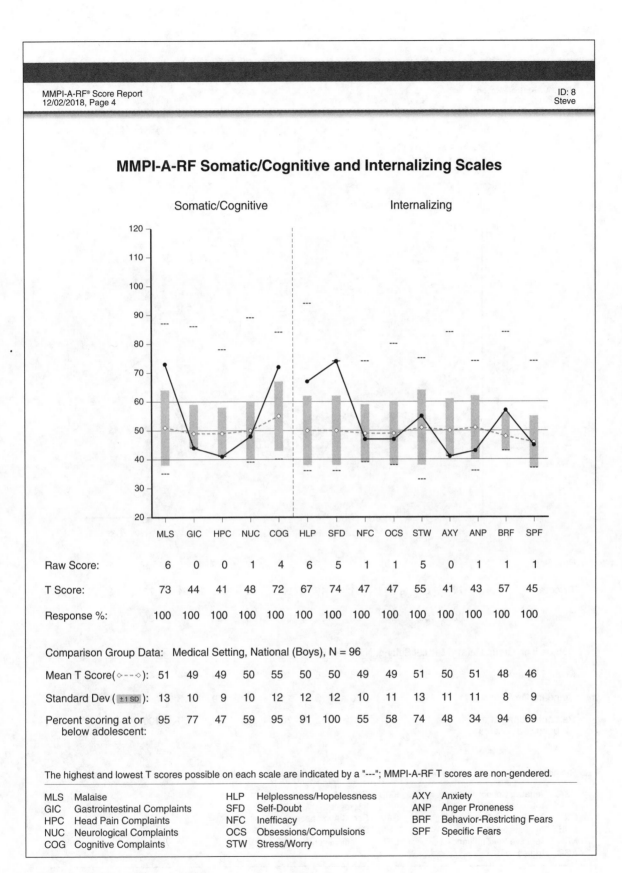

MMPI-A-RF Somatic/Cognitive and Internalizing Scales

	Somatic/Cognitive	Internalizing

	MLS	GIC	HPC	NUC	COG	HLP	SFD	NFC	OCS	STW	AXY	ANP	BRF	SPF
Raw Score:	6	0	0	1	4	6	5	1	1	5	0	1	1	1
T Score:	73	44	41	48	72	67	74	47	47	55	41	43	57	45
Response %:	100	100	100	100	100	100	100	100	100	100	100	100	100	100

Comparison Group Data: Medical Setting, National (Boys), N = 96

Mean T Score(◇- - -◇):	51	49	49	50	55	50	50	49	49	51	50	51	48	46
Standard Dev (±1 SD):	13	10	9	10	12	12	12	10	11	13	11	11	8	9
Percent scoring at or below adolescent:	95	77	47	59	95	91	100	55	58	74	48	34	94	69

The highest and lowest T scores possible on each scale are indicated by a "---"; MMPI-A-RF T scores are non-gendered.

MLS	Malaise	HLP	Helplessness/Hopelessness	AXY	Anxiety
GIC	Gastrointestinal Complaints	SFD	Self-Doubt	ANP	Anger Proneness
HPC	Head Pain Complaints	NFC	Inefficacy	BRF	Behavior-Restricting Fears
NUC	Neurological Complaints	OCS	Obsessions/Compulsions	SPF	Specific Fears
COG	Cognitive Complaints	STW	Stress/Worry		

FIGURE 8 Steve's MMPI-A-RF Score Report, continued.

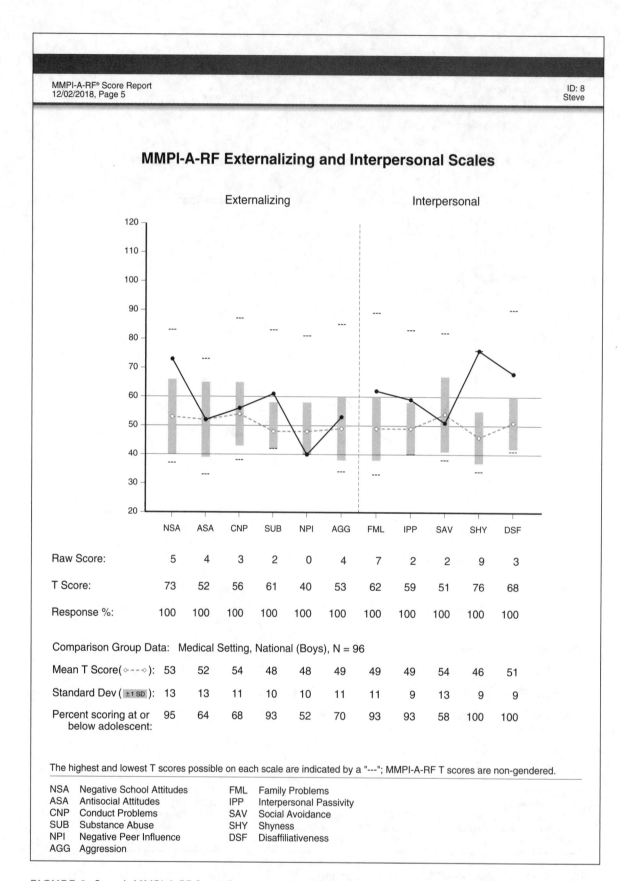

MMPI-A-RF Externalizing and Interpersonal Scales

Externalizing   Interpersonal

	NSA	ASA	CNP	SUB	NPI	AGG	FML	IPP	SAV	SHY	DSF
Raw Score:	5	4	3	2	0	4	7	2	2	9	3
T Score:	73	52	56	61	40	53	62	59	51	76	68
Response %:	100	100	100	100	100	100	100	100	100	100	100

Comparison Group Data: Medical Setting, National (Boys), N = 96

	NSA	ASA	CNP	SUB	NPI	AGG	FML	IPP	SAV	SHY	DSF
Mean T Score(◇---◇):	53	52	54	48	48	49	49	49	54	46	51
Standard Dev (±1 SD):	13	13	11	10	10	11	11	9	13	9	9
Percent scoring at or below adolescent:	95	64	68	93	52	70	93	93	58	100	100

The highest and lowest T scores possible on each scale are indicated by a "---"; MMPI-A-RF T scores are non-gendered.

NSA	Negative School Attitudes		FML	Family Problems
ASA	Antisocial Attitudes		IPP	Interpersonal Passivity
CNP	Conduct Problems		SAV	Social Avoidance
SUB	Substance Abuse		SHY	Shyness
NPI	Negative Peer Influence		DSF	Disaffiliativeness
AGG	Aggression			

FIGURE 8 Steve's MMPI-A-RF Score Report, continued.

120

MMPI-A-RF Personality Psychopathology Five (PSY-5) Scales

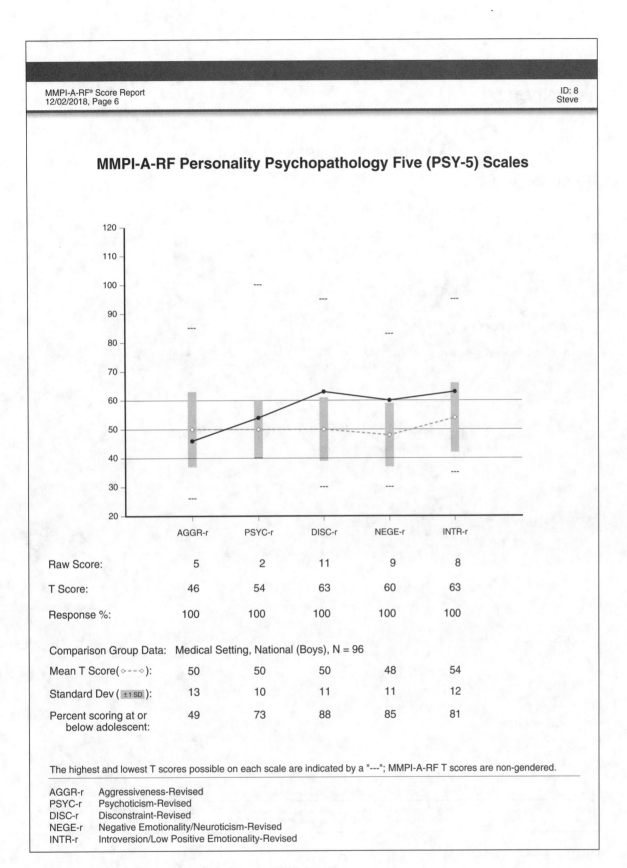

	AGGR-r	PSYC-r	DISC-r	NEGE-r	INTR-r
Raw Score:	5	2	11	9	8
T Score:	46	54	63	60	63
Response %:	100	100	100	100	100

Comparison Group Data: Medical Setting, National (Boys), N = 96

	AGGR-r	PSYC-r	DISC-r	NEGE-r	INTR-r
Mean T Score(◇- - -◇):	50	50	50	48	54
Standard Dev (±1 SD):	13	10	11	11	12
Percent scoring at or below adolescent:	49	73	88	85	81

The highest and lowest T scores possible on each scale are indicated by a "---"; MMPI-A-RF T scores are non-gendered.

AGGR-r   Aggressiveness-Revised
PSYC-r   Psychoticism-Revised
DISC-r   Disconstraint-Revised
NEGE-r   Negative Emotionality/Neuroticism-Revised
INTR-r   Introversion/Low Positive Emotionality-Revised

FIGURE 8 Steve's MMPI-A-RF Score Report, continued.

121

MMPI-A-RF T SCORES (BY DOMAIN)

PROTOCOL VALIDITY

Content Non-Responsiveness

0	47	73 T	54
CNS	VRIN-r	TRIN-r	CRIN

Over-Reporting

48
F-r

Under-Reporting

38	48
L-r	K-r

SUBSTANTIVE SCALES

Somatic/Cognitive Dysfunction

49	73	44	41	48	72
RC1	MLS	GIC	HPC	NUC	COG

Emotional Dysfunction — EID 64

77	67	74	47
RCd	HLP	SFD	NFC

49	63
RC2	INTR-r

49	47	55	41	43	57	45	60
RC7	OCS	STW	AXY	ANP	BRF	SPF	NEGE-r

Thought Dysfunction — THD 51

53
RC6

42
RC8

54
PSYC-r

Behavioral Dysfunction — BXD 59

55	73	52	56	61	40
RC4	NSA	ASA	CNP	SUB	NPI

50	53	46	63
RC9	AGG	AGGR-r	DISC-r

Interpersonal Functioning

62	59	59	51	76	68
FML	RC3	IPP	SAV	SHY	DSF

Note. This information is provided to facilitate interpretation following the recommended structure for MMPI-A-RF interpretation in Chapter 7 of the *MMPI-A-RF Administration, Scoring, Interpretation, and Technical Manual*, which provides details in the text and an outline in Table 7-1.

FIGURE 8 Steve's MMPI-A-RF Score Report, continued.

academically and has poor study habits and difficulty with school authority figures.

Steve is at risk for substance abuse problems. He acknowledges problematic use and the elevation on SUB (Substance Abuse) is at a level found in youth who may require treatment for substance abuse.

Interpersonally, Steve reports considerable family discord and that he does not feel supported by his family. His responses reflect his history of oppositional and defiant behavior at home.

Steve's elevations on SHY (Shyness) and DSF (Disaffiliativeness) indicate that he feels shy, easily embarrassed, and uncomfortable around others. He tends to be introverted and socially isolated. Steve reports not enjoying being around others and that he has trouble trusting others. He most likely has difficulty dealing with his emotions.

Steve's protocol indicated that diagnoses of emotional/internalizing disorders such as depression be considered. He has several physical problems related to his diabetes, but he should be further assessed to ascertain if some of his symptoms are the result of his psychological problems or the degree to which his psychological symptoms exacerbate his physical symptoms.

Steve's scores also indicate the need to consider a diagnosis of ADHD given the elevation on COG and DISC-r. However, depression should also be considered as contributing to his attentional deficits given the elevation seen on INTR-r and the general sense of unhappiness and dissatisfaction indicated by the RCd scale. Also, although his scores are similar to those of youth who have externalizing diagnoses such as Oppositional Defiant Disorder and Substance Use Disorders, the extent to which depression contributes to these problems should be further assessed. Finally, the diagnosis of a Social Anxiety Disorder should be considered.

A potential treatment asset seen in Steve's protocol was that although he has had behavioral problems at home, his protocol is unlike that of youth whose behaviors have gotten them into legal trouble. Steve did not report antisocial attitudes. Because Steve reported being interested in a career in public service, this lack of conduct-disordered orientation could be built upon in a way to increase his self-esteem and further association with positive adult mentors.

Diagnosis

Steve was diagnosed with Unspecified Depressive Disorder, Attention Deficit Hyperactivity Disorder, Predominantly Inattentive Type by history, and Psychological Factors Affecting Other Medical Conditions.

OUTCOME

Following the administration of the MMPI-A-RF, the psychologist reviewed the critical items with Steve. He continued to affirm the items he answered True. Steve agreed to allowing his parents to be informed of his risk of self-harm and a family session was held. As the therapy progressed, the psychologist had another session to review his critical item statements. Steve said that he no longer felt as he did before and stated specifically that the statements related to self-harm risk were no longer true.

Steve was treated using a primarily motivational interviewing model. He was placed back on an SSRI for his depression. Initially, he did not attend therapy sessions regularly, but became more compliant as he developed a specific public-service career focus that required him to be medically stable. Steve was also linked with a mentor who worked in the career that he desired. He agreed to regular drug testing and no positive findings were reported. Steve was also seen in family therapy. The therapist coordinated treatment with his endocrinologist. He was successfully discharged from therapy after being compliant both with his diabetes treatment and his psychotherapy.

Terry

A Male Referred for Self-Injurious Behaviors

BACKGROUND

Terry is a 17-year-old boy who was referred by his therapist for consultation after it was discovered that he was cutting himself.

Terry reported a positive relationship with his family. He indicated having two brothers and a sister. His father is a firefighter and his mother is a full-time mother. In specific reference to the cutting behaviors, he said that they began about a year ago, citing an argument with his mother about cleaning his room and her touching some of his belongings. He said that he had not cut himself for the past 2 months but began again approximately 2 weeks ago. In response to a question about his specific self-injurious behaviors, he said that he stabbed himself in the arm, not deeply but enough to break the skin. Terry estimated that he cut himself about 10 times before his father made him promise to stop. He described the behavior as resulting from anxiety and as "ritualistic" in nature.

Terry is homeschooled and is in the 11th grade. He has completed all of his credits required for graduation and is now taking college-level classes. He has a goal of work in aerospace. Terry denied, and there is no indication of substance abuse, according to his mother. He also denied any history of child welfare involvement or out-of-home placement in residential treatment. He also denied any history of fire-setting or animal cruelty. Terry said that he has no juvenile court contacts.

COLLATERAL INFORMATION

Terry's mother said that her health was good when she gave birth to Terry but that he was born with nuchal cord and had fetal distress. Delivery was induced. He also suffered from jaundice and dehydration and was hospitalized at 6 months. He obtained developmental milestones nonremarkably but did not sleep for more than 10 to 20 minutes until he was 20 months old.

Terry's mother noted that he has always been a high achiever and academically advanced, which has led to some social problems, as he was the youngest child in his peer groups. Terry would often be picked on by his peers and would become so upset that he would run home crying. He developed separation problems that have continued even into high school, resulting in his mom choosing to homeschool Terry. She noted that he tends to associate more with adults and tends to be anxious in social situations.

Terry was diagnosed with ADHD at the age of 7 and was once in speech therapy. He was treated with stimulant medication but developed side effects and is not taking medications at this time. His mother and Terry both said that he is "adamantly against medication." He also received occupational therapy for 3 months at about the age of 10. The neuropsychological evaluation that resulted in a diagnosis of ADHD also produced diagnoses of Developmental Coordination Disorder and Communication Disorder. A provisional reading disorder diagnosis was also assigned. His mother noted that he has been seen "by various counselors" since the age of 12.

Medical History

Terry said that he is in good general health. He denied any history of head trauma, seizures, concussions, or loss of consciousness. An audiological evaluation noted that he had difficulty with the task of auditory closure. His pediatrician reported that Terry has been treated for allergies, recurring ear infections, flu, and pneumonia; has fractured a thumb, sustained minor head injuries without unconsciousness but has not had seizures.

Current Behavioral Status

Terry appeared to be about his stated age. His hygiene and grooming were adequate, and he wore clothing that was appropriately arranged, suitable for the season, and clean. His attention and cooperation were adequate. His eye contact was direct. His gait and posture were nonremarkable. There were no overt indications of gross or fine motor dysfunction. His speech was not markedly variable in tone, pacing, or volume. There were no overt indications of loosening of associations, flight of ideas, or tangentiality. His manner of social interaction was noticeably reserved.

Terry presented with appropriate affect and euthymic normal mood, and he denied any present problems with his temper or mood instability. He denied and gave no evidence of other symptoms associated with mood disorders in adolescents such as racing thoughts, grandiosity, and manic or hypomanic periods.

Terry denied, and there were no overt indications of hallucinations, delusions, organized paranoid ideation, or other symptoms of serious psychotic mental illnesses.

Terry denied present experiences of depression. He stated that his sleep was presently "good" as was his appetite. He also denied any current suicidal or homicidal ideation, plan, intent, or means. He denied feelings of hopelessness, problems in concentration, chronic dysphoria, loss of interest or pleasure in things, or loss of sexual interest.

There were no clinical indications of specific phobias, obsessions, or compulsions and Terry denied general anxiety. He denied any flashbacks or intrusive thoughts of past events in his life as well as any episodes of disassociation.

Terry's thinking indicated the capacity for verbal abstract reasoning as demonstrated by his ability to identify similarities between related and increasingly complex concepts. He gave adequate and age-appropriate answers to basic questions of general knowledge.

Terry was oriented to situation, time, place, and person. His long-term, short-term, and immediate recall functions were intact. His focused concentration also appeared to be adequate. He had no marked difficulties with short-term recall. His insight and judgment appeared to be somewhat less than typical for his age as ascertained by situational questions and his history.

Both parents completed the Conners Comprehensive Behavior Rating Scales. The instrument contains validity scales and there were no indications of either under- or overreporting or of inconsistent responding.

Terry's father's ratings were clinically significant for emotional distress, social problems, and defiant/aggressive behavior. The ratings by his mother were identical.

Both parents rated him as similar to youth diagnosed with an anxiety disorder, depression, social anxiety, and an autism spectrum disorder.

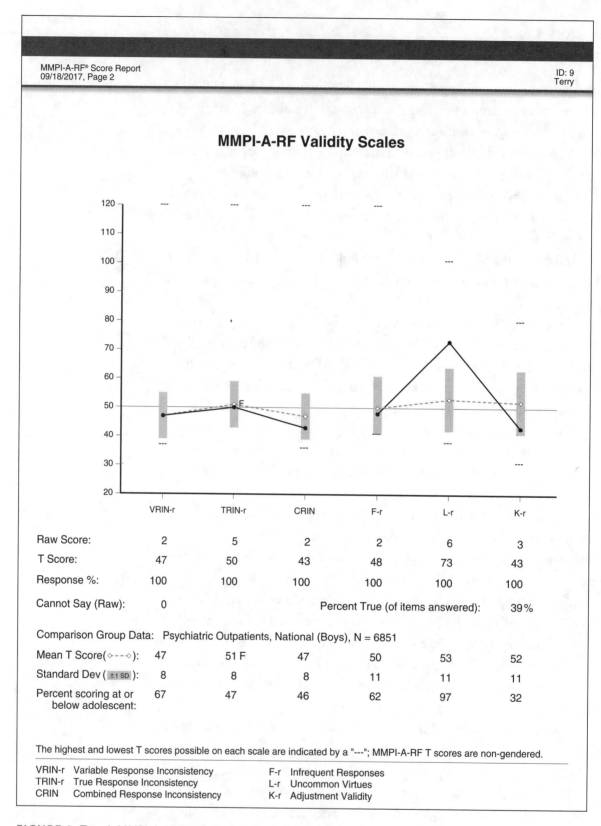

MMPI-A-RF Validity Scales

	VRIN-r	TRIN-r	CRIN	F-r	L-r	K-r
Raw Score:	2	5	2	2	6	3
T Score:	47	50	43	48	73	43
Response %:	100	100	100	100	100	100

Cannot Say (Raw): 0   Percent True (of items answered): 39%

Comparison Group Data: Psychiatric Outpatients, National (Boys), N = 6851

Mean T Score(◇--◇):	47	51 F	47	50	53	52
Standard Dev (±1 SD):	8	8	8	11	11	11
Percent scoring at or below adolescent:	67	47	46	62	97	32

The highest and lowest T scores possible on each scale are indicated by a "---"; MMPI-A-RF T scores are non-gendered.

VRIN-r Variable Response Inconsistency	F-r Infrequent Responses
TRIN-r True Response Inconsistency	L-r Uncommon Virtues
CRIN Combined Response Inconsistency	K-r Adjustment Validity

FIGURE 9 Terry's MMPI-A-RF Score Report. Copyright 2016 by the Regents of the University of Minnesota. All rights reserved.

MMPI-A-RF Higher-Order (H-O) and Restructured Clinical (RC) Scales

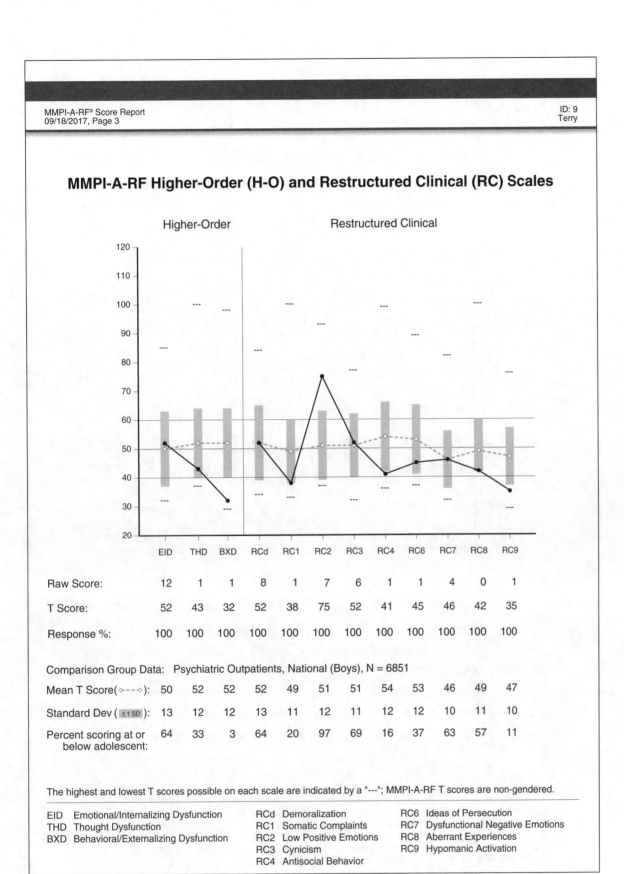

	EID	THD	BXD	RCd	RC1	RC2	RC3	RC4	RC6	RC7	RC8	RC9
Raw Score:	12	1	1	8	1	7	6	1	1	4	0	1
T Score:	52	43	32	52	38	75	52	41	45	46	42	35
Response %:	100	100	100	100	100	100	100	100	100	100	100	100

Comparison Group Data: Psychiatric Outpatients, National (Boys), N = 6851

Mean T Score(◇--◇):	50	52	52	52	49	51	51	54	53	46	49	47
Standard Dev (±1 SD):	13	12	12	13	11	12	11	12	12	10	11	10
Percent scoring at or below adolescent:	64	33	3	64	20	97	69	16	37	63	57	11

The highest and lowest T scores possible on each scale are indicated by a "---"; MMPI-A-RF T scores are non-gendered.

EID   Emotional/Internalizing Dysfunction
THD   Thought Dysfunction
BXD   Behavioral/Externalizing Dysfunction

RCd   Demoralization
RC1   Somatic Complaints
RC2   Low Positive Emotions
RC3   Cynicism
RC4   Antisocial Behavior

RC6   Ideas of Persecution
RC7   Dysfunctional Negative Emotions
RC8   Aberrant Experiences
RC9   Hypomanic Activation

FIGURE 9   Terry's MMPI-A-RF Score Report, continued.

129

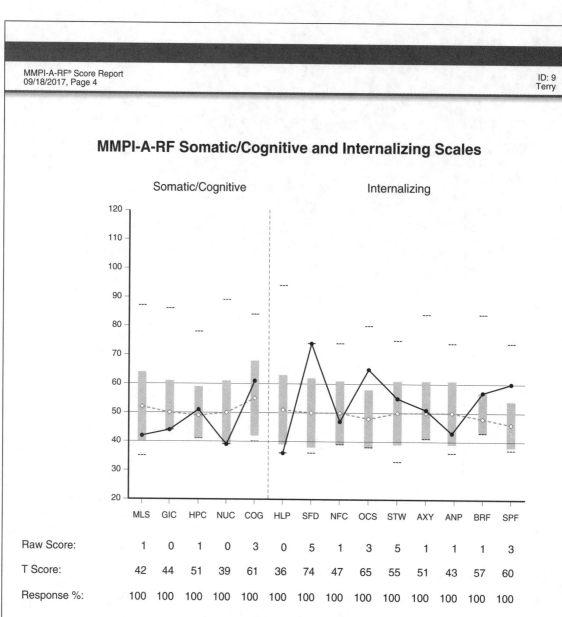

MMPI-A-RF Somatic/Cognitive and Internalizing Scales

Somatic/Cognitive   Internalizing

	MLS	GIC	HPC	NUC	COG	HLP	SFD	NFC	OCS	STW	AXY	ANP	BRF	SPF
Raw Score:	1	0	1	0	3	0	5	1	3	5	1	1	1	3
T Score:	42	44	51	39	61	36	74	47	65	55	51	43	57	60
Response %:	100	100	100	100	100	100	100	100	100	100	100	100	100	100

Comparison Group Data: Psychiatric Outpatients, National (Boys), N = 6851

Mean T Score(◇- - -◇):	52	50	49	50	55	51	50	50	48	50	50	50	48	46
Standard Dev (±1 SD):	12	11	10	11	13	12	12	11	10	11	11	11	9	8
Percent scoring at or below adolescent:	28	73	77	34	81	18	100	56	97	79	75	36	92	98

The highest and lowest T scores possible on each scale are indicated by a "---"; MMPI-A-RF T scores are non-gendered.

MLS	Malaise	HLP	Helplessness/Hopelessness	AXY	Anxiety
GIC	Gastrointestinal Complaints	SFD	Self-Doubt	ANP	Anger Proneness
HPC	Head Pain Complaints	NFC	Inefficacy	BRF	Behavior-Restricting Fears
NUC	Neurological Complaints	OCS	Obsessions/Compulsions	SPF	Specific Fears
COG	Cognitive Complaints	STW	Stress/Worry		

FIGURE 9 Terry's MMPI-A-RF Score Report, continued.

MMPI-A-RF Externalizing and Interpersonal Scales

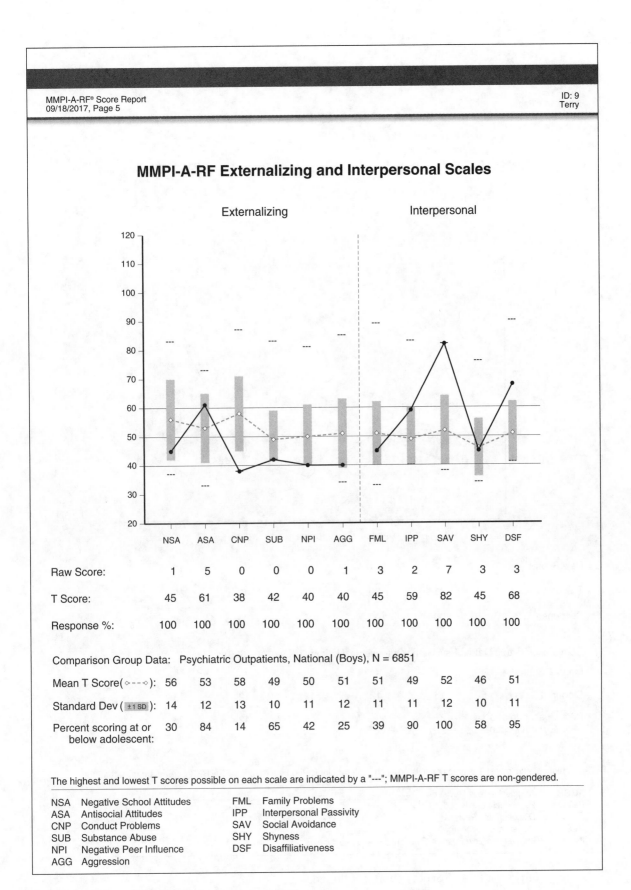

	NSA	ASA	CNP	SUB	NPI	AGG	FML	IPP	SAV	SHY	DSF
Raw Score:	1	5	0	0	0	1	3	2	7	3	3
T Score:	45	61	38	42	40	40	45	59	82	45	68
Response %:	100	100	100	100	100	100	100	100	100	100	100

Comparison Group Data: Psychiatric Outpatients, National (Boys), N = 6851

	NSA	ASA	CNP	SUB	NPI	AGG	FML	IPP	SAV	SHY	DSF
Mean T Score(◇- - -◇):	56	53	58	49	50	51	51	49	52	46	51
Standard Dev (±1 SD):	14	12	13	10	11	12	11	11	12	10	11
Percent scoring at or below adolescent:	30	84	14	65	42	25	39	90	100	58	95

The highest and lowest T scores possible on each scale are indicated by a "---"; MMPI-A-RF T scores are non-gendered.

NSA	Negative School Attitudes		FML	Family Problems
ASA	Antisocial Attitudes		IPP	Interpersonal Passivity
CNP	Conduct Problems		SAV	Social Avoidance
SUB	Substance Abuse		SHY	Shyness
NPI	Negative Peer Influence		DSF	Disaffiliativeness
AGG	Aggression			

FIGURE 9 Terry's MMPI-A-RF Score Report, continued.

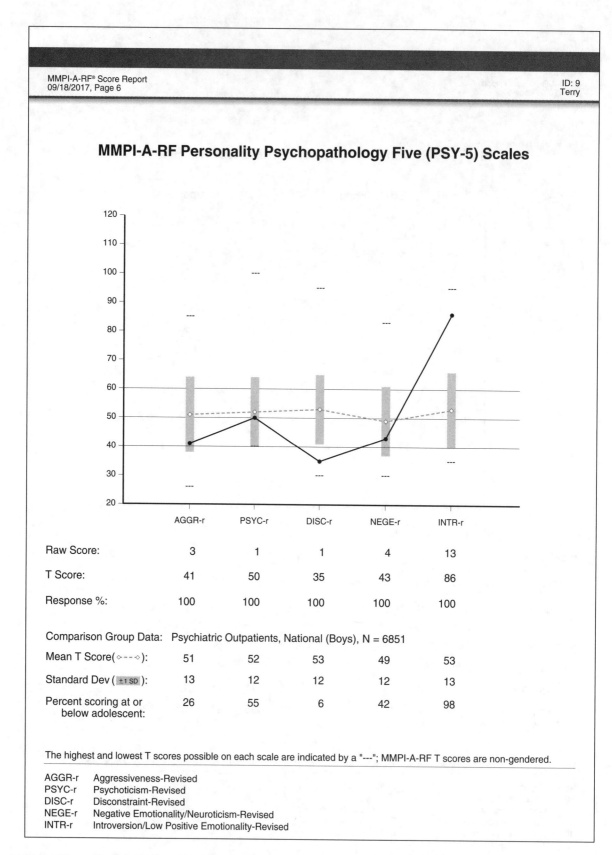

MMPI-A-RF Personality Psychopathology Five (PSY-5) Scales

	AGGR-r	PSYC-r	DISC-r	NEGE-r	INTR-r
Raw Score:	3	1	1	4	13
T Score:	41	50	35	43	86
Response %:	100	100	100	100	100

Comparison Group Data: Psychiatric Outpatients, National (Boys), N = 6851

	AGGR-r	PSYC-r	DISC-r	NEGE-r	INTR-r
Mean T Score(◇--◇):	51	52	53	49	53
Standard Dev (±1 SD):	13	12	12	12	13
Percent scoring at or below adolescent:	26	55	6	42	98

The highest and lowest T scores possible on each scale are indicated by a "---"; MMPI-A-RF T scores are non-gendered.

AGGR-r   Aggressiveness-Revised
PSYC-r   Psychoticism-Revised
DISC-r   Disconstraint-Revised
NEGE-r   Negative Emotionality/Neuroticism-Revised
INTR-r   Introversion/Low Positive Emotionality-Revised

FIGURE 9   Terry's MMPI-A-RF Score Report, continued.

MMPI-A-RF T SCORES (BY DOMAIN)

PROTOCOL VALIDITY

Content Non-Responsiveness

0	47	50	43
CNS	VRIN-r	TRIN-r	CRIN

Over-Reporting

48
F-r

Under-Reporting

73	43
L-r	K-r

SUBSTANTIVE SCALES

Somatic/Cognitive Dysfunction

38	42	44	51	39	61
RC1	MLS	GIC	HPC	NUC	COG

Emotional Dysfunction

52		52	36	74	47		
EID		RCd	HLP	SFD	NFC		

75	86
RC2	INTR-r

46	65	55	51	43	57	60	43
RC7	OCS	STW	AXY	ANP	BRF	SPF	NEGE-r

Thought Dysfunction

43		45
THD		RC6

42
RC8

50
PSYC-r

Behavioral Dysfunction

32		41	45	61	38	42	40
BXD		RC4	NSA	ASA	CNP	SUB	NPI

35	40	41	35
RC9	AGG	AGGR-r	DISC-r

Interpersonal Functioning

45	52	59	82	45	68
FML	RC3	IPP	SAV	SHY	DSF

Note. This information is provided to facilitate interpretation following the recommended structure for MMPI-A-RF interpretation in Chapter 7 of the *MMPI-A-RF Administration, Scoring, Interpretation, and Technical Manual*, which provides details in the text and an outline in Table 7-1.

FIGURE 9 Terry's MMPI-A-RF Score Report, continued.

MMPI-A-RF

Terry's protocol indicated that he presented himself in a very positive light by denying minor faults to which most adolescents readily admit. This response style can, to a certain degree, reflect a background that represents traditional values, which describes his family accurately according to Terry's therapist. However, a traditional upbringing is insufficient to account for this elevation, which indicates that Terry is likely reticent to acknowledge problems. The protocol should therefore be interpreted with caution. The absence of elevations on any Substantive scales cannot be interpreted as indicating the absence of problems assessed by those scales, and any elevations may underestimate the actual level of difficulties.

Terry's protocol was compared to a sample group of 6,851 boys who were psychiatric outpatients. Of note, the elevation on L-r was significantly above the mean of the comparison group.

Of immediate concern in Terry's protocol was that he responded to certain MMPI-A-RF items that are keyed in the direction of suicide risk and had elevations on scales RC2 and INT-r that are correlated with the risk of suicide. Terry's risk for self-harm should be closely monitored.

Although none of the Higher-Order scales (H-O) was elevated, perhaps due to the underreporting reflected on L-r, Terry did produce substantial elevations on some of the Substantive scales.

As can be seen in the elevations on RC2 (Low Positive Emotions), SFD (Self-Doubt), and INTR-r (Introversion/Low Positive Emotionality-Revised), Terry describes a significant lack of positive emotions and being socially distant from others. He reports a lack of positive emotional experiences and being socially disengaged. Terry acknowledges several symptoms associated with depression. He most likely experiences anhedonia, feels hopeless, lacks energy, and experiences fatigue. His dysphoria may make it difficult for his therapist to motivate him and he can be self-punishing. Terry reports self-doubt, feeling useless, and has a very poor self-image. He tends to be passive, self-defeating, and degrading.

Terry's OCS (Obsessions/Compulsions) and SPF (Specific Fears) scores indicate that he is anxious, and that he reports an above-average level of obsessive and compulsive symptoms. These problems may rise to a level that interferes with his thinking. Terry also reports experiencing multiple fears and phobias.

Terry's protocol indicated that he reports experiencing a diffuse pattern of cognitive complaints, and likely has difficulties with concentration and poor sleep.

There are no indications of disordered thinking in this protocol. However, because of indications of underreporting described earlier, such problems cannot be ruled out.

Terry reported several antisocial attitudes (ASA), which are associated with a history of conduct problems and behavioral acting out. However, he also generated low scores on BXD (Behavioral/Externalizing Dysfunction) and DISC-r (Disconstraint-Revised). While interpretation should be tempered by the L-r elevation of 73, the T scores are very low (32 and 35) and even with possible underreporting, this may indicate the likelihood of over-constrained behavior. Terry's anxiety may be keeping him from acting on his antisocial attitudes.

Socially, Terry reports significant social problems characterized by social avoidance and withdrawal. There were considerable elevations on SAV (Social Avoidance) and DSF (Disaffiliativeness). He likely has very few or no friends and is introverted and socially withdrawn. Terry likely is very socially awkward, isolated, and bullied by peers. He may be very uncomfortable with girls. Terry reports that he does not like being around others. He also has considerable difficulty trusting others. Terry is also likely very uncomfortable when he must deal with emotions.

The diagnostic considerations indicated by Terry's MMPI-A-RF results include depression-related disorders or others characterized by anhedonia as well as disorders involving obsessions and compulsions and specific phobias. Given his cognitive problems, he should be evaluated for possible ADHD or other neurodevelopmental disorders. Other considerations include disruptive behavior disorders as well as disorders involving social avoidance.

Regarding treatment intervention, beyond his need for an evaluation of his risk for self-harm, Terry's level of depression requires intensive treatment. He should be evaluated for both a need for inpatient treatment as well as antidepressant medications. In addition, he likely will require treatment for obsessive-compulsive symptoms, anxiety, fears, and phobias. Terry would also benefit from interventions designed to increase his social skills.

Treatment may be challenged by Terry's pronounced anhedonia and social isolation and difficulties establishing a therapeutic relationship because of his tendencies for disaffiliation.

Potential treatment assets that can be used in treatment are that Terry was willing to complete the test and did so in a consistent manner. His level of emotional distress may, at least initially, motivate him to be engaged in treatment aimed at relief of emotional discomfort. Because of his very poor self-esteem, Terry may be responsive to supportive interventions focused on the skills that he has rather than addressing his deficits.

Diagnosis

Terry was diagnosed with Social Anxiety Disorder, Unspecified Depressive Disorder, Attention Deficit Hyperactivity Disorder by history, Developmental Coordination Disorder by history, and Communication Disorder by history. The need to rule out Autistic Spectrum Disorder and Social Communication Disorder was also indicated.

OUTCOME

In light of the possibility of an Autistic Spectrum Disorder, Terry was referred to a specialized clinic for further assessment. He was diagnosed with Social Pragmatic Communication Disorder, which qualified him for services with the local agency for developmental disabilities. Home-based services were initiated. They included cognitive-behavioral therapy and family therapy. He was seen by a psychiatrist and placed on an SSRI. Terry was referred to a speech therapist who developed a treatment plan for enhancing his social communication skills.

The Forensic Cases

Carl

A Male Referred for a Juvenile Sex Offender Risk Assessment

BACKGROUND

Carl is a 16-year-old male who was referred for a juvenile sex offender risk assessment by his attorney. He had entered a plea of admission to a charge of rape and had been adjudicated delinquent. At the time that he was examined, he was in foster care following placement in a group home. Carl was seen twice and in the second interview, portions of his MMPI-A-RF were reviewed with him.

Juvenile court records state that Carl had his younger stepbrother (age 8) perform oral sex on him. Carl's stepmother, the mother of the victim, discovered the abuse and confronted Carl. Carl was subsequently removed from home and put into out-of-home placement.

Interview With Youth

Carl described his upbringing in very negative terms. He indicated that his parents were never married and that his mother primarily raised him during his childhood. His father had some visitation. Carl reported that he had a good relationship with his mother but described his father as being verbally abusive. He recounted that his parents did not get along and he often felt in the middle. Carl said that he grew up mostly in the Midwest, but that his mother moved to California when he was in middle school and took him with her. However, he alleged that her boyfriend "mentally" abused him and that his mother and her boyfriend lived with the boyfriend's parents, who would not allow Carl to live there.

Carl moved to live with his father at about the age of 14. He was living there at the time of the instant offense. Carl reported that he did not get along with his stepmother and made allegations that his father was threatening and verbally abusive. Carl said that he has four half-siblings, two with his mother and two with his father. His father is employed in construction and his mother works in a factory. He said that owing to his frequent moves, he has few friends. He stays in touch online with the few friends that he does have. He does not have a girlfriend. Following the alleged instant offense, Carl was placed in a group home and is now, as noted, in foster care.

Carl reported that he is currently in the 11th grade and was attending his fourth high school owing to frequent moves as well as his foster placement. He said that he attended three or four elementary schools and two middle schools. Carl indicated that he has never been in any type of special education but was diagnosed with ADHD in the fourth grade.

Carl reported that he did not have any significant school discipline problems and was never expelled. However, he stated that owing to his frequent change of schools, he "didn't cooperate well with others" and relates better with adults than peers. His goal is to receive training as a chef, and he has been accepted into a career center.

Carl indicated that he does not drink alcohol. He said that he began smoking marijuana in the eighth grade and would use it frequently "to forget" about his childhood. He said that he stopped about 3 months ago after his father began drug testing him. He denied any other substance abuse.

Carl alleged that when he was younger, about 7 or 8 years old, a paternal uncle sexually abused him. He would not reveal any details but said that he has informed his caseworker and his attorney. Carl alleged that his birth father was verbally abusive and hit him with belts and spoons. He said that this is his first contact with the juvenile justice system.

Carl indicated that he briefly saw a therapist for depression but could not recall the name and did not feel that it was especially helpful. He denied any history of fire-setting or animal cruelty. He has never been psychiatrically hospitalized. He denied any history of suicidal behaviors but said that while he was living with his father, he would "not often" superficially cut himself. Carl said that he believes that there is a history of mood disorder in his mother's family.

When he was younger, Carl was prescribed medication for ADHD, but he no longer takes it. He has never been prescribed any other mental health medications but said that he has an upcoming appointment for evaluation of medication to address depression and anxiety.

Carl denied any significant present medical problems. He has not had any surgeries. Carl said that he suffered one concussion in a fight when he was 13 years old and was evaluated and released. Otherwise, he denied any history of head trauma, loss of consciousness, seizures, or other neurological involvement.

Regarding his sexual history, Carl has had sexual intercourse three times, each at the age of 14. Each encounter was with a female of about the same age and consensual. He denied ever forcing or coercing sex. He stated that his sexual preference is heterosexual and denied any interest in younger female or male children, especially prepubescent. He denied any fetishes or aberrant sexual behaviors or interests. He reported that he would masturbate regularly to a *Playboy* or *Hustler* that his father had given to him (confirmed by his father). Otherwise, he does not use pornography and denied any interest in or use of child pornography.

COLLATERAL INFORMATION

Carl's father said that Carl had a very difficult childhood owing to the frequent moves of Carl's mother, estimating that Carl may have been to at least 16 different schools. During the time that Carl lived with him, Carl had a difficult time adjusting to structure but seemed to be doing well, until the alleged offense was discovered. He reported that he believes that Carl has been depressed for a number of years, citing his mother's reported instability in lifestyle. When Carl lived with him and his wife, he was able to complete the credits needed to bring him up to the appropriate grade level, but had behavioral problems such as smoking marijuana, leading him to be drug tested.

His father briefly took Carl to a therapist, for about 10 sessions, to address Carl's early experiences but felt that the therapist was not helpful. Carl's father also said that he could not recall the name or address of this therapist.

Although the father said that Carl could be manipulative and untruthful, Carl was not physically aggressive. He observed no significant mood swings (with the exception of after he would speak with his mother) nor any unusual or bizarre behavior, including that of a sexual nature. He acknowledged giving Carl a *Playboy* as he felt this to be an appropriate outlet and he was limiting Carl's phone usage. Carl did have problems with his stepmother and could also be very difficult with his younger siblings. His father believes that Carl needs both mental health treatment and a consequence for the alleged instant offense.

Numerous unsuccessful attempts were made to contact Carl's mother.

Records obtained from Carl's current school report no disciplinary contacts. He is not receiving any special educational services. His grades are generally poor. The information obtained may, however, be limited owing to the number of schools that he has attended.

Current Behavioral Status

Carl appeared to be his stated age. His hygiene and grooming were adequate. He displayed no unusual mannerisms and maintained direct eye contact throughout the examination. His speech was normal in tone, rhythm, volume, and pacing. His approach to the evaluation was cooperative.

Overall, Carl's flow of conversation and thought was understandable. His responses were goal-directed and responsive to the examiner's questions. His speech was not pressured, slow, or rapid in pacing. He did not exhibit disturbances of thought typically associated with serious mental illnesses such as rambling, circumstantial ideation, fragmented ideation, flight of ideas, poverty of speech, or perseveration. There were no disturbances in the form of his thinking; he did not have loose associations or tangential thinking and his cognitions appeared to be well organized overall.

Carl's affect was appropriate and reactive to a reported generally depressed state. He described himself as "irritated" and rated his current level of psychological distress as a "5" out of a possible 10. His emotional presentation was appropriate to his stated emotional state and it was controlled. Often, when asked about things in his past, he would begin to cry but was able to compose himself.

Carl denied and gave no behavioral evidence of visual, gustatory, olfactory, or tactile hallucinations. He further gave no behavioral evidence of hearing or responding to hallucinations during any of the examinations. As such, there were no observable indications of the types of perceptual abnormalities typically associated with psychosis.

Carl denied and gave no evidence of specific delusional thinking. There was no evidence of systematic paranoid delusions or grandiosity. Accordingly, there appears to be no indication in his thought content that would typically be seen with seriously mentally ill persons.

Interpersonally, Carl described himself as generally guarded and distrustful, citing his past as the reason he feels this way. He indicated that he is generally uncomfortable around people and tries to stay vigilant for any potential harm or negative consequence.

Carl reported a number of symptoms typically associated with depression such as limited appetite, hopelessness, and loss of interest or pleasure, loss of sexual interest, sleep problems, poor concentration, and irritability. When specifically asked, he denied active suicidal ideation, intent, or plan but indicated that he has had episodic thoughts of killing himself adding, "I couldn't do it." He denied homicidal ideation.

Carl denied any history of bipolar disorder or manic episodes such as marked agitation, extreme loss of the need for sleep, racing thoughts, or rapid mood swings. Carl described himself as chronically anxious and especially fearful in confined spaces. He denied any other specific phobias as well as any intrusive obsessive thinking or compulsive behavior but described himself as being very orderly. He denied any history of "flashbacks," intrusive thoughts, or other psychological consequences of trauma exposure.

Carl was alert and responsive to his environment and there were no problems observed with his attention or concentration. He was mildly distractible but could be refocused. He was oriented to time, place, person, and situation. His concentration was intact as evidenced by his attention and focus in the conversation with the examiner. His immediate recall was also intact as demonstrated by his ability to recall five digits forward and three in reverse order. His short-term recall was also adequate as demonstrated by his ability to recall three of three items from memory after a 10-minute distraction. His concentration was adequate as demonstrated in his ability for serial and simple mental calculations. He had an adequate capacity for verbal abstract reasoning as demonstrated in his ability to state conceptual similarities between related objects and concepts, including complex abstractions. This was also demonstrated in his ability to interpret commonly used proverbs. His insight and judgment appeared to be fair, as determined by both his history and in response to situational questions.

On the K-BIT 2, Carl earned a Vocabulary standard score of 94. Carl earned a Nonverbal standard score of 106. His overall Composite IQ standard score was 100.

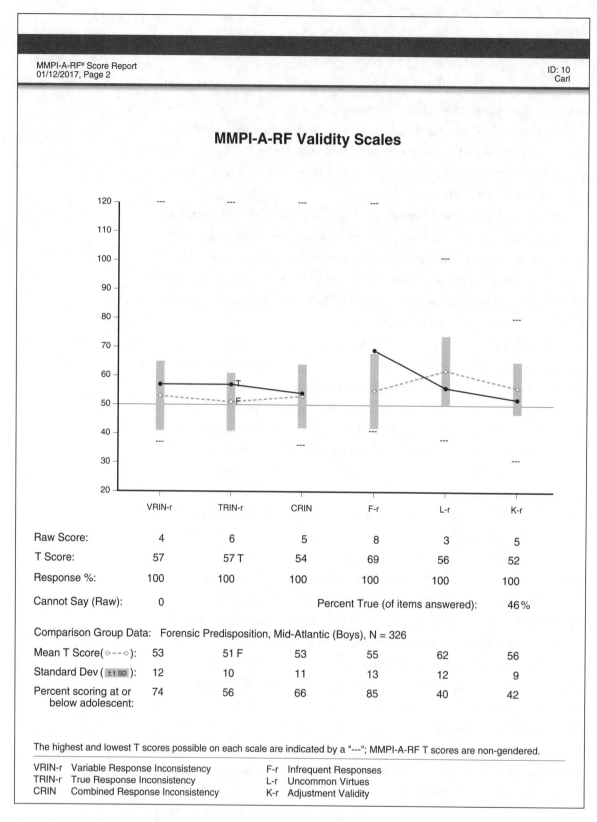

MMPI-A-RF Validity Scales

	VRIN-r	TRIN-r	CRIN	F-r	L-r	K-r
Raw Score:	4	6	5	8	3	5
T Score:	57	57 T	54	69	56	52
Response %:	100	100	100	100	100	100

Cannot Say (Raw): 0   Percent True (of items answered): 46%

Comparison Group Data: Forensic Predisposition, Mid-Atlantic (Boys), N = 326

	VRIN-r	TRIN-r	CRIN	F-r	L-r	K-r
Mean T Score(◇--◇):	53	51 F	53	55	62	56
Standard Dev (±1 SD):	12	10	11	13	12	9
Percent scoring at or below adolescent:	74	56	66	85	40	42

The highest and lowest T scores possible on each scale are indicated by a "---"; MMPI-A-RF T scores are non-gendered.

VRIN-r   Variable Response Inconsistency   F-r   Infrequent Responses
TRIN-r   True Response Inconsistency   L-r   Uncommon Virtues
CRIN   Combined Response Inconsistency   K-r   Adjustment Validity

FIGURE 10 Carl's MMPI-A-RF Score Report. Copyright 2016 by the Regents of the University of Minnesota. All rights reserved.

142

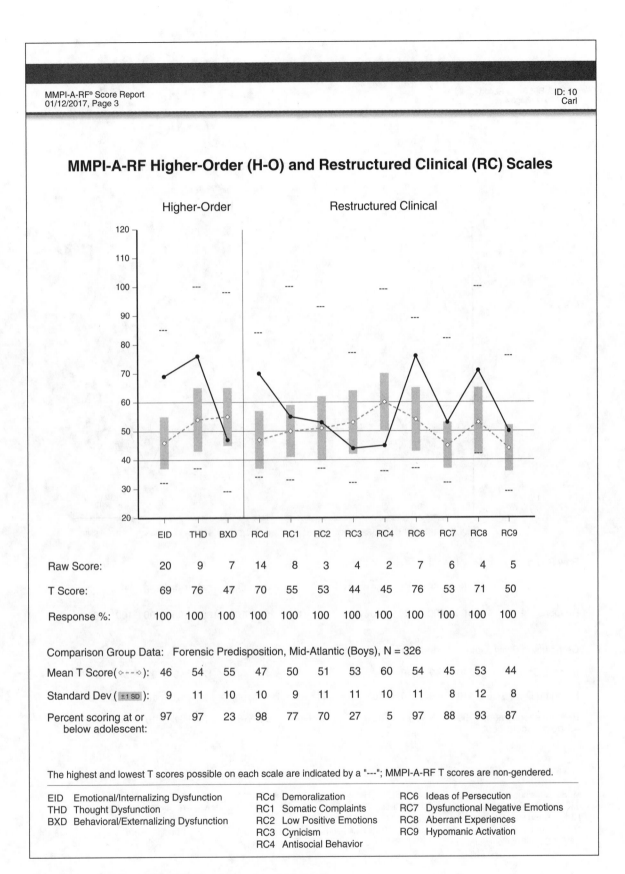

MMPI-A-RF Higher-Order (H-O) and Restructured Clinical (RC) Scales

Higher-Order   Restructured Clinical

	EID	THD	BXD	RCd	RC1	RC2	RC3	RC4	RC6	RC7	RC8	RC9
Raw Score:	20	9	7	14	8	3	4	2	7	6	4	5
T Score:	69	76	47	70	55	53	44	45	76	53	71	50
Response %:	100	100	100	100	100	100	100	100	100	100	100	100

Comparison Group Data: Forensic Predisposition, Mid-Atlantic (Boys), N = 326

Mean T Score(◇--◇):	46	54	55	47	50	51	53	60	54	45	53	44
Standard Dev (±1 SD):	9	11	10	10	9	11	11	10	11	8	12	8
Percent scoring at or below adolescent:	97	97	23	98	77	70	27	5	97	88	93	87

The highest and lowest T scores possible on each scale are indicated by a "---"; MMPI-A-RF T scores are non-gendered.

EID	Emotional/Internalizing Dysfunction	RCd	Demoralization
THD	Thought Dysfunction	RC1	Somatic Complaints
BXD	Behavioral/Externalizing Dysfunction	RC2	Low Positive Emotions
		RC3	Cynicism
		RC4	Antisocial Behavior

RC6	Ideas of Persecution
RC7	Dysfunctional Negative Emotions
RC8	Aberrant Experiences
RC9	Hypomanic Activation

FIGURE 10   Carl's MMPI-A-RF Score Report, continued.

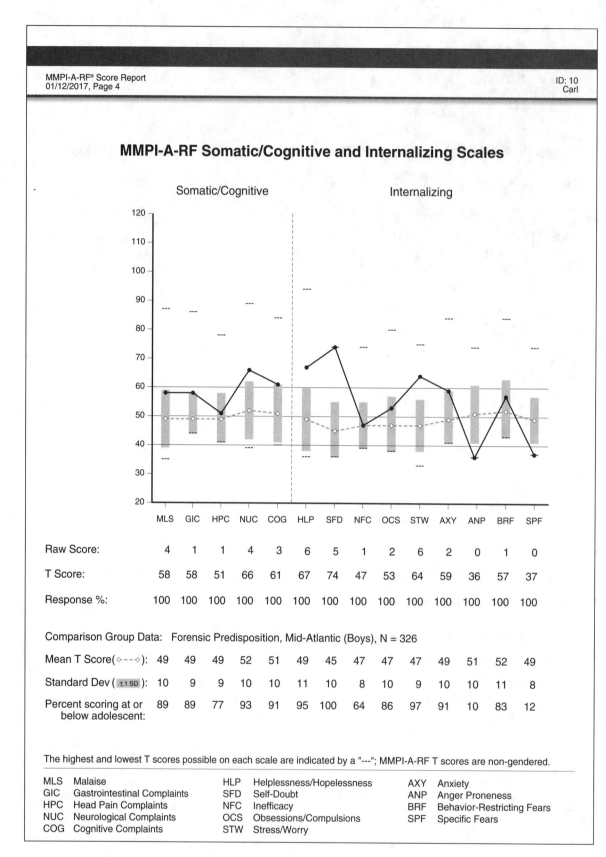

MMPI-A-RF Somatic/Cognitive and Internalizing Scales

Somatic/Cognitive   Internalizing

	MLS	GIC	HPC	NUC	COG	HLP	SFD	NFC	OCS	STW	AXY	ANP	BRF	SPF
Raw Score:	4	1	1	4	3	6	5	1	2	6	2	0	1	0
T Score:	58	58	51	66	61	67	74	47	53	64	59	36	57	37
Response %:	100	100	100	100	100	100	100	100	100	100	100	100	100	100

Comparison Group Data: Forensic Predisposition, Mid-Atlantic (Boys), N = 326

Mean T Score(◇--◇):	49	49	49	52	51	49	45	47	47	47	49	51	52	49
Standard Dev (±1 SD):	10	9	9	10	10	11	10	8	10	9	10	10	11	8
Percent scoring at or below adolescent:	89	89	77	93	91	95	100	64	86	97	91	10	83	12

The highest and lowest T scores possible on each scale are indicated by a "---"; MMPI-A-RF T scores are non-gendered.

MLS	Malaise	HLP	Helplessness/Hopelessness
GIC	Gastrointestinal Complaints	SFD	Self-Doubt
HPC	Head Pain Complaints	NFC	Inefficacy
NUC	Neurological Complaints	OCS	Obsessions/Compulsions
COG	Cognitive Complaints	STW	Stress/Worry

AXY	Anxiety
ANP	Anger Proneness
BRF	Behavior-Restricting Fears
SPF	Specific Fears

FIGURE 10 Carl's MMPI-A-RF Score Report, continued.

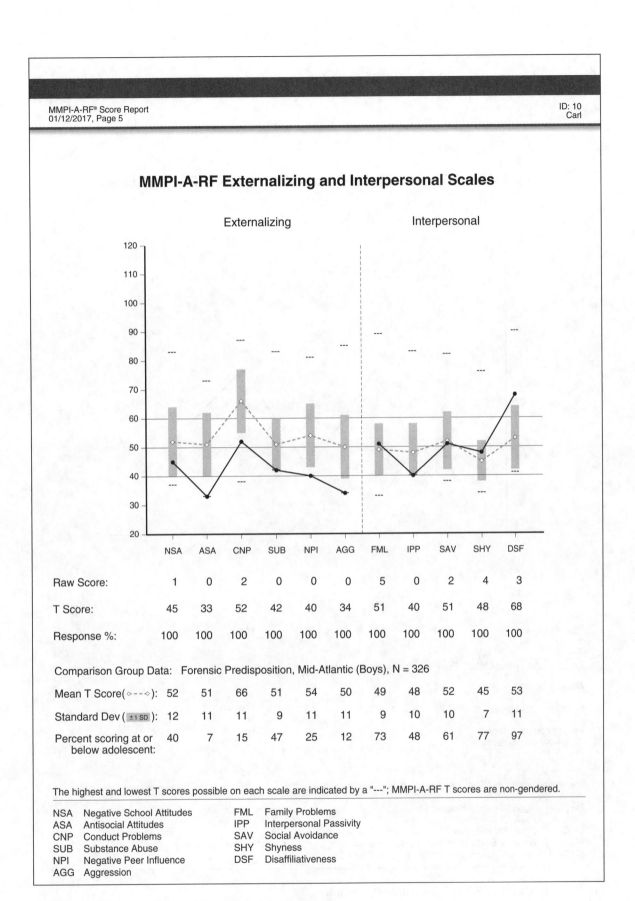

MMPI-A-RF Externalizing and Interpersonal Scales

Externalizing | Interpersonal

	NSA	ASA	CNP	SUB	NPI	AGG	FML	IPP	SAV	SHY	DSF
Raw Score:	1	0	2	0	0	0	5	0	2	4	3
T Score:	45	33	52	42	40	34	51	40	51	48	68
Response %:	100	100	100	100	100	100	100	100	100	100	100

Comparison Group Data: Forensic Predisposition, Mid-Atlantic (Boys), N = 326

	NSA	ASA	CNP	SUB	NPI	AGG	FML	IPP	SAV	SHY	DSF
Mean T Score(◇---◇):	52	51	66	51	54	50	49	48	52	45	53
Standard Dev (±1 SD):	12	11	11	9	11	11	9	10	10	7	11
Percent scoring at or below adolescent:	40	7	15	47	25	12	73	48	61	77	97

The highest and lowest T scores possible on each scale are indicated by a "---"; MMPI-A-RF T scores are non-gendered.

NSA	Negative School Attitudes	FML	Family Problems
ASA	Antisocial Attitudes	IPP	Interpersonal Passivity
CNP	Conduct Problems	SAV	Social Avoidance
SUB	Substance Abuse	SHY	Shyness
NPI	Negative Peer Influence	DSF	Disaffiliativeness
AGG	Aggression		

FIGURE 10 Carl's MMPI-A-RF Score Report, continued.

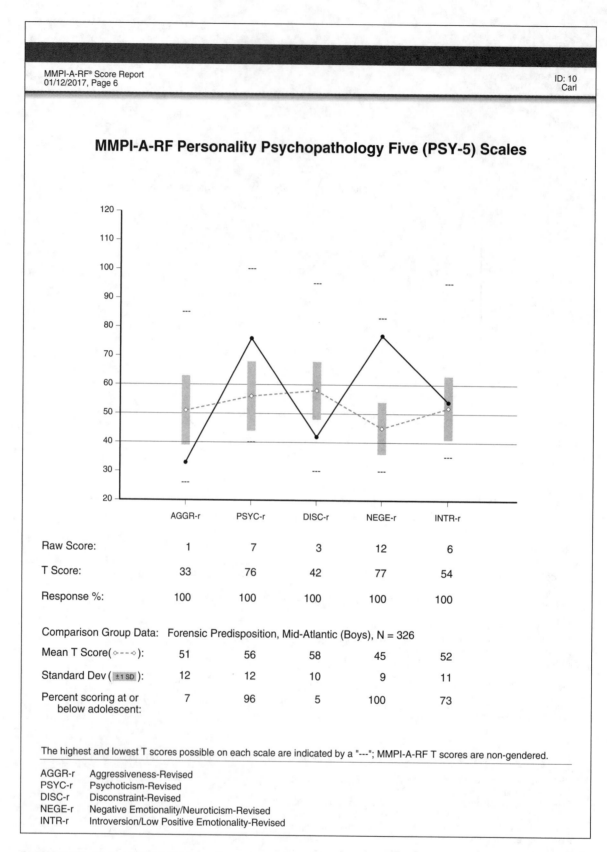

MMPI-A-RF Personality Psychopathology Five (PSY-5) Scales

	AGGR-r	PSYC-r	DISC-r	NEGE-r	INTR-r
Raw Score:	1	7	3	12	6
T Score:	33	76	42	77	54
Response %:	100	100	100	100	100

Comparison Group Data: Forensic Predisposition, Mid-Atlantic (Boys), N = 326

	AGGR-r	PSYC-r	DISC-r	NEGE-r	INTR-r
Mean T Score(◇--◇):	51	56	58	45	52
Standard Dev (±1 SD):	12	12	10	9	11
Percent scoring at or below adolescent:	7	96	5	100	73

The highest and lowest T scores possible on each scale are indicated by a "---"; MMPI-A-RF T scores are non-gendered.

AGGR-r	Aggressiveness-Revised
PSYC-r	Psychoticism-Revised
DISC-r	Disconstraint-Revised
NEGE-r	Negative Emotionality/Neuroticism-Revised
INTR-r	Introversion/Low Positive Emotionality-Revised

FIGURE 10 Carl's MMPI-A-RF Score Report, continued.

146

MMPI-A-RF T SCORES (BY DOMAIN)

PROTOCOL VALIDITY

Content Non-Responsiveness

0	57	57 T	54
CNS	VRIN-r	TRIN-r	CRIN

Over-Reporting

69
F-r

Under-Reporting

56	52
L-r	K-r

SUBSTANTIVE SCALES

Somatic/Cognitive Dysfunction

55	58	58	51	66	61
RC1	MLS	GIC	HPC	NUC	COG

Emotional Dysfunction

69		70	67	74	47		
EID		RCd	HLP	SFD	NFC		

		53	54				
		RC2	INTR-r				

		53	53	64	59	36	57	37	77
		RC7	OCS	STW	AXY	ANP	BRF	SPF	NEGE-r

Thought Dysfunction

76		76
THD		RC6

		71
		RC8

		76
		PSYC-r

Behavioral Dysfunction

47		45	45	33	52	42	40
BXD		RC4	NSA	ASA	CNP	SUB	NPI

		50	34	33	42
		RC9	AGG	AGGR-r	DISC-r

Interpersonal Functioning

51	44	40	51	48	68
FML	RC3	IPP	SAV	SHY	DSF

Note. This information is provided to facilitate interpretation following the recommended structure for MMPI-A-RF interpretation in Chapter 7 of the *MMPI-A-RF Administration, Scoring, Interpretation, and Technical Manual,* which provides details in the text and an outline in Table 7-1.

FIGURE 10 Carl's MMPI-A-RF Score Report, continued.

MMPI-A-RF

Carl's protocol was valid. He appeared to understand the test items and responded appropriately. There were no indications of either under- or overreporting of problems. His protocol was compared to a reference group of 326 Mid-Atlantic Forensic Predisposition boys.

Carl responded to several of the MMPI-A-RF items in a direction indicating suicidal thoughts and he also may be at risk for self-injurious behavior. In his second interview, Carl was asked about this and denied presently feeling suicidal or experiencing impulses to hurt himself. Nevertheless, he should be monitored and appropriate precautions taken as needed.

Carl's scores indicate significant thought dysfunction. Specifically, he reports significant persecutory ideation and is likely to experience auditory and visual hallucinations and other psychotic symptoms. He likely engages in aggressive and oppositional behavior as well as fighting and truancy. He is likely to have a history of school suspensions. Carl also reported unusual thought processes and perceptual experiences. He is likely to have poor reality testing, to be disoriented, and to daydream. When asked about these findings, Carl denied having the experiences just described and he did not give evidence of a paranoid psychosis or poor ties with reality. He related his feelings of persecution both to his current legal situation as well as his life experiences.

Carl's responses also indicate that he is experiencing significant emotional distress. He reports feeling sad, dissatisfied with his life experiences, and overwhelmed by life. He appears to feel quite inferior, degrades himself, and feels hopeless and that he is a failure in life. He believes that he has gotten a raw deal out of life so far and he may tend to give up easily.

Carl reports vague neurological complaints and a diffuse pattern of cognitive difficulties. He likely presents with multiple somatic complaints, has problems with concentration and attention, has academic problems, and presents with slow speech.

Socially, Carl reports some dislike of being around others and he likely has few or no friends, is socially withdrawn, is uncomfortable dealing with emotions, and has difficulty trusting others.

Carl did not have problems related to maladaptive externalizing behavior such as theft or physical aggression. He actually reported a below-average number of antisocial attitudes.

Risk Assessment

As a general cautionary note, youth who have sexually offended are heterogeneous. There is no single type of an adolescent with sexual behavioral problems. Teenagers are not merely "small adults" and have very different neurodevelopmental functioning. Many (but not all) adolescents who have sexual behavioral problems have a history of trauma that can negatively impact the developing brain.

In evaluating youth who have sexually offended, it is imperative to note that research indicates that adolescents are more responsive to treatment than are adult sex offenders. They do not necessarily continue reoffending into adulthood, especially when provided with adequate treatment (ASTA, 2012). Moreover, the overall rate of recidivism of adolescent sexual offenders who receive treatment is low as compared to adults (Alexander, 1999) and is lower when compared to other delinquent behavior (Caldwell, 2010; Worling & Curwin, 2000). Youth who have sexually offended do not fit one particular personality typology. Research reviewing a 10-year period found that differences exist between juvenile sex offenders and nonsexual offenders on personality characteristics of behavioral problems, history of sexual abuse, nonsexual offending, and peer functioning. Inconsistent results were found for demographic factors, family factors, antisocial attitudes, and intellectual and neurological functioning (Wijk et al., 2006).

There are multiple pathways to sex offending behaviors in juveniles. Juveniles who have sexually offended are not monolithic and should be assessed in a manner that is responsive to needs and risk (Prentky, 2017). Most important in the critical difference between adult and juvenile sex offender risk assessment is the focus of the juvenile justice system on treatment and rehabilitation. Risk assessment of juveniles should focus not only on risk factors, but also on treatment needs and protective factors. Given the dynamic nature of youth, risk assessments must never be seen as final and should be redone periodically.

JUVENILE SEX OFFENDER ASSESSMENT PROTOCOL-II (J-SOAP)

Carl was assessed using the J-SOAP-II (Prentky & Righthand, 2003), a measure designed to aid in the systematic review of risk factors that have been identified in the professional literature as being associated with sexual and criminal offending. The J-SOAP-II is appropriate for use with both adjudicated and nonadjudicated youth but does not provide a "cut-off" or "score." Rather, the J-SOAP-II provides a ratio-based analysis of risk factors that can be utilized as part of, but not the total, assessment of risk. The J-SOAP-II consists of scales measuring static (unchangeable), historical, and dynamic (fluid and changeable) factors empirically supported as potential risk factors for sexual offending in youth.

In the Static/Historical scales, Carl was found to have 3 out of 16 possible items. He did not have any of the 16 Impulsive/Antisocial Behavior indicators. Carl does not have a documented history of other prior legally charged sex offenses nor a reported strong sexual drive history. Factors that increase his risk are that his alleged victim is a male, the duration of the alleged offending behavior, and that there may have been some degree of nonopportunistic behavior. Although he alleges that he was sexually abused by an uncle, there is no documentation that such abuse took place. Further, although it is often thought that a history of sexual abuse victimization increases risk (and has erroneously been reported as a significant factor in both assessment and treatment), recidivism research has not shown this to be the case. Carl does not appear to have a substantial history of other antisocial behavior or antisocial attitudes that support crime and violence.

On the Dynamic scales portion of the J-SOAP-II, Carl had 9 of 14 items on the Intervention scale and 6 of 10 items on the Community Stability scale. In these areas, he demonstrates a higher risk. The factors identified are his history of poor peer relationships as well as a lack of understanding of risk factors, which can be addressed in treatment. Carl's risk is increased owing to his instability of living situations (both past and current), poor school stability, and a lack of positive support system. Overall, his Static score was 3 out of 32 items, his Dynamic score was 15 out of 24 items, and his Total J-SOAP-II score was 18 out of 56.

PROFESOR

Carl was also assessed using the Protective and Risk Observations for Eliminating Sexual Offense Recidivism (Worling, 2017). The PROFESOR is designed for use as a structured checklist to assist professionals in identifying and summarizing protective and risk factors for adolescents and emerging adults (ages 12–25) who have sexually offended. It is intended to assist with planning interventions that can help individuals enhance their capacity for sexual and relationship health and thus eliminate sexual recidivism. It contains 20 bipolar factors that are based on review of the available literature and clinical experience with adolescents and emerging adults. Items are assessed as either protective (P), neutral (N), or risk (R). These ratings are then summarized in five categories: Predominantly Protective; More Protective than Risk; Predominantly Balanced; More Risk than Protective; and Predominantly Risk. These ratings can then guide the nature and intensity of treatment to reduce recidivism. In this youth's case, he is rated overall as in the Predominantly Balanced category, having more neutral ratings overall and an equal number of risk and protective factors.

Using the J-SOAP-II, Carl was found to have more lower than higher identified risk factors. On the PROFESOR, he was identified as having about the same level of risk and protective factors with a number of factors being neutral. Protective factors identified in each included the lack of tendencies for maladaptive externalizing behavior identified in the MMPI-A-RF, his intelligence, and his emotional distress (reflected in his MMPI-A-RF scores), which may be a motivating factor in the initial parts of his treatment.

Diagnosis

Carl was given the diagnoses of Major Depressive Disorder, Severe, without psychotic features (rule out emerging psychotic features), Unspecified Trauma and Stressor Related Disorder and Unspecified Disruptive, Impulse-Control and Conduct Disorder. The MMPI-A-RF indicated the potential for an underlying thought disorder which was not seen in the clinical and follow-up interviews. The MMPI-A-RF can be sensitive to emerging serious mental illness that may not initially be seen in an interview. Therefore, he should be monitored for possible psychotic decompensation. This was also the case for the potential risk of suicide identified on the MMPI-A-RF.

OUTCOME

It was recommended that Carl continue in his treatment foster home placement. In addition, it was recommended that he begin both individual and group sexual offender therapies using evidence-based models that are trauma informed. It was recommended that the juvenile court initiate a treatment team consisting of his providers from mental health, school, and probation. These services were implemented, and Carl did not reoffend.

FORENSIC CONTRIBUTIONS OF THE MMPI-A-RF

In cases of assessment of youth who sexually offend, the MMPI-A-RF provides the clinician the ability to assess if there are underlying psychological problems that should be addressed in treatment. Especially in the case of juveniles, the focus should be on not simply a prediction of risk—but what is more important, how to manage that risk in the future and build on the strengths and protective factors that reduce the risk of reoffending.

The MMPI-A-RF Validity scales can provide insight into potential defensiveness in treatment. As an example, the L-r scale can provide the clinician with important hypotheses about readiness for treatment as well as possible sociocultural factors (high L-r scores can be associated with traditional and conforming values). Substantive scale scores can provide insight into the potential for psychological dysfunctions that could impede treatment, especially if there is the potential for a thought or mood disorder. Risk factors that have been shown to correlate with negative outcomes are those generally seen in delinquent populations such as early onset antisocial behavior. The MMPI-A-RF behavioral-externalizing measures can serve to alert the examiner if the youth is at risk for the types of behaviors most often seen in poor outcomes.

Although often thought of as a measure to identify psychopathology, the MMPI-A-RF can also provide important clues to the treatment assets or positive qualities of a youth. This focus on treatment assets is of immeasurable importance in the treatment of all youth but has critical implications for youth who offend. In Carl's case, his protocol suggested an absence of antisocial attitudes or tendencies for maladaptive behavior, which form an important asset in his treatment, and which were identified as protective factors against reoffending.

David

A Youth Evaluated for Competency to Waive His Miranda Rights

BACKGROUND

David is a 17-year-old male who was seen for an evaluation of his competency to waive his *Miranda* rights. He had been arrested on a charge of murder. Following his arrest, he was taken to a juvenile correctional facility where he attempted suicide by hanging and was taken to a psychiatric hospital. Due to concerns about his emotional state at the time he was interviewed by the police, his attorney requested an evaluation of his ability to knowingly and intelligently waive his rights. He was assessed at the psychiatric hospital about 8 weeks after the alleged offense.

Interview With Youth

Prior to the offense, David lived with his mother and stepfather. His birth father had been incarcerated when David was very young and has had little involvement in David's life. David's mother reported that her pregnancy and delivery of him were nonremarkable. He was a healthy infant who obtained developmental milestones normally. There is no history of abuse or neglect.

David socialized easily and had no behavioral problems at home or in elementary school. However, when his family moved to another, more rural area when he was in the seventh grade, he began to withdraw and associated with a peer group that he described as social misfits. He became more socially active after joining basketball and track teams.

David had a history of using marijuana but not on a regular basis. He would also periodically take methylphenidate, a psychostimulant that he would obtain from a peer and use while studying. He had no history of abuse victimization. He had never been in any type of mental health services and there is no known family history of mental illness.

David had a history of three concussions from sports. A neuropsychological evaluation had found evidence of mild neurocognitive disorder about 6 months prior to the alleged offense.

David had no prior contact with the juvenile justice system and was not seen as a behavioral problem either at home or in middle or high school. He had no known history of fire-setting or animal cruelty. He earned average to above-average grades and was never in any form of special education. Prior to the alleged offense, he had broken up with his girlfriend. He reported that he had not slept the night before the alleged offense and had thoughts of suicide.

COLLATERAL INFORMATION

Since being admitted to the hospital about 2 weeks prior to the examination, David was diagnosed with Major Depression, single episode, severe, with psychotic features; Mild Neurocognitive Disorder owing to multiple concussions; and Cannabis Use Disorder.

In a telephone interview with the examiner, David's mother reported he had never been aggressive and had not shown fascination with violent media. David's mother said that he related well to her and to his stepfather, whom he considered his functional father. She said that he had no problems with peers or siblings. She reported that he had become increasingly depressed after breaking up with his girlfriend in the weeks before the alleged offense and had also become very withdrawn.

Current Behavioral Status

David was dressed in street clothing that was neat, clean, and properly arranged. He maintained generally good eye contact and demonstrated no unusual behavioral mannerisms. His attention span was adequate. His manner of social interaction was polite and cooperative. His speech was normal in tone, pacing, and volume. No disturbances in the form of his speech such as pressure of speech, flight of ideas, loosening of associations, or of abnormal tone or volume were observed. His answers to questions were appropriate and relevant.

David reported a chronically depressed mood, describing his present level of emotional distress as an 8 out of a possible 10, citing the alleged instant offense as well as his separation from his family as his primary sources of stress. His emotional presentation was appropriate to his stated mood. David described periods of rapid mood changes in which he would feel "hopped up" and then would rapidly become depressed for no apparent reason, telling me that he has experienced this for some time prior to his arrest for the alleged charges and that these experiences have continued. He denied and gave no observable indications of any visual, auditory, gustatory, tactile, or olfactory hallucinations, but said that in the past he has heard what he thought was a voice but believes the phenomenon to be his own thoughts. At the time of this examination, no delusional thoughts were elicited.

Regarding symptoms often associated with depression, David reported that even with medication he experiences difficulty falling asleep. However, he does not have problems with his appetite. He indicated that he had thoughts of stabbing himself to death as recently as the day before the examination. He denied any thoughts of wanting to hurt others. He reported feeling hopeless about his future, having difficulty concentrating, and feeling increasingly irritable. He also reported significant anhedonia. David denied any history of manic episodes or racing thoughts. He also denied other symptoms often associated with mania such as extreme recklessness, racing thoughts, impulsivity, or grandiosity.

Although he denied any specific phobias, David described himself as chronically anxious, indicating that he can sometimes be fairly obsessive in his thinking and compulsive in how he organizes his clothing. Since the alleged offense, he has had frequent nightmares about what happened as well as intrusive thoughts. He denied any "flashbacks" or psychological reexperiencing of the event.

David was alert with adequate concentration. He was oriented to time, place, person, and situation. He was able to correctly answer questions concerning commonly known general information. His immediate, short- and long-term memory functions were intact upon formal testing. He was very capable of abstract reasoning. His insight and judgment, as ascertained by situational questions and his history, were somewhat impaired.

COMPETENCY TO WAIVE *MIRANDA* CONSIDERATIONS

The determination of the competency to make a statement or to waive one's rights is a legal determination that is only the province of the legal trier of fact. The examiner provides the judge with an expert opinion regarding psychological factors relevant to the determination of competency. A comprehensive evaluation must address relevant psychological factors using both test data and relevant collateral data (Frumkin, 2000, 2014).

Relevant Legal Knowledge

David was able to accurately name the charges he faces, and the potential consequences associated with conviction. He was aware of the roles of major courtroom figures as well as the available plea options. He was able to provide an understandable and internally consistent response to the charges against him and adequately answer questions about them. Overall, the examiner did not find any significant impairment in his present competence related to functional abilities.

Review of Interview Recording

The examiner reviewed a DVD of the interview that was made by the police following the alleged offense. David was handcuffed throughout the interview. The examiner observed him to be very respectful, often answering "Yes Sir" to the detective's questions. When the detective began to explain his *Miranda* rights, he initially asked David to state them in his own words. David did so until he was told that he had a right to terminate the interview. At that point, the detective asked whether David understands what was being told to him. David responded affirmatively without restating what was said. When the detective finished reading David his rights, he asked David to say out loud "I understand and know what I am doing." David responded by saying, "I know what you are doing."

During the interview, David did not exhibit behaviors indicative of responding to nonobservable stimuli. He did not exhibit bizarre or unusual behaviors, expressions, or other actions. He did not appear to be distracted and appeared to be able to maintain attention. His speech was understandable and relevant to the questions asked of him.

The examiner observed that David told the interviewer that he had not slept prior to the alleged offense and that he also stated that he had wanted to die and related an "urge" that he experienced concerning the alleged behavior. About halfway through the interview, David began to cry but later stopped and continued with the interview. He would, at other points during the interview, become tearful and would need to calm himself and then would go on with the interview.

Defendant's Account of Police Interview

David recalled being taken to a police station. After a short while, a detective came into the room. David said that he "thought" that the detective read him his rights after he introduced himself to David and that he held up a piece of paper. When asked, David described his emotions at the time as feeling "in shock." He said that he felt that he had to talk to the police because he had done something "horrible" and that he had to talk because it was the police. He also indicated that he believed that by "telling them what happened, it would help me."

On the K-BIT 2, David earned a Vocabulary standard score of 112. He earned a Nonverbal standard score of 120. His overall Composite IQ was 119. These results indicate that, in comparison to persons his age, David has the intellectual capacity to understand and comprehend his *Miranda* rights.

David was also administered the Repeatable Battery for the Assessment of Neuropsychological Status. The RBANS is a neurocognitive instrument that assesses immediate and short-term memory, visuospatial constructional abilities, attention, and language. David's scores were all within normal limits.

Comprehension of *Miranda* Rights

MIRANDA RIGHTS COMPREHENSION INSTRUMENTS (MRCI)

The MRCI (Goldstein et al., 2011) is a set of instruments designed to assist mental health professionals in assessments of juveniles' and adults' ability to

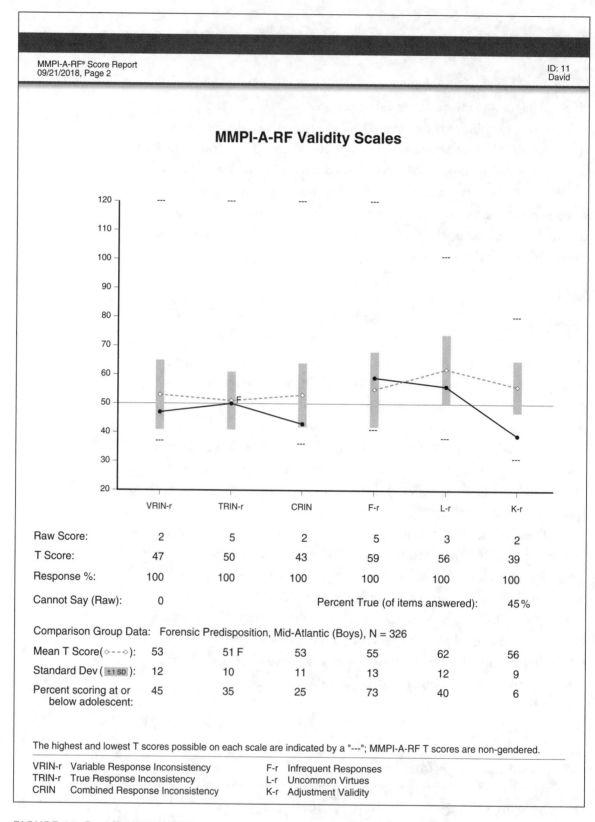

MMPI-A-RF Validity Scales

	VRIN-r	TRIN-r	CRIN	F-r	L-r	K-r
Raw Score:	2	5	2	5	3	2
T Score:	47	50	43	59	56	39
Response %:	100	100	100	100	100	100

Cannot Say (Raw): 0   Percent True (of items answered): 45%

Comparison Group Data: Forensic Predisposition, Mid-Atlantic (Boys), N = 326

	VRIN-r	TRIN-r	CRIN	F-r	L-r	K-r
Mean T Score(◇- - -◇):	53	51 F	53	55	62	56
Standard Dev (±1 SD):	12	10	11	13	12	9
Percent scoring at or below adolescent:	45	35	25	73	40	6

The highest and lowest T scores possible on each scale are indicated by a "---"; MMPI-A-RF T scores are non-gendered.

VRIN-r	Variable Response Inconsistency	F-r	Infrequent Responses
TRIN-r	True Response Inconsistency	L-r	Uncommon Virtues
CRIN	Combined Response Inconsistency	K-r	Adjustment Validity

FIGURE 11 David's MMPI-A-RF Score Report. Copyright 2016 by the Regents of the University of Minnesota. All rights reserved.

MMPI-A-RF Higher-Order (H-O) and Restructured Clinical (RC) Scales

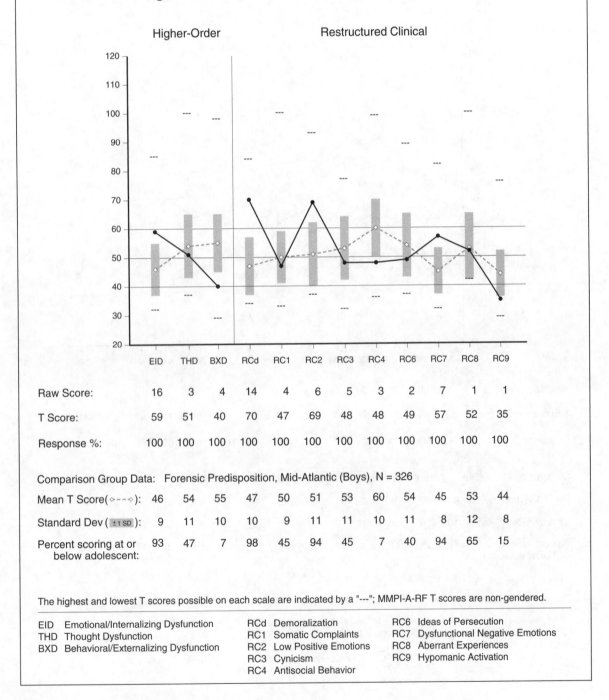

	EID	THD	BXD	RCd	RC1	RC2	RC3	RC4	RC6	RC7	RC8	RC9
Raw Score:	16	3	4	14	4	6	5	3	2	7	1	1
T Score:	59	51	40	70	47	69	48	48	49	57	52	35
Response %:	100	100	100	100	100	100	100	100	100	100	100	100

Comparison Group Data: Forensic Predisposition, Mid-Atlantic (Boys), N = 326

Mean T Score(◇- - -◇):	46	54	55	47	50	51	53	60	54	45	53	44
Standard Dev (±1 SD):	9	11	10	10	9	11	11	10	11	8	12	8
Percent scoring at or below adolescent:	93	47	7	98	45	94	45	7	40	94	65	15

The highest and lowest T scores possible on each scale are indicated by a "---"; MMPI-A-RF T scores are non-gendered.

EID Emotional/Internalizing Dysfunction	RCd Demoralization	RC6 Ideas of Persecution
THD Thought Dysfunction	RC1 Somatic Complaints	RC7 Dysfunctional Negative Emotions
BXD Behavioral/Externalizing Dysfunction	RC2 Low Positive Emotions	RC8 Aberrant Experiences
	RC3 Cynicism	RC9 Hypomanic Activation
	RC4 Antisocial Behavior	

FIGURE 11 David's MMPI-A-RF Score Report, continued.

MMPI-A-RF Somatic/Cognitive and Internalizing Scales

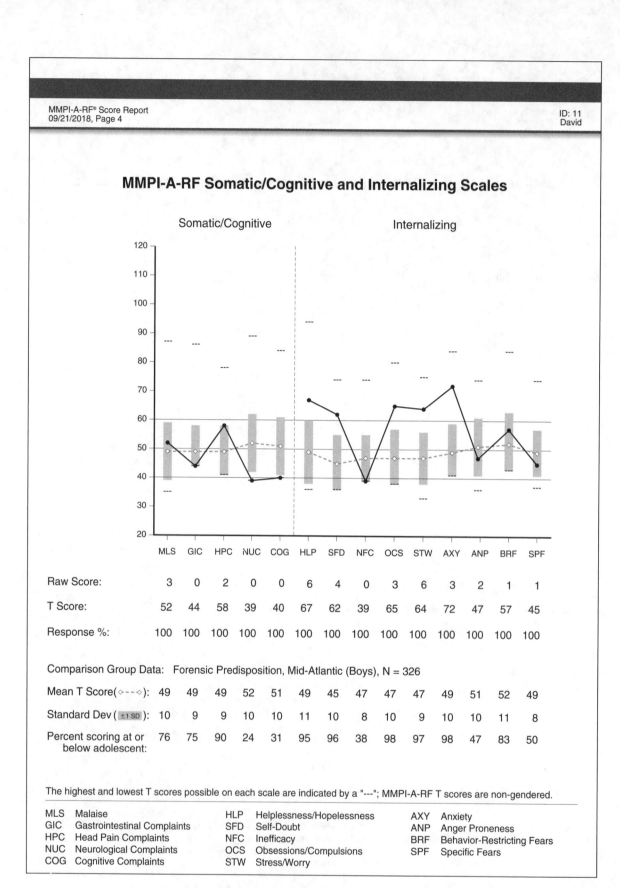

	MLS	GIC	HPC	NUC	COG	HLP	SFD	NFC	OCS	STW	AXY	ANP	BRF	SPF
Raw Score:	3	0	2	0	0	6	4	0	3	6	3	2	1	1
T Score:	52	44	58	39	40	67	62	39	65	64	72	47	57	45
Response %:	100	100	100	100	100	100	100	100	100	100	100	100	100	100

Comparison Group Data: Forensic Predisposition, Mid-Atlantic (Boys), N = 326

Mean T Score(◇- - -◇):	49	49	49	52	51	49	45	47	47	47	49	51	52	49
Standard Dev (±1 SD):	10	9	9	10	10	11	10	8	10	9	10	10	11	8
Percent scoring at or below adolescent:	76	75	90	24	31	95	96	38	98	97	98	47	83	50

The highest and lowest T scores possible on each scale are indicated by a "---"; MMPI-A-RF T scores are non-gendered.

MLS	Malaise	HLP	Helplessness/Hopelessness	AXY	Anxiety
GIC	Gastrointestinal Complaints	SFD	Self-Doubt	ANP	Anger Proneness
HPC	Head Pain Complaints	NFC	Inefficacy	BRF	Behavior-Restricting Fears
NUC	Neurological Complaints	OCS	Obsessions/Compulsions	SPF	Specific Fears
COG	Cognitive Complaints	STW	Stress/Worry		

FIGURE 11 David's MMPI-A-RF Score Report, continued.

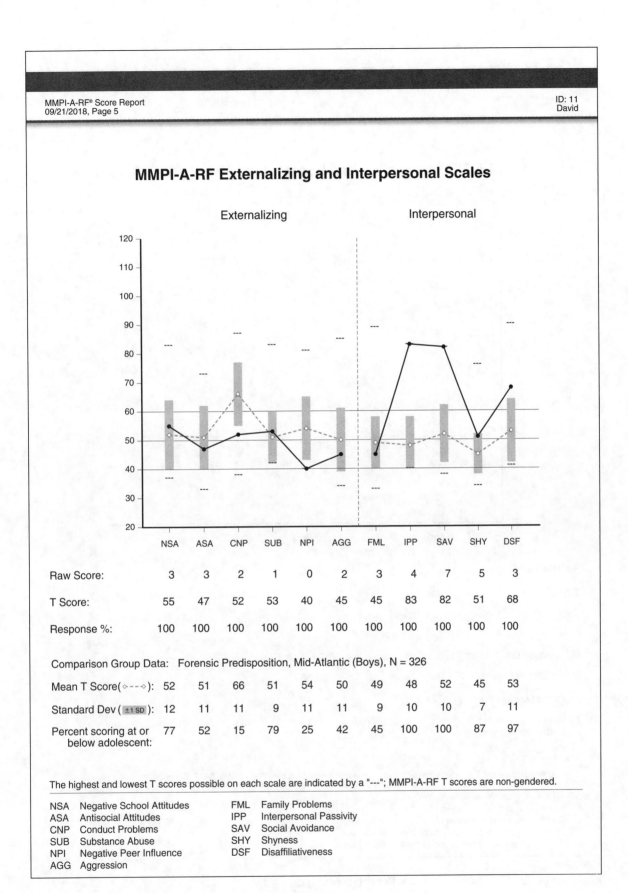

FIGURE 11 David's MMPI-A-RF Score Report, continued.

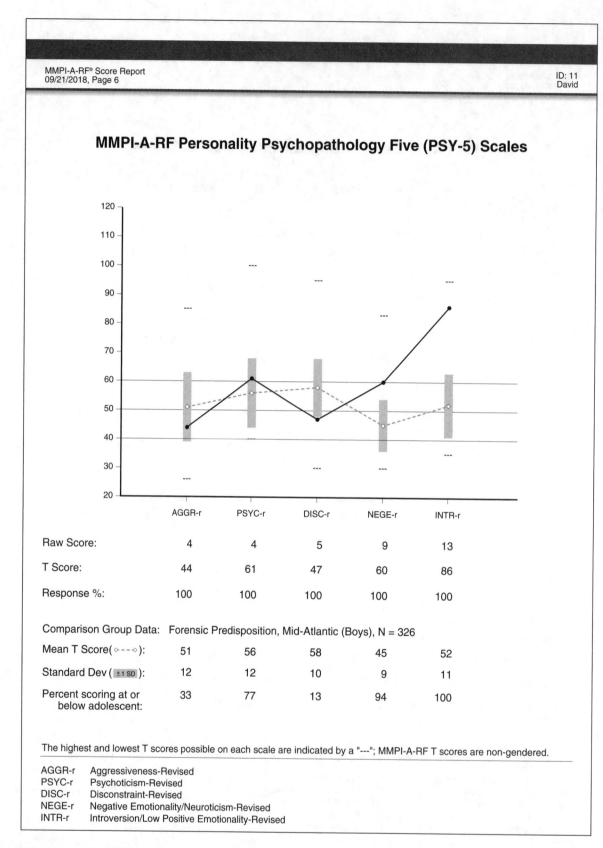

MMPI-A-RF Personality Psychopathology Five (PSY-5) Scales

	AGGR-r	PSYC-r	DISC-r	NEGE-r	INTR-r
Raw Score:	4	4	5	9	13
T Score:	44	61	47	60	86
Response %:	100	100	100	100	100

Comparison Group Data: Forensic Predisposition, Mid-Atlantic (Boys), N = 326

	AGGR-r	PSYC-r	DISC-r	NEGE-r	INTR-r
Mean T Score(◇‑‑‑◇):	51	56	58	45	52
Standard Dev (±1 SD):	12	12	10	9	11
Percent scoring at or below adolescent:	33	77	13	94	100

The highest and lowest T scores possible on each scale are indicated by a "---"; MMPI-A-RF T scores are non-gendered.

AGGR-r	Aggressiveness-Revised
PSYC-r	Psychoticism-Revised
DISC-r	Disconstraint-Revised
NEGE-r	Negative Emotionality/Neuroticism-Revised
INTR-r	Introversion/Low Positive Emotionality-Revised

FIGURE 11 David's MMPI-A-RF Score Report, continued.

162

MMPI-A-RF T SCORES (BY DOMAIN)

PROTOCOL VALIDITY

Content Non-Responsiveness

0	47	50	43
CNS	VRIN-r	TRIN-r	CRIN

Over-Reporting

59
F-r

Under-Reporting

56	39
L-r	K-r

SUBSTANTIVE SCALES

Somatic/Cognitive Dysfunction

47	52	44	58	39	40
RC1	MLS	GIC	HPC	NUC	COG

Emotional Dysfunction

59
EID

70	67	62	39
RCd	HLP	SFD	NFC

69	86
RC2	INTR-r

57	65	64	72	47	57	45	60
RC7	OCS	STW	AXY	ANP	BRF	SPF	NEGE-r

Thought Dysfunction

51
THD

49
RC6

52
RC8

61
PSYC-r

Behavioral Dysfunction

40
BXD

48	55	47	52	53	40
RC4	NSA	ASA	CNP	SUB	NPI

35	45	44	47
RC9	AGG	AGGR-r	DISC-r

Interpersonal Functioning

45	48	83	82	51	68
FML	RC3	IPP	SAV	SHY	DSF

Note. This information is provided to facilitate interpretation following the recommended structure for MMPI-A-RF interpretation in Chapter 7 of the *MMPI-A-RF Administration, Scoring, Interpretation, and Technical Manual*, which provides details in the text and an outline in Table 7-1.

FIGURE 11 David's MMPI-A-RF Score Report, continued.

understand and appreciate the significance of their *Miranda* rights. Using these instruments, no deficits were seen.

MMPI-A-RF

David's Validity scale scores indicate that he responded relevantly and appropriately to the items and appeared to comprehend them. There were no indications of random responding or of tendencies to overendorse in either an all-True or all-False direction. There were no indications of overreporting or underreporting of problems. As such, the test findings can be considered valid and reflective of his psychological functioning at the time that he was tested. His protocol was compared to a reference group of 326 Mid-Atlantic Forensic Predisposition boys.

David responded affirmatively to items indicating a history of suicidal ideation and/or attempts. He is likely to be preoccupied with suicide and death and to be at risk for current suicidal ideation and attempts. (At the time of examination, he had been admitted to the hospital owing to his suicidal risk. With his attorney's permission, the examiner communicated these findings of risk to his psychiatrist.)

David's scores indicated that he likely experiences significant emotional distress. He is likely depressed and sad. He has a very poor image of himself and feels inadequate and overwhelmed. He likely feels hopeless, that he has been treated unfairly in life, and that his problems are beyond help. David reports a number of associated symptoms of depression such as problems making decisions, procrastination, social withdrawal, inability to take pleasure in things once enjoyed, and self-punitive thoughts. He also endorsed items consistent with a risk for self-injurious behavior. David reported a significant lack of positive emotions, a pronounced lack of interest in activities he once enjoyed (anhedonia). He is likely to be very pessimistic, to lack energy, and to display vegetative symptoms of depression.

David also reports considerable symptoms of anxiety and likely has many specific fears. He also reports an above-average level of obsessive-compulsive symptoms to a degree that could affect his thinking. He experiences an above-average amount of perceived stress and worry as well as likely sleep problems.

David did not report behaviors consistent with delinquent, acting-out, or antisocial tendencies, or other indications of maladaptive externalizing behavior. Rather, his responses indicated a tendency toward overcontrolled behavior.

Interpersonally, David reports being unassertive, passive, submissive, and that he is easily dominated by others. He reports not enjoying social events and avoiding social situations. He is very likely socially inhibited in social situations. He likely has very few friends. David is very likely introverted and may have been bullied by peers. He is likely uncomfortable around the opposite sex.

MMPI-A-RF findings indicated consideration of depression-related disorders, anxiety-related disorders, disorders involving obsessions and compulsions as well as personality traits or disorders involving social avoidance, passiveness, and submissiveness. He may have some unusual thoughts and experiences.

Forensic Formulation

The following considerations were presented to the Court to assist with making the competency determination:

*Factors that would suggest that David <u>could</u> make a knowing,
intelligent and voluntary waiver are:*

Knowing

In the DVD of the interview, he was able to paraphrase what was said to him when asked to do so. He did not exhibit overt symptoms of loss of contact with reality such as appearing to respond to unobservable stimuli. While the MMPI-A-RF suggested the potential for some unusual thinking, his responses to the interviewer's questions did not appear to show overt signs of a thought disorder. On a test of knowledge and comprehension specific to *Miranda* rights, *The Miranda Rights Comprehension Instrument,* no significant impairment was seen.

Intelligent

David is of sufficient intelligence as demonstrated by the findings of current testing as well as his academic history. There is no evidence of neuropsychological dysfunction that would preclude his knowledge. He was able to understand and respond appropriately to the MMPI-A-RF items.

Voluntary

Review of the interview did not indicate that the detective made any threats, promises, or used any manner of physical coercion.

Factors that would suggest that David could <u>not</u> make a knowing, intelligent and voluntary waiver are:

Knowing

David has had no contact with either the juvenile justice or adult criminal justice system. This lack of contact can result in nonfamiliarity with his rights. Near the end of the recorded interview in which he is read his *Miranda* rights, rather than repeat back in his own words what was told to him, David simply responds that he does understand. Immediately following the reading of his rights, the detective asks him to state, "I understand and know what I am doing," he becomes seemingly confused and refers to the deputy, suggesting that he thought that he was being asked if he knew what the deputy was doing.

Intelligent

David possesses adequate intelligence to know his rights and the potential implications of waiving them. In that he was 17 at the time, there is a concern that he may still lack the foresight of a fully mature adult.

Voluntary

The MMPI-A-RF was administered after he had been hospitalized for less than a week. Prior to that, he had received no treatment. Although it is possible that aspects of the depression seen on the MMPI-A-RF could stem from his present situation, collateral data indicate that David was depressed prior to and during the alleged offense. The test findings can be seen as consistent with his self-report and his parent's description of him as being very depressed. The MMPI-A-RF results characterize David as a person who is easily overwhelmed and has limited coping skills. They also indicate that he is a passive and submissive young man, who tends to be socially avoidant and suggestible. These traits would increase the likelihood that he would not act in an assertive and self-protective manner.

David stated that on the night before the alleged offense, he was depressed and suicidal. Following the incident and arrest, he asked the police to shoot him. He has acted on his suicidal thoughts and the MMPI-A-RF continues to indicate that he is at high risk of suicide. It appears, therefore, that his suicidal thinking and depression had not abated during the time of his interview with the police. In that he was suicidal, he may have lacked the psychological energy or motivation to take steps in his own best interest, such as refusing to speak with law enforcement or requesting an attorney or his parents.

OUTCOME

After the examination was completed, a plea agreement was offered by the prosecution and accepted. No hearing was held on the potential suppression of his confession.

FORENSIC CONTRIBUTIONS OF THE MMPI-A-RF

The MMPI-A-RF contributed to this assessment in a number of different ways. As is the case in all forensic evaluations, it provides an assessment of possible response bias. In *Miranda* rights cases, the examiner seeks to determine whether the examinee's self-reported symptoms are sufficiently valid to support an opinion (in concert with other data such as recordings of the interview). Whereas the MMPI-A-RF provides a present state evaluation of possible overreporting, it can provide the examiner with reasonable hypotheses as to a defendant's general approach to the examination.

The MMPI-A-RF also provides an assessment of possible preexisting psychological problems that may have been active in the youth at the time of his *Miranda* waiver. Although this is a retrospective examination, the MMPI-A-RF allows for hypothesis generation to assist in determining whether psychological deficits existed at the time of the *Miranda* waiver. In David's case, the MMPI-A-RF suggested considerable depression that was likely present at the time of his interrogation. Conversely, it did not give evidence of any present poor ties with reality and this correlated with the observations of his interview.

A critical area of assessment is whether the waiver of rights was voluntary. Here, the MMPI-A-RF can identify personality traits of dependence, submissiveness, passivity, or deficits in social functioning that could have negatively impacted the youth's ability to waive his rights and to resist any coercive pressure to make that waiver or to make incriminating statements. The MMPI-A-RF results characterize David as a very passive and submissive person, who is easily overwhelmed and who has limited coping skills. He is also described as a person who would likely not act in an assertive or self-protective manner. These characteristics could have implications for his ability to make a voluntary statement or resist pressure to waive his rights.

Susan

A Female Arrested After Plotting to Commit a School Shooting

BACKGROUND

Susan is a 15-year-old girl referred by the juvenile court for a psychological examination after being adjudicated delinquent on a charge of soliciting terrorism. The specific request of the court was a general psychological evaluation as well as a risk assessment given the nature of her charges. Along with another female, she had approached another juvenile to help carry out a detailed plan of shooting students and staff at her high school. The juvenile that she approached reported the incident to the local police. Susan was arrested and entered a plea of admission to the charge. At the time that she was evaluated, she was in the juvenile detention facility awaiting the disposition of her case.

Interview With Youth

Susan reported that she lives with her mother, stepfather, and two younger half-siblings. She described a very positive relationship with her mother and stepfather. However, when asked about her birth father, she began to cry and said that she has very little contact with him because he has a severe substance abuse problem. She described her parents as being no more or less strict than those of her peers and said that she has chores at home and also a curfew. She denied having any behavioral problems at home. She also reported a positive relationship with siblings, describing any conflicts between them as being typical of siblings.

Susan indicated that she has friends in school and that her best friend is the codefendant in this case. Asked about how she believed that peers at school would describe her, she said, "Outgoing and friendly" and denied any history of conflict at school. In regard to community activities, she said that she plays basketball and goes to a gymnastics class. She does not date and is not sexually active.

Susan said that her grandmother passed away about a year ago and that this was a very significant loss for her (as she discussed this, she again became tearful).

Susan reported that she is in the ninth grade and said that she has had one in-school suspension for truancy. She does not have an IEP and denied any difficulties with learning or comprehension. She reported earning A's and B's except in chemistry, which she finds difficult. She is unsure of a future career.

Susan denied any history of substance abuse. She denied any history of physical, emotional, or sexual abuse or any history of child welfare involvement or out-of-home placement. She also denied any history of fire-setting or animal cruelty. She stated that the current charges are her first involvement with the juvenile court.

Susan said that she has never been in outpatient mental health counseling nor has she been psychiatrically hospitalized. She has never been prescribed psychotropic medication. Although she denied any history of suicide attempts, she acknowledged a history of suicidal ideation as well as cutting (showing scars on her arms and legs) that began in eighth grade, noting that her suicidal thoughts increased after the death of her grandmother and that her cutting behavior stopped at the beginning of this year. She is unaware of any family history of mental illness, but as noted, described her father as having substance abuse problems.

Susan stated that she is in good health and denied any significant health or developmental problems. She denied any history of seizures, head trauma, loss of consciousness, or other neurological involvement. She said that she has never been medically hospitalized and takes no medications.

COLLATERAL INFORMATION
Parent Interview

An interview with Susan's mother and stepfather revealed that they have been married for 10 years and also have two younger children. They reported that Susan's birth father has little involvement with her and that he will often not follow through on commitments to see her, which is a great source of emotional pain for Susan. They also indicated that he is in and out of jail owing to substance abuse problems.

Susan's mother said that she received regular medical care while pregnant. Susan was a healthy child who reached developmental milestones normally. There have been no significant medical, developmental, speech, hearing, language, or vision problems.

Susan's parents indicated that she has always earned above-average grades, does not have an IEP, and has not had behavioral problems at school. However, they said that toward the end of seventh grade, Susan began to have more emotional difficulties and engage in cutting behavior, which they ascribed to being influenced by her peers. They said that they were able to support Susan emotionally and that they did not take her to mental health counseling.

In the eighth grade, Susan seemed to be doing better, earning good grades and not displaying behavior problems, other than minor interpersonal conflicts via social media. They indicated that she does not date.

Susan's parents said they have always provided supervision for each child and have rules and structure at home. They said that they monitor her internet usage and have blocks on her phone. There are no firearms in the house.

Susan's parents reported that she does not exhibit any bizarre or unusual behavior at home. She is not withdrawn and does not have any fascination with guns or violence, including any fascination with school violence or attacks. She has not been aggressive and has never made threats. To the best of their knowledge, she does not have substance abuse problems and there is no history of physical or sexual abuse. They do not believe that she has been bullied either physically or socially. She has not had problems with lying, theft, or truancy. They described her peer group as stable and nondelinquent but did acknowledge that the codefendant seemed to have family problems. They believe that Susan's paternal grandfather has a history of bipolar disorder. They listed Susan's strengths as being musical.

Susan's school records indicate that she has never been in special education. There is no history of discipline problems. She earns average to above-average grades and has never failed a grade nor was she ever retained.

Current Behavioral Status

Susan was appropriately dressed and groomed in detention-issued clothing that was neat, clean, and appropriately arranged. Her hygiene and grooming were adequate.

There were no overt indications of loosening of associations, flight of ideas, or tangentiality. Susan's psychomotor activity was nonremarkable (that is to say, she was not hyperactive or agitated nor was she lethargic or nonresponsive). Her speech was normal in tone, pacing, and volume. She was not distractible throughout the examination. Her manner of social interaction was outwardly friendly, polite, and cooperative.

Susan presented with an appropriate and expressive affect to a reported anxious and worried mood, which she described as reactive to her legal and family circumstances and being placed in detention. When asked to rate her subjective level of distress (SUDS), she described her present degree of emotional upset as being a 5 out of a possible 10, describing her current distress over being incarcerated and separated from her family.

Susan denied, and there were no overt indications of hallucinations, delusions, or paranoia. She gave no behavioral evidence of visual, gustatory, olfactory, or tactile hallucinations. Susan also denied and gave no evidence of specific delusional thinking. She did not exhibit systematic paranoid delusions or grandiosity.

Susan denied some symptoms typically associated with depression such as limited appetite, hopelessness, loss of interest or pleasure, but complained of poor sleep, which has worsened since she has been incarcerated. She also reported difficulty in concentration as well as increased irritability.

Susan denied active suicidal ideation, intent, or plan. She also denied homicidal ideation.

When asked to describe her history of mood swings, Susan stated that since seventh grade, she has had rapidly changing moods and complained of racing thoughts but denied other symptoms associated with mania such as increased activity or grandiosity.

Susan reported phobias of spiders and elevators, which is normative but denied any intrusive obsessive thinking or compulsive behavior, other than to say, "I like schedules." However, she reported chronic anxiety, which she said is manifested often in worrying about her family. When asked about "flashbacks" and other symptoms associated with trauma exposure, Susan reported having flashbacks about her father.

Susan was alert and responsive to her environment and there were no problems observed with her attention or concentration. She was oriented to time, place, person, and situation. Her fund of general information suggested at least average intellectual functioning.

Susan's concentration was adequate as evidenced by her attention and focus in the conversation with the examiner. Her immediate recall was intact as demonstrated by her ability to recall six digits forward and three in reverse order. Concentration was also demonstrated to be intact by her ability to perform simple mental calculations. Her short-term recall was intact as demonstrated by her ability to recall three items from memory after a 10-minute distraction. She also demonstrated the capacity for verbal abstract reasoning through her ability to state conceptual similarities between related objects and concepts as well as more complex abstractions. This was also demonstrated in her ability to interpret commonly used proverbs. Her insight and judgment appeared to be appropriate for her age as determined by responses to situational questions.

Susan's mother completed the Conners Comprehensive Behavior Rating Scale. In this rating, her mother's rating scores on the Validity scales did not indicate a positive, negative, or inconsistent response style. The findings suggested consideration of diagnoses of an anxiety disorder, especially obsessive-compulsive disorder.

MMPI-A-RF

Susan's MMPI-A-RF protocol was valid and interpretable. Her scores were compared to a reference group of 195 Mid-Atlantic Forensic Disposition girls.

Susan's protocol was similar to youth who are at risk of suicide. She answered some test items in the direction related to a preoccupation with death or suicidal ideation and had elevated scores on specific MMPI-A-RF scales associated with suicidal risk in adolescents. In a discussion of her item responses, she acknowledged thinking about killing herself and that she often wished that she were dead. Her parents and the court mental health clinician were told of the need to monitor her safety and to provide appropriate services.

Susan's scores indicate that she experiences significant emotional distress with a greater-than-average number of negative emotional experiences that include irritability, remorse, and apprehension. She also likely has nightmares and problems with concentration as well as insecurity. Susan describes herself as being chronically anxious with an above-average level of stress and

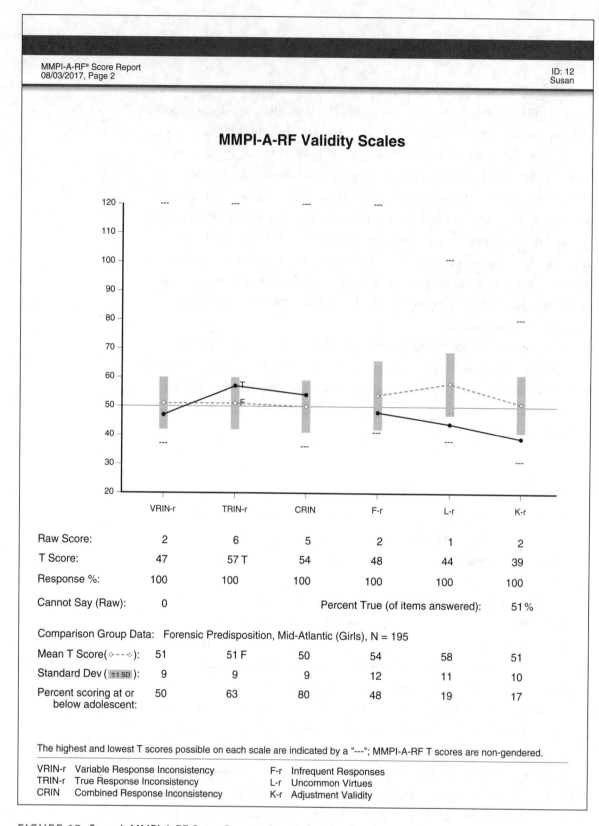

MMPI-A-RF Validity Scales

	VRIN-r	TRIN-r	CRIN	F-r	L-r	K-r
Raw Score:	2	6	5	2	1	2
T Score:	47	57 T	54	48	44	39
Response %:	100	100	100	100	100	100

Cannot Say (Raw): 0   Percent True (of items answered): 51%

Comparison Group Data: Forensic Predisposition, Mid-Atlantic (Girls), N = 195

	VRIN-r	TRIN-r	CRIN	F-r	L-r	K-r
Mean T Score(◇- - -◇):	51	51 F	50	54	58	51
Standard Dev (±1 SD):	9	9	9	12	11	10
Percent scoring at or below adolescent:	50	63	80	48	19	17

The highest and lowest T scores possible on each scale are indicated by a "---"; MMPI-A-RF T scores are non-gendered.

VRIN-r	Variable Response Inconsistency	F-r	Infrequent Responses
TRIN-r	True Response Inconsistency	L-r	Uncommon Virtues
CRIN	Combined Response Inconsistency	K-r	Adjustment Validity

FIGURE 12 Susan's MMPI-A-RF Score Report. Copyright 2016 by the Regents of the University of Minnesota. All rights reserved.

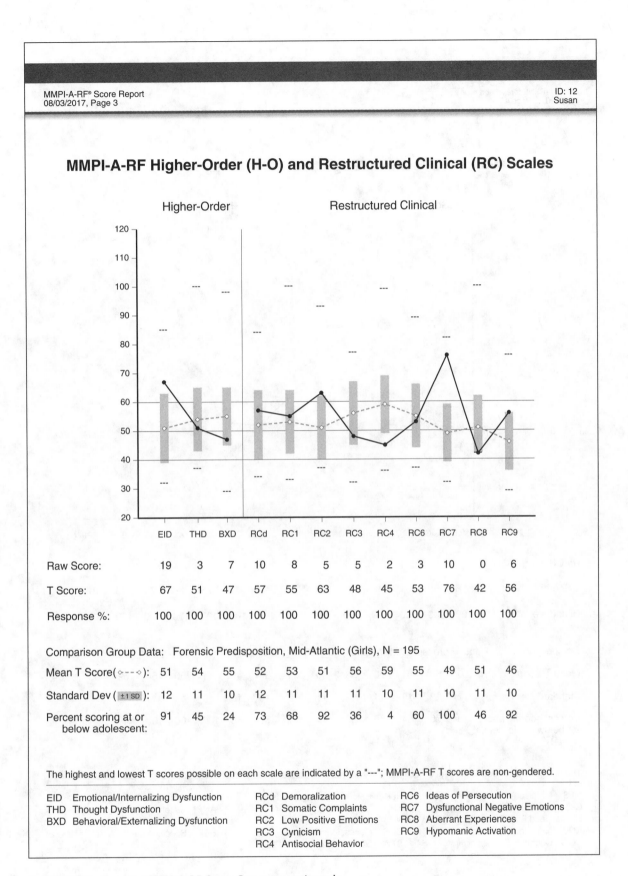

MMPI-A-RF Higher-Order (H-O) and Restructured Clinical (RC) Scales

	EID	THD	BXD	RCd	RC1	RC2	RC3	RC4	RC6	RC7	RC8	RC9
Raw Score:	19	3	7	10	8	5	5	2	3	10	0	6
T Score:	67	51	47	57	55	63	48	45	53	76	42	56
Response %:	100	100	100	100	100	100	100	100	100	100	100	100

Comparison Group Data: Forensic Predisposition, Mid-Atlantic (Girls), N = 195

Mean T Score(◇---◇):	51	54	55	52	53	51	56	59	55	49	51	46
Standard Dev (±1 SD):	12	11	10	12	11	11	11	10	11	10	11	10
Percent scoring at or below adolescent:	91	45	24	73	68	92	36	4	60	100	46	92

The highest and lowest T scores possible on each scale are indicated by a "---"; MMPI-A-RF T scores are non-gendered.

EID Emotional/Internalizing Dysfunction	RCd Demoralization	RC6 Ideas of Persecution
THD Thought Dysfunction	RC1 Somatic Complaints	RC7 Dysfunctional Negative Emotions
BXD Behavioral/Externalizing Dysfunction	RC2 Low Positive Emotions	RC8 Aberrant Experiences
	RC3 Cynicism	RC9 Hypomanic Activation
	RC4 Antisocial Behavior	

FIGURE 12 Susan's MMPI-A-RF Score Report, continued.

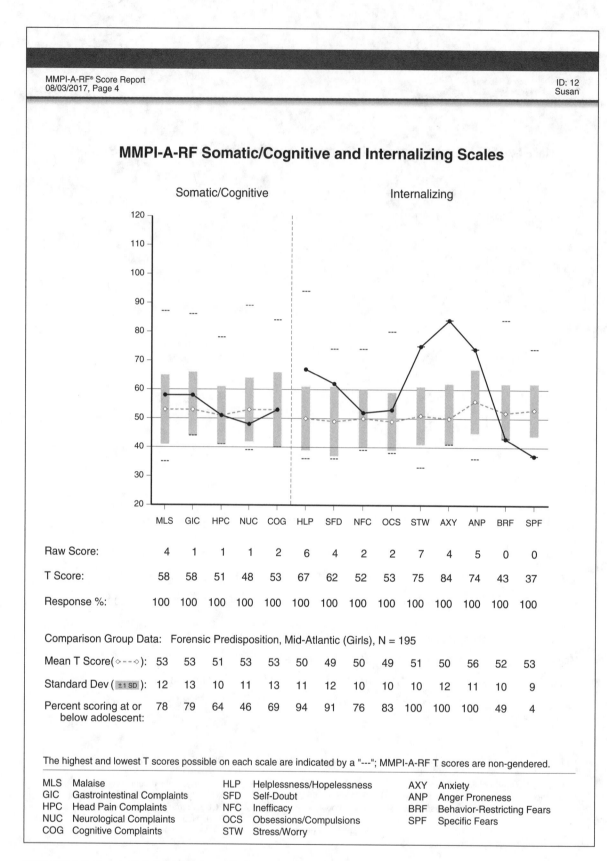

MMPI-A-RF Somatic/Cognitive and Internalizing Scales

Somatic/Cognitive   Internalizing

	MLS	GIC	HPC	NUC	COG	HLP	SFD	NFC	OCS	STW	AXY	ANP	BRF	SPF
Raw Score:	4	1	1	1	2	6	4	2	2	7	4	5	0	0
T Score:	58	58	51	48	53	67	62	52	53	75	84	74	43	37
Response %:	100	100	100	100	100	100	100	100	100	100	100	100	100	100

Comparison Group Data: Forensic Predisposition, Mid-Atlantic (Girls), N = 195

Mean T Score(◇--◇):	53	53	51	53	53	50	49	50	49	51	50	56	52	53
Standard Dev (±1 SD):	12	13	10	11	13	11	12	10	10	10	12	11	10	9
Percent scoring at or below adolescent:	78	79	64	46	69	94	91	76	83	100	100	100	49	4

The highest and lowest T scores possible on each scale are indicated by a "---"; MMPI-A-RF T scores are non-gendered.

MLS	Malaise	HLP	Helplessness/Hopelessness	AXY	Anxiety
GIC	Gastrointestinal Complaints	SFD	Self-Doubt	ANP	Anger Proneness
HPC	Head Pain Complaints	NFC	Inefficacy	BRF	Behavior-Restricting Fears
NUC	Neurological Complaints	OCS	Obsessions/Compulsions	SPF	Specific Fears
COG	Cognitive Complaints	STW	Stress/Worry		

FIGURE 12 Susan's MMPI-A-RF Score Report, continued.

176

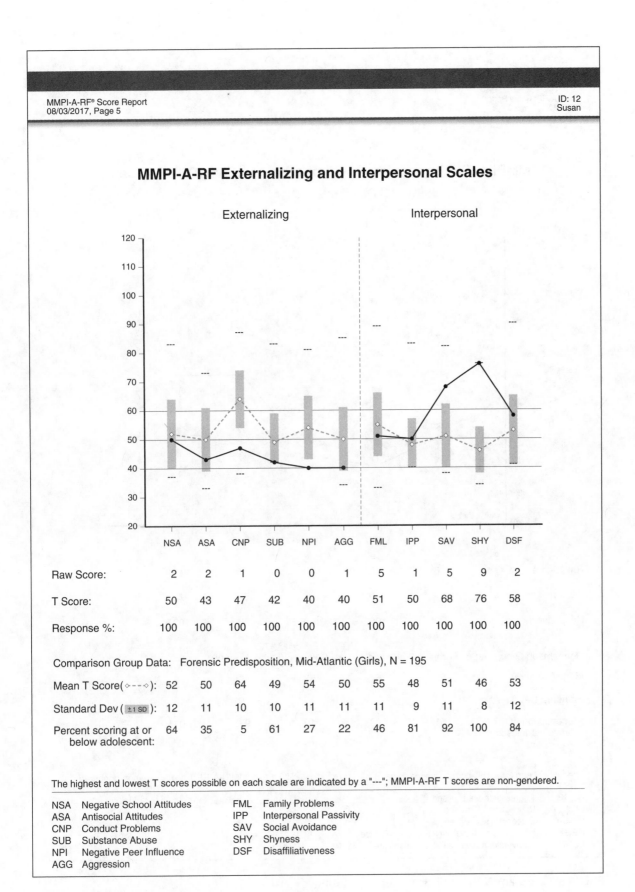

MMPI-A-RF Externalizing and Interpersonal Scales

	NSA	ASA	CNP	SUB	NPI	AGG	FML	IPP	SAV	SHY	DSF
Raw Score:	2	2	1	0	0	1	5	1	5	9	2
T Score:	50	43	47	42	40	40	51	50	68	76	58
Response %:	100	100	100	100	100	100	100	100	100	100	100

Comparison Group Data: Forensic Predisposition, Mid-Atlantic (Girls), N = 195

Mean T Score(◇- - -◇):	52	50	64	49	54	50	55	48	51	46	53
Standard Dev (±1 SD):	12	11	10	10	11	11	11	9	11	8	12
Percent scoring at or below adolescent:	64	35	5	61	27	22	46	81	92	100	84

The highest and lowest T scores possible on each scale are indicated by a "---"; MMPI-A-RF T scores are non-gendered.

NSA   Negative School Attitudes
ASA   Antisocial Attitudes
CNP   Conduct Problems
SUB   Substance Abuse
NPI   Negative Peer Influence
AGG   Aggression

FML   Family Problems
IPP   Interpersonal Passivity
SAV   Social Avoidance
SHY   Shyness
DSF   Disaffiliativeness

FIGURE 12   Susan's MMPI-A-RF Score Report, continued.

177

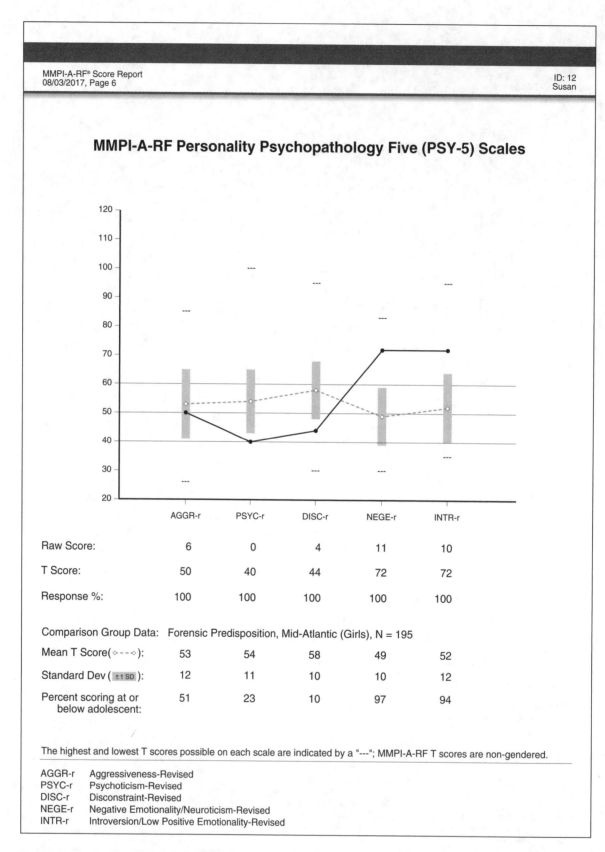

MMPI-A-RF Personality Psychopathology Five (PSY-5) Scales

	AGGR-r	PSYC-r	DISC-r	NEGE-r	INTR-r
Raw Score:	6	0	4	11	10
T Score:	50	40	44	72	72
Response %:	100	100	100	100	100

Comparison Group Data: Forensic Predisposition, Mid-Atlantic (Girls), N = 195

	AGGR-r	PSYC-r	DISC-r	NEGE-r	INTR-r
Mean T Score(◇---◇):	53	54	58	49	52
Standard Dev (±1 SD):	12	11	10	10	12
Percent scoring at or below adolescent:	51	23	10	97	94

The highest and lowest T scores possible on each scale are indicated by a "---"; MMPI-A-RF T scores are non-gendered.

AGGR-r   Aggressiveness-Revised
PSYC-r   Psychoticism-Revised
DISC-r   Disconstraint-Revised
NEGE-r   Negative Emotionality/Neuroticism-Revised
INTR-r   Introversion/Low Positive Emotionality-Revised

FIGURE 12 Susan's MMPI-A-RF Score Report, continued.

MMPI-A-RF T SCORES (BY DOMAIN)

PROTOCOL VALIDITY

Content Non-Responsiveness

0	47	57 T	54
CNS	VRIN-r	TRIN-r	CRIN

Over-Reporting

48
F-r

Under-Reporting

44	39
L-r	K-r

SUBSTANTIVE SCALES

Somatic/Cognitive Dysfunction

55	58	58	51	48	53
RC1	MLS	GIC	HPC	NUC	COG

Emotional Dysfunction

67		57	67	62	52		
EID		RCd	HLP	SFD	NFC		

63	72
RC2	INTR-r

76	53	75	84	74	43	37	72
RC7	OCS	STW	AXY	ANP	BRF	SPF	NEGE-r

Thought Dysfunction

51		53
THD		RC6

42
RC8

40
PSYC-r

Behavioral Dysfunction

47		45	50	43	47	42	40
BXD		RC4	NSA	ASA	CNP	SUB	NPI

56	40	50	44
RC9	AGG	AGGR-r	DISC-r

Interpersonal Functioning

51	48	50	68	76	58
FML	RC3	IPP	SAV	SHY	DSF

Note. This information is provided to facilitate interpretation following the recommended structure for MMPI-A-RF interpretation in Chapter 7 of the *MMPI-A-RF Administration, Scoring, Interpretation, and Technical Manual*, which provides details in the text and an outline in Table 7-1.

FIGURE 12 Susan's MMPI-A-RF Score Report, continued.

worry as well as likely sleep difficulties. She reported a high level of anger problems involving being irritable and impatient. She likely has a history of making verbal threats.

Susan has a number of symptoms associated with depression such as a lack of positive emotional experiences, psychomotor retardation, low energy, and fatigue and is likely difficult to motivate and self-punishing.

Susan reports feeling hopeless and helpless, a critical risk factor in suicide risk in adolescents. Susan sees herself as being a failure, as a person who cannot be helped, and who has been treated unfairly in life. Her self-esteem is likely poor, and she also likely gives up easily in the face of challenges. She is also at risk for self-harming behaviors.

Interpersonally, Susan reports avoiding some social events and that she has very few or no friends. She is likely introverted, withdrawn, isolated, and sonically awkward. She may feel that she has been bullied by other youth and she is likely uncomfortable around boys. Others may see her as being very shy.

Susan's protocol did not indicate any maladaptive externalizing behaviors. There were also no indications of disordered thinking nor of cognitive problems.

Compared to the reference group of forensic disposition, Susan has greater tendencies for social avoidance and shyness. She is also experiencing a greater degree of negative emotions. More generally, Susan scored considerably higher than the comparison group on Emotionalizing-Internalizing Dysfunction.

CLINICAL IMPRESSION

Susan was diagnosed with Unspecified Anxiety Disorder and Unspecified Depressive Disorder.

Risk Assessment

Susan was assessed using different methodologies. The majority of violence risk research has been done on males and may not apply to females and may in fact underestimate risk of future violence because the risk factors do not apply in the same manner. To illustrate, the following factors described by

Odgers et al. (2005) in their review of the research literature discuss the substantial differences between risk assessment of adolescent males and females. Females are more likely to become involved in relational violence, less likely to be involved in actual physical aggressing with the exception of within the context of a relationship. Whereas in males a clear association exists between early onset of aggressive behaviors and future violent behavior, this correlation is much less robust in females. Consequently, the majority of females are "under the radar" when traditional models of risk assessment are used. Compared to males, girls who are aggressive are significantly more likely to have a history of severe abuse and maltreatment. Violent girls in juvenile justice settings are more likely to have diagnoses of mental disorders than males in similar settings. Specifically, rates of PTSD, depression, and attention deficit disorders are higher in females. Consequently, any risk assessment of females, including the following, must be understood within the context of the limited research and unclear differences between violent male and violent female adolescents. This fact must also be communicated clearly to the court.

Another significant limitation is that the majority of research concerning violence risk in youth does not address school or rampage shooters (Bushman et al., 2016). The research discussed will be done to provide an empirical understanding for the court. However, such research is inherently limited in application to one individual because all of the factors (present or absent) unique to that person may not be reflected in the literature. In addition, any behavior, including violent behavior, has multiple determinants and differential impacts of those determinants on the person(s). Further, although there are considerable data on violence as well as recidivism of youthful offenders, there are few data on persons who perpetrate school shootings.

School shootings do not occur with great frequency, especially when compared to other violent acts. It is challenging to predict such a low base-rate. Finally, the research concerning recidivism of school shooters is limited owing to a number of factors. First, school or mass shooters often commit suicide or are killed in the act itself. Second, school shootings remain a relatively new phenomenon with most research beginning in the latter part of the 20th century and continuing. Many of the surviving perpetrators were young at the time of the offense and remain incarcerated, limiting the number of offenders who are released and can be followed. In addition, specific to school shootings, most offenders are incarcerated for a significant period of time and when and if they are released, by definition are no longer students and do not have the same opportunity for similar reoffending behavior.

This leaves the existing data on youth violence and recidivism as the best potential source of inferential data to be applied to the particular person or defendant before the court.

STRUCTURED PROFESSIONAL JUDGMENT—RISK ASSESSMENT

Susan was assessed using the Structured Assessment of Violence Risk in Youth. The SAVRY is a structured professional judgment rating of risk factors that are empirically associated with risk of violent behavior in adolescents. However, any such instrument should be used with caution because of the limited research on violence prediction on youth owing to the inherent "dynamism" or change of adolescents and, as noted earlier, the even more limited research on female adolescents.

The SAVRY is composed of 24 items in three risk domains (Historical Risk Factors, Social/Contextual Risk Factors, and Individual/Clinical Risk Factors), drawn from existing research and the professional literature on adolescent development as well as on violence and aggression in youth. Each risk item has a three-level rating structure with specific rating guidelines (Low, Moderate, or High). In addition to the 24 risk factors, the SAVRY also includes six Protective Factor items. The SAVRY is not designed to be a formal test or scale; there are no assigned numerical values nor are there any specified cutoff scores.

Within the group of *Historical Risk Factors,* Susan has no known prior episode of aggressive behavior and no known history of nonviolent offending. She denies she was the victim of abuse (and there are no substantiations or official documentation of abuse).

In the next area, *Social/Contextual Risk Factors,* Susan has not been described in the past as associating to a great extent with delinquent or negative peers with the exception of the codefendant, who is reported to have emotional problems and who is this examinee's best friend. Susan does have poor coping skills (cutting/suicidal ideation) but has not experienced significant peer rejection and does have a present consistent source of personal or social support. Youth who have experienced considerable stress and who have limited coping skills are often seen as being at greater risk for aggressive behavior. The community Susan is from does not appear to suffer significant disorganization and she does not have a high potential for exposure to crime, poverty, and violence, which is an asset.

Within the subset of *Individual/Clinical Risk Factors,* she voices a positive attitude toward treatment, and this is also seen on the MMPI-A-RF. She does not have a clear pattern of involvement in substance abuse and on the MMPI-A-RF she did not have indications of personality characteristics of adolescents at risk for substance abuse. She does not have a history of anger management problems and also appears to be significantly impaired in her capacity for age-appropriate empathy. She has been stable in the detention center and is described as being compliant with parental attempts at supervision and behavioral management.

In terms of *Protective Factors* (those qualities or aspects that might mitigate against violent acting out), Susan does verbalize a strong commitment to school.

Overall, given the limited number of risk factors identified and the identified protective factors, Susan would be rated on this instrument as being at low to moderate risk for continued aggressive behavior. Should there be significant changes in the contextual or clinical or dynamic risk factors, then the overall risk assessment could change as well. Finally, any risk assessment of adolescents must include the caveat that by nature they are changeable and dynamic and that some degree of antisocial behavior and aggression is statistically normative in adolescents and that the majority of adolescents do not continue antisocial behavior into adulthood.

Threat Assessment

Threat assessment differs significantly from a risk assessment for future aggression (Meloy & Hoffmann, 2014). Threat assessment focuses on the risk posed by a student or another person in response to an actual or perceived threat. Various models have been developed for use in the school setting. Susan was assessed utilizing a model developed specifically for this purpose. Using a threat assessment model developed by Meloy and O'Toole (2011), the following areas are addressed:

PATHWAY WARNING BEHAVIORS *Any behavior that is part of research, planning, preparation or implementation of attack.* In Susan's case, she and Sadie had made detailed plans and then sought out another student to assist.

FIXATION WARNING BEHAVIORS *Any behavior that indicates a pathological preoccupation with a person or a cause.* On the basis of the information provided, it appears that Susan was motivated by postings on social media. This apparently evolved into a discussion with Sadie as to how an attack could take place. There appears to be no other clearly stated motivation, such as revenge against another person or persons or the general institution of the school. She denies any specific grievances against the school and her school records indicate that she does not have a significant disciplinary history.

IDENTIFICATION WARNING BEHAVIOR *Any behavior that indicates a pathological desire to be a "pseudo-commando."* There appears to be no evidence of an attempt to engage in such behavior.

NOVEL AGGRESSIVE WARNING BEHAVIORS *An act of violence that appears unrelated to any targeted violence pathway warning behavior.* There appears to be, to the best of my knowledge, no indication of any aggressive warning behaviors in this case.

ENERGY BURST WARNING BEHAVIORS *An increase in the frequency or variety of any noted activities related to the target, even if the activities themselves are relatively innocuous, usually in the days or weeks prior to the attack.* In this case, these communications had taken place over a long period of time. Some indications of an increase are suggested by their approaching a third student.

LEAKAGE WARNING BEHAVIOR *The communication to a third party of an attempt to do harm through an attack.* Prior to the alleged offense, the two youths exchanged very specific and detailed communication about how such an attack could be developed and carried out. They then approached another youth about assisting. Whereas Susan maintained that she was not serious in her intent, the youth whom they approached was convinced enough that she determined it to be a serious threat and contacted authorities.

LAST RESORT WARNING BEHAVIOR *Evidence of a violent crime imperative and time imperative; increasing desperation or distress forcing a person into a position of last resort for which there is no alternative but violence.* There appears to be in the materials that I reviewed no indications of an increasing imperative.

DIRECTLY COMMUNICATED THREAT WARNING *The communication of a direct threat to the target or to law enforcement behavior.* There is no evidence in the materials that I reviewed of such a communication.

OUTCOME

Susan was seen as a moderate risk of threat in the school setting and low to moderate risk for general aggression. She was recommended for intensive home-based intervention, intense supervision, random drug testing, Dialectical Behavioral Therapy, psychiatric consultation, and use of either inpatient or residential treatment if she was noncompliant or showed a worsening of symptoms. Supervision requirements included no access to weapons, monitored internet and social media use, and coordination with all providers.

The court placed Susan on intensive supervision and placed the recommendations of the examination in a journal entry. A treatment team, chaired by a court clinician, monitored her progress for 2 years, after which she was successfully discharged from court supervision.

FORENSIC CONTRIBUTIONS OF THE MMPI-A-RF

School shootings and threats of school violence have become an increasing area of assessment in juvenile forensic psychology. As the case above illustrates, youth who commit acts of school violence or who threaten such acts are extremely complex and heterogeneous. As noted earlier, there is no "profile" or common model of school shooters. For this reason, use of an instrument such as the MMPI-A-RF is of considerable importance. As has long been the case with each version of the MMPI, the test can be used to identify disturbances in thinking and perception as well as personality traits that can increase the risk of violence. Also, the MMPI-A-RF can identify those personality factors that are protective against risk. Finally, the MMPI-A-RF can identify treatment needs for the youth that can be targeted to reduce the potential for future threats or violence.

Sadie

Susan's Codefendant in a School Shooting Plot

BACKGROUND

Sadie plotted the school shooting with Susan.[1] Together with Susan, Sadie had approached another juvenile to assist in carrying out a detailed plan of shooting students and staff at her high school. The youth who was approached reported the incident to the local police. The specific request of the court was a general psychological evaluation as well as a risk assessment given the nature of her charges. Following a plea of admission, Sadie was adjudicated and was placed in a residential treatment center pending disposition of her case.

Interview With Youth

Sadie stated that she is 14 years old and was living with her mother at the time of the alleged offense. She indicated that her parents divorced when she was an infant. She reported a positive relationship with both parents, who have a shared parenting agreement. She alleged that her paternal step-uncle sexually abused her at the age of 11.

Sadie said that about 3 years ago, her mother became very ill and was hospitalized for about a week. They then lived with her mother's family, then with her stepfather, but now that her mother's divorce is finalized her mother plans to find her own home.

Sadie said that she has a very good relationship with her mother. She said that her birth father and she also get along well. Sadie is the only child born to her biological parents. She has three stepsisters by her ex-stepfather, and had a negative relationship with each of them.

Sadie indicated that she was in the ninth grade and will be going to a different school. She described herself as musical and said she has career aspirations in music. She said that in elementary school and eighth grade years, her grades went down, attributing this to the abuse she allegedly suffered. She denied any history of prior disciplinary problems but was expelled for the instant incident. She denied any history of substance abuse, indicating that she is "scared of getting into trouble."

Sadie said that she disclosed the alleged abuse when she was initially hospitalized and alleged that it was not reported to the proper authorities. However, she also told a therapist at a residential center where she was placed after being hospitalized. This therapist contacted child welfare authorities and the matter is currently under investigation. Outside of that, she denied any history of child welfare involvement or out-of-home placement. She also denied any history of fire-setting or animal cruelty. She indicated that the current charges are her first involvement with the juvenile court.

Sadie said that she was first psychiatrically hospitalized because she told her mother that she was cutting herself. She remained in the hospital for 12 days and had 2 weeks of follow-up services. Shortly thereafter she was admitted to another psychiatric hospital for cutting as well as suicidal ideation. She was hospitalized for 2 weeks and was discharged but did not follow through with aftercare.

Sadie was admitted to residential treatment by her parents after the school-shooting plot was discovered. She said that she has been diagnosed with "Situational Depression, Anxiety, PTSD and Bipolar Disorder" and is medicated with Geodon, Wellbutrin, and Prazosin. Sadie said that following discharge from the residential program, she would be admitted to an intensive outpatient program.

Sadie reported that although she has never attempted suicide, she began cutting about 1 month after she and her mother left her stepfather.

Sadie stated that she is in good health and denied any significant health or developmental problems. She denied any history of seizures, head trauma, loss of consciousness, or other problems suggestive of neurological impairment. She said that she has never been medically hospitalized.

COLLATERAL INFORMATION
Parent Interview
An interview with her parents and review of a developmental history that they completed indicated that Sadie's mother's pregnancy was complicated by

toxemia and sinus infections. Sadie was born 6 weeks early by a noncompli-cated C-section and was in the NICU for 5 days owing to low birthweight. Developmental milestones were obtained normally but she suffered from asthma as a young child, with migraines developing at age 7. Her parents divorced shortly after she was born but have maintained a cordial relationship with shared parenting. Both parents subsequently remarried. The alleged sexual abuse by her step-uncle is under investigation by the police and child welfare authorities.

Sadie did well in elementary school but when she began the seventh grade, she became the target of social bullying both at the school and online. During that time, her mother left her marriage fairly suddenly. Sadie struggled in ninth grade and has now been expelled. She has an intervention plan for anxiety and migraines.

Sadie's parents noted that at the time of the incident, her mood had become darker and withdrawn with increasing isolation. They deny that she had any fascination with weapons, mass murder, or violence, and she was not aggressive. She was, however, burning items such as photographs and journal entries in the basement. She was also increasingly fascinated with the occult and they noted that there was a "rash of suicide attempts" by other youth at the high school.

Her parents reported that Sadie will be living with her father and that there are no weapons in the house. Her internet access is restricted, and she will be on electronic monitoring and always supervised by adults. She will be taking classes online for the rest of the school year.

Educational Records

High school records indicated that she was on an intervention plan for anxiety and depression. She had no prior disciplinary problems. Her grades had suddenly dropped about 8 weeks prior to the plot being discovered.

Mental Health Records

In each of her psychiatric hospitalizations as well as when she was in residential treatment, Sadie was diagnosed with Bipolar II Disorder as well as Posttraumatic Stress Disorder. While in residential treatment, she was also diagnosed with emerging Borderline Personality Traits.

Current Behavioral Status

Sadie was appropriately dressed and groomed in clothing that was neat, clean, and appropriately arranged. Her hygiene and grooming were without any noticeable problems. There were no overt indications of loosening of associations, flight of ideas, or tangentiality. Her psychomotor activity was nonremarkable. Her speech was normal in tone, pacing, and volume. Her attention span was adequate. Her manner of social interaction was outwardly friendly, polite, and cooperative.

Sadie presented with an appropriate and expressive affect and reported an anxious and worried mood described as reactive to her legal and family circumstances and being placed in detention. When asked to rate her subjective level of distress (SUDS), Sadie described her present degree of emotional upset as being a 3 out of a possible 10, describing her current distress as stemming from being separated from her family.

Sadie denied and there were no overt indications of hallucinations, delusions, or paranoia. She gave no behavioral evidence of visual, gustatory, olfactory, or tactile hallucinations. She gave no evidence of systematic paranoid delusions or grandiosity, other than to say that she believes that she is being followed. Accordingly, there appears to be no overt clinical or behavioral evidence in the content of thought as would be typically seen with seriously mentally ill adolescents. It should be noted, however, that overt symptoms of serious mental illness are fairly rare in adolescents.

Sadie denied symptoms typically associated with depression such as limited appetite, hopelessness, loss of interest or pleasure, and poor sleep; and also denied loss of sexual desire or difficulty in concentration but did complain of some increased irritability, which can be associated with depression. However, she reported that this has improved.

In response to specific questions, Sadie denied active suicidal ideation, intent, or plan. She also denied homicidal ideation. However, as noted, she acknowledged a history of cutting herself.

When asked to describe her history of mood swings, Sadie stated that for much of her adolescence she has had rapidly changing moods and complained of racing thoughts and hypomania, but denied other symptoms associated with mania such as increased activity or grandiosity. She said that placement on medication has helped these symptoms greatly and that she no longer has the "big highs and lows" that she used to experience.

Sadie reported phobias of small places but denied any intrusive obsessive thinking or compulsive behavior, other than to say, "It used to be worse." However, she reported chronic anxiety, which she said is manifested often in worrying about her mother and also about again seeing her step-uncle. She said that when her mother started to date again, she was very fearful of men but has a positive relationship with her mother's current boyfriend. When I asked her about "flashbacks" and other symptoms associated with trauma exposure, she reported having flashbacks about her alleged abuse by her step-uncle and said that a few nights ago, she had nightmares and a "panic attack" and was helped by the nurse.

Sadie was alert and responsive to her environment and there were no problems observed with her attention or concentration. She was oriented to time, place, person, and situation. Her fund of general information suggested at least average intellectual functioning.

Sadie's concentration was also demonstrated to be adequate by her ability to perform simple mental calculations. Her short-term recall was adequate as demonstrated by her ability to recall three items from memory after a 10-minute distraction. She had the capacity for verbal abstract reasoning as demonstrated in her ability to state conceptual similarities between related objects and concepts, as well as more complex abstractions. This was also demonstrated in her ability to interpret commonly used proverbs. Her insight and judgment were seen as possibly improving owing to her answers to situational questions and her response to treatment-related questions.

Asked what she could do in the future to avoid situations such as her current one, Sadie indicated she felt she needed to continue treatment and that it was a good idea for her to change schools and to live with her father. She said that she does not want to live in her mother's house, as that is where the alleged abuse took place and it is an emotional "trigger" for her. She also said that she needs to stay away from her former peers and should avoid weapons and media that references violence.

On the K-BIT 2, Sadie earned a Vocabulary standard score of 103. She earned a Nonverbal standard score of 120. Her overall Composite IQ score was 114.

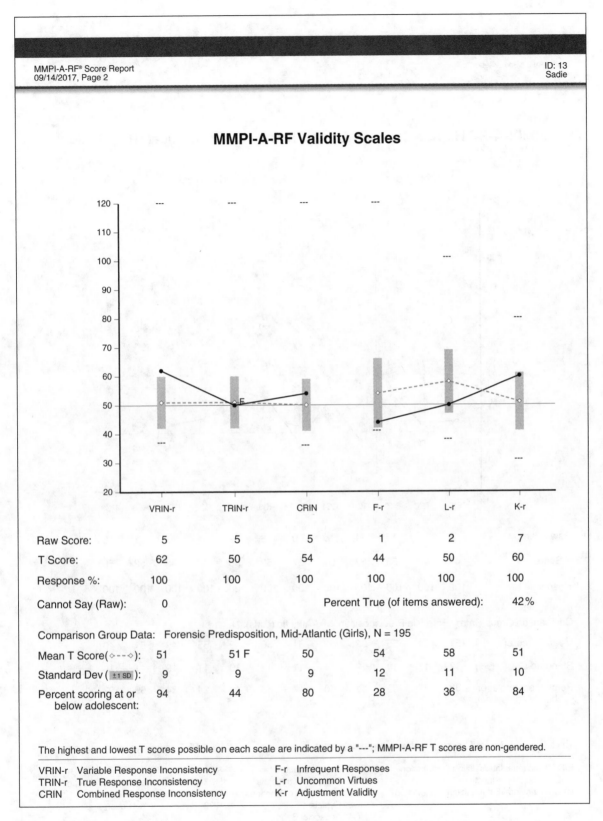

MMPI-A-RF Validity Scales

	VRIN-r	TRIN-r	CRIN	F-r	L-r	K-r
Raw Score:	5	5	5	1	2	7
T Score:	62	50	54	44	50	60
Response %:	100	100	100	100	100	100

Cannot Say (Raw):	0		Percent True (of items answered):	42%

Comparison Group Data: Forensic Predisposition, Mid-Atlantic (Girls), N = 195

	VRIN-r	TRIN-r	CRIN	F-r	L-r	K-r
Mean T Score(◇- - -◇):	51	51 F	50	54	58	51
Standard Dev (±1 SD):	9	9	9	12	11	10
Percent scoring at or below adolescent:	94	44	80	28	36	84

The highest and lowest T scores possible on each scale are indicated by a "---"; MMPI-A-RF T scores are non-gendered.

VRIN-r	Variable Response Inconsistency		F-r	Infrequent Responses
TRIN-r	True Response Inconsistency		L-r	Uncommon Virtues
CRIN	Combined Response Inconsistency		K-r	Adjustment Validity

FIGURE 13 Sadie's MMPI-A-RF Score Report. Copyright 2016 by the Regents of the University of Minnesota. All rights reserved.

MMPI-A-RF Higher-Order (H-O) and Restructured Clinical (RC) Scales

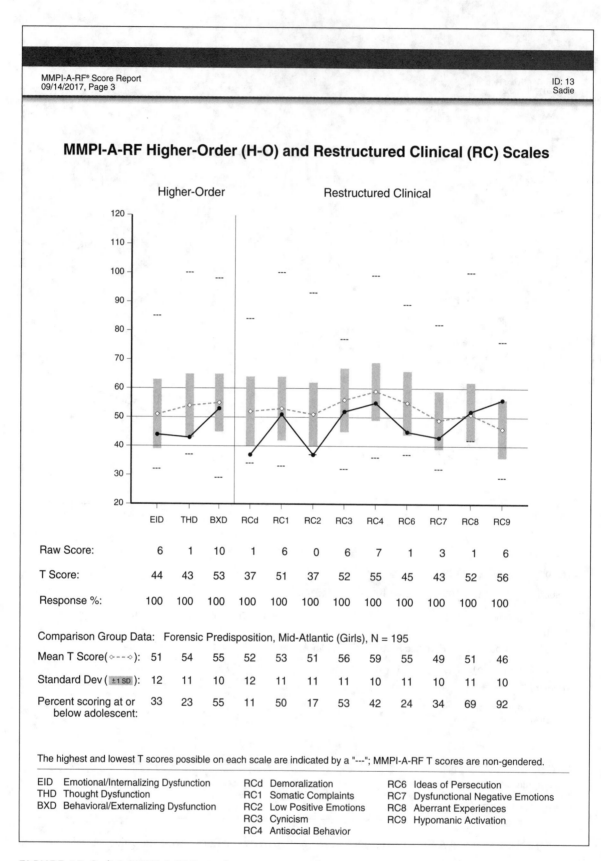

	EID	THD	BXD	RCd	RC1	RC2	RC3	RC4	RC6	RC7	RC8	RC9
Raw Score:	6	1	10	1	6	0	6	7	1	3	1	6
T Score:	44	43	53	37	51	37	52	55	45	43	52	56
Response %:	100	100	100	100	100	100	100	100	100	100	100	100

Comparison Group Data: Forensic Predisposition, Mid-Atlantic (Girls), N = 195

Mean T Score(◇---◇):	51	54	55	52	53	51	56	59	55	49	51	46
Standard Dev (±1 SD):	12	11	10	12	11	11	11	10	11	10	11	10
Percent scoring at or below adolescent:	33	23	55	11	50	17	53	42	24	34	69	92

The highest and lowest T scores possible on each scale are indicated by a "---"; MMPI-A-RF T scores are non-gendered.

EID Emotional/Internalizing Dysfunction
THD Thought Dysfunction
BXD Behavioral/Externalizing Dysfunction

RCd Demoralization
RC1 Somatic Complaints
RC2 Low Positive Emotions
RC3 Cynicism
RC4 Antisocial Behavior

RC6 Ideas of Persecution
RC7 Dysfunctional Negative Emotions
RC8 Aberrant Experiences
RC9 Hypomanic Activation

FIGURE 13 Sadie's MMPI-A-RF Score Report, continued.

192

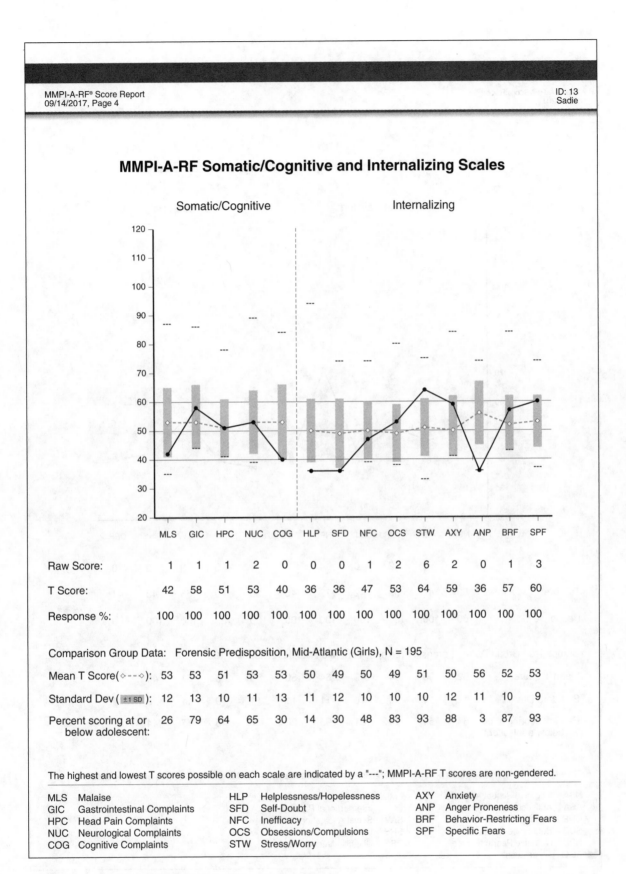

MMPI-A-RF Somatic/Cognitive and Internalizing Scales

Somatic/Cognitive   Internalizing

	MLS	GIC	HPC	NUC	COG	HLP	SFD	NFC	OCS	STW	AXY	ANP	BRF	SPF
Raw Score:	1	1	1	2	0	0	0	1	2	6	2	0	1	3
T Score:	42	58	51	53	40	36	36	47	53	64	59	36	57	60
Response %:	100	100	100	100	100	100	100	100	100	100	100	100	100	100

Comparison Group Data: Forensic Predisposition, Mid-Atlantic (Girls), N = 195

Mean T Score(◇--◇):	53	53	51	53	53	50	49	50	49	51	50	56	52	53
Standard Dev (±1 SD):	12	13	10	11	13	11	12	10	10	10	12	11	10	9
Percent scoring at or below adolescent:	26	79	64	65	30	14	30	48	83	93	88	3	87	93

The highest and lowest T scores possible on each scale are indicated by a "---"; MMPI-A-RF T scores are non-gendered.

MLS	Malaise	HLP	Helplessness/Hopelessness	AXY	Anxiety
GIC	Gastrointestinal Complaints	SFD	Self-Doubt	ANP	Anger Proneness
HPC	Head Pain Complaints	NFC	Inefficacy	BRF	Behavior-Restricting Fears
NUC	Neurological Complaints	OCS	Obsessions/Compulsions	SPF	Specific Fears
COG	Cognitive Complaints	STW	Stress/Worry		

FIGURE 13 Sadie's MMPI-A-RF Score Report, continued.

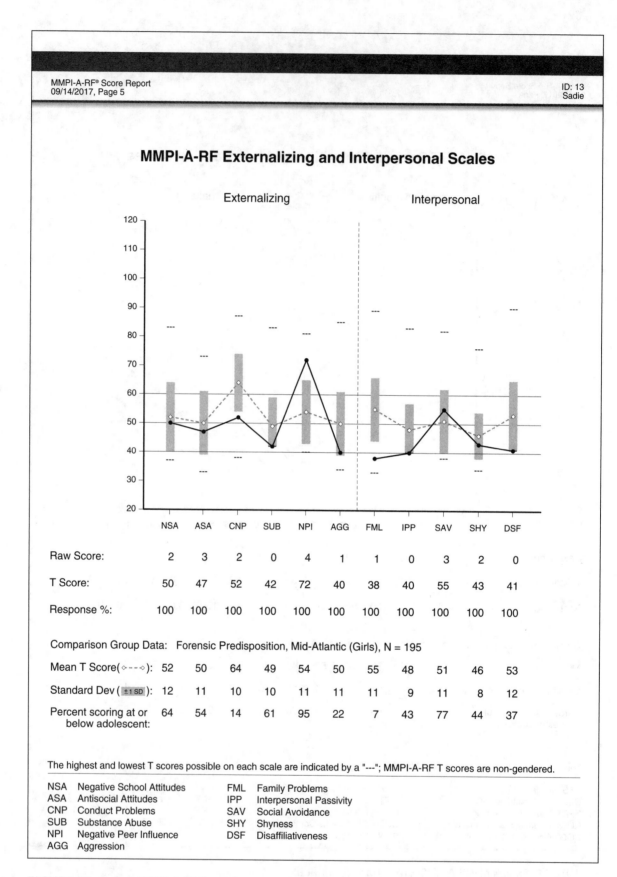

MMPI-A-RF Externalizing and Interpersonal Scales

	NSA	ASA	CNP	SUB	NPI	AGG	FML	IPP	SAV	SHY	DSF
Raw Score:	2	3	2	0	4	1	1	0	3	2	0
T Score:	50	47	52	42	72	40	38	40	55	43	41
Response %:	100	100	100	100	100	100	100	100	100	100	100

Comparison Group Data: Forensic Predisposition, Mid-Atlantic (Girls), N = 195

	NSA	ASA	CNP	SUB	NPI	AGG	FML	IPP	SAV	SHY	DSF
Mean T Score(◇- - -◇):	52	50	64	49	54	50	55	48	51	46	53
Standard Dev (±1 SD):	12	11	10	10	11	11	11	9	11	8	12
Percent scoring at or below adolescent:	64	54	14	61	95	22	7	43	77	44	37

The highest and lowest T scores possible on each scale are indicated by a "---"; MMPI-A-RF T scores are non-gendered.

NSA	Negative School Attitudes		FML	Family Problems
ASA	Antisocial Attitudes		IPP	Interpersonal Passivity
CNP	Conduct Problems		SAV	Social Avoidance
SUB	Substance Abuse		SHY	Shyness
NPI	Negative Peer Influence		DSF	Disaffiliativeness
AGG	Aggression			

FIGURE 13 Sadie's MMPI-A-RF Score Report, continued.

194

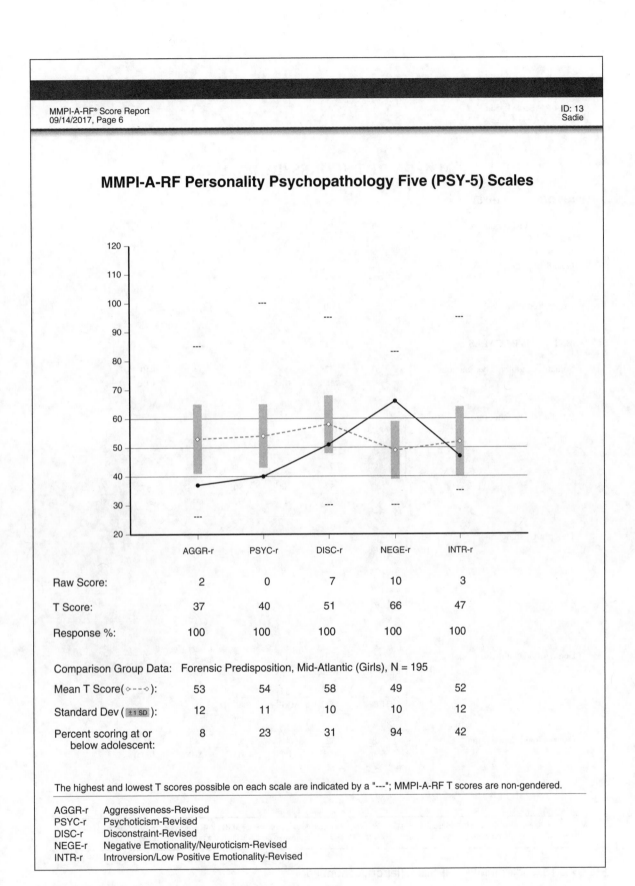

MMPI-A-RF Personality Psychopathology Five (PSY-5) Scales

	AGGR-r	PSYC-r	DISC-r	NEGE-r	INTR-r
Raw Score:	2	0	7	10	3
T Score:	37	40	51	66	47
Response %:	100	100	100	100	100

Comparison Group Data: Forensic Predisposition, Mid-Atlantic (Girls), N = 195

	AGGR-r	PSYC-r	DISC-r	NEGE-r	INTR-r
Mean T Score(◇- - -◇):	53	54	58	49	52
Standard Dev (±1 SD):	12	11	10	10	12
Percent scoring at or below adolescent:	8	23	31	94	42

The highest and lowest T scores possible on each scale are indicated by a "---"; MMPI-A-RF T scores are non-gendered.

AGGR-r   Aggressiveness-Revised
PSYC-r   Psychoticism-Revised
DISC-r   Disconstraint-Revised
NEGE-r   Negative Emotionality/Neuroticism-Revised
INTR-r   Introversion/Low Positive Emotionality-Revised

FIGURE 13 Sadie's MMPI-A-RF Score Report, continued.

MMPI-A-RF T SCORES (BY DOMAIN)

PROTOCOL VALIDITY

Content Non-Responsiveness

0	62	50	54
CNS	VRIN-r	TRIN-r	CRIN

Over-Reporting

44
F-r

Under-Reporting

50	60
L-r	K-r

SUBSTANTIVE SCALES

Somatic/Cognitive Dysfunction

51	42	58	51	53	40
RC1	MLS	GIC	HPC	NUC	COG

Emotional Dysfunction

44
EID

37	36	36	47
RCd	HLP	SFD	NFC

37	47
RC2	INTR-r

43	53	64	59	36	57	60	66
RC7	OCS	STW	AXY	ANP	BRF	SPF	NEGE-r

Thought Dysfunction

43
THD

45
RC6

52
RC8

40
PSYC-r

Behavioral Dysfunction

53
BXD

55	50	47	52	42	72
RC4	NSA	ASA	CNP	SUB	NPI

56	40	37	51
RC9	AGG	AGGR-r	DISC-r

Interpersonal Functioning

38	52	40	55	43	41
FML	RC3	IPP	SAV	SHY	DSF

Note. This information is provided to facilitate interpretation following the recommended structure for MMPI-A-RF interpretation in Chapter 7 of the *MMPI-A-RF Administration, Scoring, Interpretation, and Technical Manual,* which provides details in the text and an outline in Table 7-1.

FIGURE 13 Sadie's MMPI-A-RF Score Report, continued.

MMPI-A-RF

Sadie's protocol was compared to 195 forensic predisposition girls in the Mid-Atlantic. Sadie's Validity scale scores indicated that her protocol was valid and interpretable, with no indications of inconsistent responding, overreporting, or underreporting.

Sadie reported a number of negative emotional experiences including stress and worry. She is likely to be anxious, to complain of sleeplessness, and to have problems concentrating. She also reports multiple fears and phobias.

Sadie acknowledged that she tends to affiliate with a negative peer group. She likely has a history of school suspensions. Sadie is most probably oppositional and defiant with persons whom she perceives as authority figures. In addition, she likely has a history of rule breaking that may be of a level that brings her to the attention of the juvenile court. Likely behaviors include running away from home, school truancy, and substance abuse.

CONNERS COMPREHENSIVE BEHAVIOR RATING SCALE

A youth leader on the unit familiar with Sadie completed the Conners Comprehensive Behavior Rating Scale, a standardized measure of psychological problems in youth.[2] The scores on the Validity scales do not indicate a positive, negative, or inconsistent response style. The T scores for the following Conners CBRS-P Content scales were very elevated in the areas of Emotional Distress, Social Problems, Worrying, Separation Fears, Perfectionistic and Compulsive Behaviors, and Physical Symptoms.

Diagnostic similarities were found between Sadie's scores and ADHD Predominantly Inattentive Type, Major Depressive Episode, Manic Episode, Generalized Anxiety Disorder, Separation Anxiety Disorder, Social Phobia Obsessive-Compulsive Disorder, Autistic Disorder, and Asperger's Disorder.

CLINICAL IMPRESSION

Sadie was given diagnoses of Bipolar II Disorder Most Recent Episode Depressed, Unspecified Anxiety Disorder, Rule Out Posttraumatic Stress Disorder, and Emerging Borderline Personality Traits.

Risk Assessment

STRUCTURED PROFESSIONAL JUDGMENT— RISK ASSESSMENT

This youth was assessed using the Structured Assessment of Violence Risk in Youth (SAVRY). Within the group of *Historical Risk Factors,* it is noted that she shows no known prior episode of aggressive behavior and no known history of nonviolent offending. She alleges that she was the victim of abuse (which is apparently under investigation by child welfare authorities).

In the area of *Social/Contextual Risk Factors,* she has not been described in the past as associating to a great extent with delinquent or negative peers with the exception of the codefendant, who is reported to have emotional issues and who is this examinee's best friend. However, the MMPI-A-RF reports a significant tendency for affiliation with a negative peer group. She does have poor coping skills (cutting/suicidal ideation) but has not experienced significant peer rejection and does have a present consistent source of personal and social support. Youth who have experienced considerable stress and who have limited coping skills are often seen as being at greater risk for aggressive behavior. She does not appear to be from a community that suffers from significant disorganization and does not have a high potential for exposure to crime, poverty, and violence, which is an asset.

Within the subset of *Individual/Clinical Risk Factors,* she voices a positive attitude toward treatment. She does not have a clear pattern of involvement in substance abuse and on the MMPI-A-RF did not have personality characteristics of adolescents at risk for substance abuse. She does not have a history of anger management problems and also appears significantly impaired in her capacity for age-appropriate empathy. She has been stable in the residential center and is described as being willing to continue treatment.

In terms of *Protective Factors* (those qualities or aspects that might mitigate against violent acting out), it is noted that she does verbalize a strong commitment to school.

Overall, given the limited number of risk factors identified and the identified protective factors, she would be rated on this instrument as being a low to moderate risk for continued aggressive behavior. Naturally, should there be significant changes in the contextual or clinical or dynamic risk factors then the overall risk assessment could change as well. Finally, any risk assessment of adolescents must include the caveat that adolescents by nature are changeable and dynamic and that some degree of antisocial behavior and aggression is statistically normative in adolescents and the majority of adolescents do not continue antisocial behavior into adulthood.

Structured Inquiry

In Sadie's case, using a threat assessment model, the following areas are addressed:

PATHWAY WARNING BEHAVIORS *Any behavior that is part of research, planning, preparation or implementation of attack.* In Sadie's case, she and Susan had made detailed plans and then sought out another student to assist them. After the plan was discovered, Sadie told the police that she was "interested" in how school shooters thought. In addition, she acknowledged that she has thoughts about being violent but denied ever actually wanting to hurt a specific person. She said that she felt that only Sarah understood how she felt about Columbine. Sadie denied spending time on the internet searching for content about Columbine and school shooters. A subsequent search of her electronic media by law enforcement found no evidence of searches related to school violence.

FIXATION WARNING BEHAVIORS *Any behavior that indicates a pathological preoccupation with a person or a cause.* On the basis of the information provided, it appears that Sadie had developed an interest in Columbine. This apparently evolved into a discussion of how an attack could take place and also how to avoid getting caught. There appears to be no other clearly stated motivation, such as revenge against another person or persons or the general institution of the school. She denies any specific grievances against the school and her school records indicate that she does not have a significant disciplinary history.

IDENTIFICATION WARNING BEHAVIOR *Any behavior that indicates a pathological desire to be a "pseudo-commando."* There appears to be no evidence of an attempt to engage in such behavior.

NOVEL AGGRESSIVE WARNING BEHAVIORS *An act of violence that appears unrelated to any targeted violence pathway warning behavior.* There appears to be, to the best of my knowledge, no indication of any aggressive warning behaviors in this case.

ENERGY BURST WARNING BEHAVIORS *An increase in the frequency or variety of any noted activities related to the target, even if the activities themselves are relatively innocuous, usually in the days or weeks prior to the attack.* In this case, these communications had taken place over a long period of time. Some indications of an increase are suggested by their approaching a third student.

LEAKAGE WARNING BEHAVIOR *The communication to a third party of an attempt to do harm through an attack.* Prior to the alleged offense, the two youths exchanged very specific and detailed communication about how such an attack could be developed and carried out. They then approached another youth to join them. Whereas Sadie maintained that she was not serious in her intent, the youth whom they approached was convinced enough that she determined it to be a serious threat and contacted authorities.

LAST RESORT WARNING BEHAVIOR *Evidence of a violent crime imperative and time imperative; increasing desperation or distress forcing a person into a position of last resort for which there is no alternative but violence.* There appears to be in the materials that I reviewed no indications of an increasing imperative.

DIRECTLY COMMUNICATED THREAT WARNING *The communication of a direct threat to the target or to law enforcement behavior.* There is no evidence in the materials that I reviewed of such a communication.

OUTCOME

Sadie was viewed as having substantial treatment needs and was in continued need of residential treatment. She was also seen as being a moderate risk of violence in the school setting and a low to moderate risk of general aggression in the community. It was recommended that when released from the residential center she be transferred to a partial hospitalization program. She would also require intensive supervision with no access to weapons, supervised internet and social media access, random drug testing, Dialectal Behavioral Therapy, and intensive home-based services following discharge from partial hospitalization. It was also recommended that treatment be trauma informed and coordinated through the court by forming a treatment team of all involved providers.

Sadie was discharged but began cutting herself once more. She was not returned to residential care but was placed in a partial hospitalization program and showed gradual improvement. She successfully completed intensive probation and attends a different school, which was notified of her offense history.

FORENSIC CONTRIBUTIONS OF THE MMPI-A-RF

In Sadie's case, the MMPI-A-RF findings guided her treatment needs to reduce potential risk factors. In particular, her elevation on the negative peer influences provided direction into both helping her form positive relationships and also monitoring for a return to negative peer associations which, given the circumstances of the case, was a particular vulnerability and potential risk factor. Her continued level of negative emotional experiences pointed out her need to continue in treatment. In that her Higher-Order scales were not significantly elevated and that the principal elevations were on the Internalizing scales, a phased transition to a community-based setting was not contradicted by the MMPI-A-RF data.

Jordan
A Male Sexual Abuse Victim in a Civil Damages Case

BACKGROUND

Jordan, a 17-year-old boy, was referred for a psychological evaluation of possible emotional harm following a prolonged period of sexual abuse. The perpetrator of the abuse, a prominent attorney, had already entered a plea of guilty to a charge of unlawful sexual contact with a minor and is incarcerated.

Interview With Youth

Jordan indicated that he was "sort of shy growing up" and "liked to do my own thing," noting that he still sees himself that way. To the best of his knowledge, he did not have any significant medical or developmental problems as a young child.

Jordan stated that his father died in an automobile accident when Jordan was 1 year old. Jordan lives at home with his mother. He reported a positive relationship with his family members. He described his peers as being generally "good students" who are involved in some sports. He is not dating and does not have a girlfriend. Other than the instant incidents, which he indicated were against his will, he has not been sexually active.

As noted, Jordan is in the 11th grade. He reported earning average grades in elementary school, "B's and C's" in 9th and 10th grades, noting, "Last year was rough." He said that he is now earning A's and B's. His career goal is to become a physician.

Jordan denied any significant disciplinary problems during elementary school and some "class disruption" in middle school as well as some in-school suspensions for tardiness. He denied any significant disciplinary problems in high school and denied any history of physical abuse victimization.

Jordan described himself as being generally healthy but indicated that he does suffer from seasonal allergies. He is not currently taking any medications. He denied any significant childhood injuries or accidents and said that he had never undergone surgery. He noted a history of a concussion playing basketball in the seventh grade but was not medically treated. Otherwise, he denied any history of seizures, loss of consciousness, head trauma, or other neurological complications.

Jordan reported a normal appetite but complained of chronic sleep problems that began last year.

Prior to the instant events, Jordan had never received mental health services. He had never been psychiatrically hospitalized. Jordan denied current use of any substances but said that in the eighth grade, he began smoking marijuana, with his highest level of usage being about 2 or 3 times per week. He said that he stopped about 9 months ago because "It was a waste of money." He denied use of any other illicit drugs, ever drinking alcohol, or abuse of prescription drugs. He does not gamble and denied any other problems with impulse control.

Jordan has a history of contact with child welfare authorities owing to the instant incidents but prior to that, he had had no such contact. He has never been in out-of-home placement. He has been seen at, and currently receives services from, a specialized trauma treatment program following the instant incidents. There, he sees an individual counselor, first on a weekly and now every other week basis.

Jordan denied any history of suicidal behaviors but said that he has, since the instant incident, thought of suicide, telling me that the thought of his family keeps him from acting on these urges. However, he said that after the abuse, he has burned himself three times on his arm, beginning in the summer between the 9th and 10th grades. Asked why he did that, he said, "I don't know why. I felt so much coming on me." He said that he has also slept with a knife under his bed, thinking of either cutting or killing himself; the last such incident being before the start of the 10th grade.

Jordan reported that he was seen in the juvenile court in the eighth grade on a charge of possession of marijuana when he was caught with peers at a local park. He entered a plea of guilty and was sent to a substance abuse treatment program for drug testing and an educational class. He has never been in the juvenile detention center and has never been incarcerated.

COLLATERAL INFORMATION

In an interview with Jordan's mother, she reported that her pregnancy and delivery were unremarkable. He was an "easy" temperament infant who obtained developmental milestones nonremarkably. He has had no significant childhood illnesses, injuries, or neurological problems. He is not currently a behavioral problem at home. The mother said that prior to the instant incident, he had no significant behavioral problems at school, but noted that he had been suspended for the incident involving marijuana.

Jordan's mother said that after she began to work for the perpetrator, he began to act in a mentor role with Jordan. He would often spend time "tutoring" Jordan. Jordan revealed the abuse just before the beginning of his 10th-grade year, after he was taken to an emergency room for suicidal thoughts. The abuse was reported to the police.

Treatment records indicate that Jordan has been seen for over a year with a diagnosis of Posttraumatic Stress Disorder. He participates in treatment but continues to exhibit considerable anxiety as well as avoidance behaviors.

A review of Jordan's school records indicates that he has not received special educational services. He was never held back and has only the marijuana incident on his disciplinary records. His grades are poor, with a 1.89 GPA on a 0 to 4.0 scale.

Current Behavioral Status

Jordan was dressed in street clothing that was neat, clean, and appropriate. His hygiene and grooming were adequate. He displayed no unusual mannerisms and maintained direct eye contact throughout the examination. His speech was normal in tone, rhythm, volume, and pacing. His approach to the evaluation was initially a bit shy but as the examination progressed, he became more interactive, suggesting that his shyness was likely a socially appropriate response to his circumstances. His attention span was adequate, and he was neither hyperactive nor easily distracted. He completed all tasks requested of him and remained pleasant and cooperative throughout the examination.

Overall, Jordan's flow of conversation and thought was responsive to the questions and was understandable. He did not exhibit disturbances of thought typically associated with serious mental illnesses such as rambling, circumstantial ideation, fragmented ideation, flight of ideas, poverty of speech, or perseveration. There were no disturbances in the form of his thinking; that is to say, he did not have loose associations or tangential thinking and his cognitions appeared to be well organized overall. Generally, there appeared to be no abnormalities in the form of thought typically associated with the types of serious mental illness associated with loss of contact with reality.

Jordan's affect was appropriate and reactive to his generally neutral emotional state, which he described as "good." Jordan characterized his subjective level of emotional distress as a "4" out of a possible 10, saying that he does become upset when the discussion turns either to his abuse or to his deceased father. He reported that since the abuse, he has had episodic mood swings, saying that the changes in mood "come out of nowhere" and move his "happy" mood to "sad." He indicated that this phenomenon did not happen prior to the abuse.

Jordan denied and demonstrated no behavioral evidence of visual, gustatory, olfactory, or tactile hallucinations and further gave no behavioral evidence of hearing or responding to hallucinations during any of the examinations. If he did, in fact, have active symptoms of psychosis, it is likely that they would have been observed during the interviews, which they were not. Overall, there were no observable indications of the types of perceptual abnormalities typically associated with serious mental illness.

Jordan denied and exhibited no evidence of specific delusional thinking or grandiosity. Accordingly, there appeared to be no evidence in the content of thought as would typically be seen with seriously mentally ill persons. However, he reported a sense of hypervigilance, noting that subsequent to the sexual abuse, he continues to "Worry that [his abuser] will come back in my life" and that he is "Afraid of just seeing him."

Jordan denied certain symptoms typically associated with depression such as limited appetite, hopelessness, loss of interest or pleasure, loss of sexual interest, poor concentration, or irritability. However, since the abuse, he reports problems sleeping, saying that he will have much difficulty falling asleep, because of his anxiety about the perpetrator. He also reported periodic nightmares about the abuse incidents and said, "It's like he is wanting to find me."

In response to specific inquiry, Jordan denied active suicidal ideation, intent, or plan. He also denied homicidal ideation. He denied current self-injurious behavior, but as noted, reported a history of burning himself.

Jordan denied any history of bipolar disorder or manic episodes characterized by marked agitation, extreme loss of the need for sleep, racing thoughts, or rapid mood swings.

Jordan denied any specific phobias as well as any intrusive obsessive thinking (prior to the abuse incident) or compulsive behavior. Jordan said that since the abuse, he "worries about the future—what's it going to be." He reported he still experiences intrusive memories about the abuse, noting however that this has improved, that he still has them, "but not as much." He indicated that last year, "Health class was awful" when the sexual subjects were studied. In addition, when talk with his peers turns to sexual matters, Jordan reported he will become anxious, sometimes angry, and will attempt to leave. He said that while studying sexuality in school, the classes would trigger memories of his victimization. He said that also in Health class, he would have flashbacks, describing them as "Pictures in my head. I would gaze off and would think about it and become depressed." He complained that he would still have nightmares about the abuse, and fears, as noted, about the perpetrator coming into his room. He also reported that after the abuse, he became much more irritable but that he is "calmer, not as angry now."

Jordan was alert and responsive to his environment. He was oriented to time, place, person, and situation. His fund of general information suggested fair to adequate intellectual functioning for his age.

Jordan's concentration was age appropriate as evidenced by a lack of fluctuations in his attention and focus in the conversation with the examiner. His immediate recall was adequate as demonstrated by his ability to recall eight digits forward and five in reverse order. His short-term recall was also adequate as demonstrated by his ability to recall three of three items from memory after a 10-minute distraction, as well as simple mental calculations and serial mental subtractions. He also demonstrated an adequate capacity for verbal abstract reasoning; for example, by his ability to state conceptual similarities between simply related objects and concepts and increasingly abstract ones in a way that would be expected for a youth his age. This level of age-appropriate cognitive functioning was also demonstrated in his ability to interpret commonly used proverbs. His insight and judgment were within general age expectations as determined by both his history and response to situational questions.

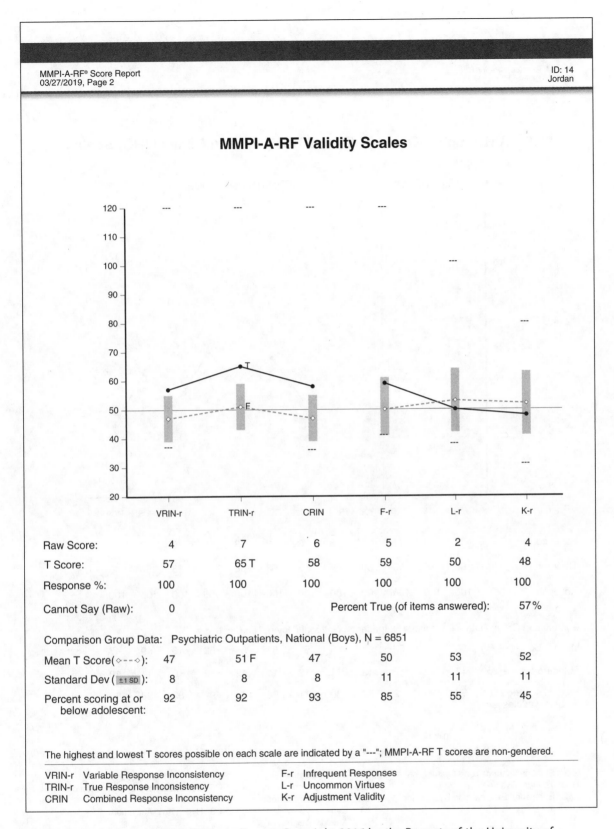

MMPI-A-RF Validity Scales

	VRIN-r	TRIN-r	CRIN	F-r	L-r	K-r
Raw Score:	4	7	6	5	2	4
T Score:	57	65 T	58	59	50	48
Response %:	100	100	100	100	100	100

Cannot Say (Raw):   0   Percent True (of items answered):   57%

Comparison Group Data: Psychiatric Outpatients, National (Boys), N = 6851

	VRIN-r	TRIN-r	CRIN	F-r	L-r	K-r
Mean T Score(◇- - -◇):	47	51 F	47	50	53	52
Standard Dev (±1 SD):	8	8	8	11	11	11
Percent scoring at or below adolescent:	92	92	93	85	55	45

The highest and lowest T scores possible on each scale are indicated by a "---"; MMPI-A-RF T scores are non-gendered.

VRIN-r	Variable Response Inconsistency	F-r	Infrequent Responses
TRIN-r	True Response Inconsistency	L-r	Uncommon Virtues
CRIN	Combined Response Inconsistency	K-r	Adjustment Validity

FIGURE 14 Jordan's MMPI-A-RF Score Report. Copyright 2016 by the Regents of the University of Minnesota. All rights reserved.

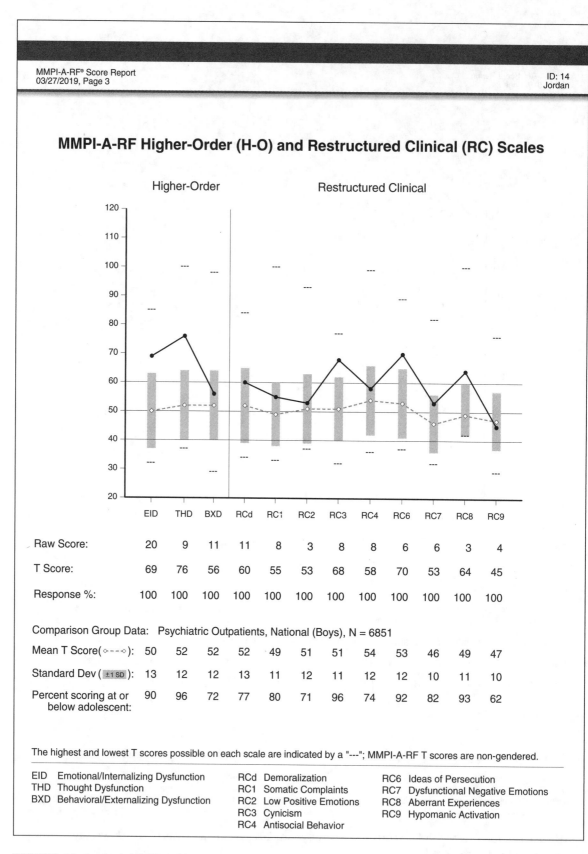

MMPI-A-RF Higher-Order (H-O) and Restructured Clinical (RC) Scales

	Higher-Order			Restructured Clinical								
	EID	THD	BXD	RCd	RC1	RC2	RC3	RC4	RC6	RC7	RC8	RC9
Raw Score:	20	9	11	11	8	3	8	8	6	6	3	4
T Score:	69	76	56	60	55	53	68	58	70	53	64	45
Response %:	100	100	100	100	100	100	100	100	100	100	100	100

Comparison Group Data: Psychiatric Outpatients, National (Boys), N = 6851

Mean T Score(◇--◇):	50	52	52	52	49	51	51	54	53	46	49	47
Standard Dev (±1 SD):	13	12	12	13	11	12	11	12	12	10	11	10
Percent scoring at or below adolescent:	90	96	72	77	80	71	96	74	92	82	93	62

The highest and lowest T scores possible on each scale are indicated by a "---"; MMPI-A-RF T scores are non-gendered.

EID Emotional/Internalizing Dysfunction	RCd Demoralization	RC6 Ideas of Persecution
THD Thought Dysfunction	RC1 Somatic Complaints	RC7 Dysfunctional Negative Emotions
BXD Behavioral/Externalizing Dysfunction	RC2 Low Positive Emotions	RC8 Aberrant Experiences
	RC3 Cynicism	RC9 Hypomanic Activation
	RC4 Antisocial Behavior	

FIGURE 14 Jordan's MMPI-A-RF Score Report, continued.

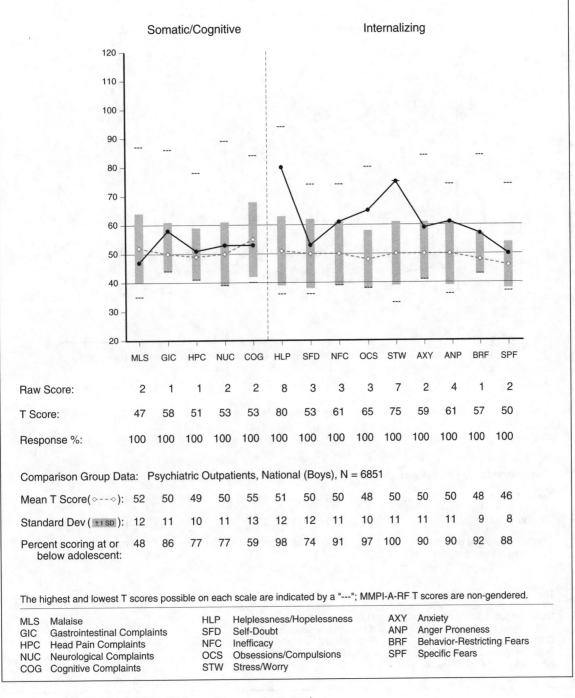

MMPI-A-RF Somatic/Cognitive and Internalizing Scales

Somatic/Cognitive   Internalizing

	MLS	GIC	HPC	NUC	COG	HLP	SFD	NFC	OCS	STW	AXY	ANP	BRF	SPF
Raw Score:	2	1	1	2	2	8	3	3	3	7	2	4	1	2
T Score:	47	58	51	53	53	80	53	61	65	75	59	61	57	50
Response %:	100	100	100	100	100	100	100	100	100	100	100	100	100	100

Comparison Group Data: Psychiatric Outpatients, National (Boys), N = 6851

Mean T Score(◇--◇):	52	50	49	50	55	51	50	50	48	50	50	50	48	46
Standard Dev (±1 SD):	12	11	10	11	13	12	12	11	10	11	11	11	9	8
Percent scoring at or below adolescent:	48	86	77	77	59	98	74	91	97	100	90	90	92	88

The highest and lowest T scores possible on each scale are indicated by a "---"; MMPI-A-RF T scores are non-gendered.

MLS	Malaise	HLP	Helplessness/Hopelessness	AXY	Anxiety
GIC	Gastrointestinal Complaints	SFD	Self-Doubt	ANP	Anger Proneness
HPC	Head Pain Complaints	NFC	Inefficacy	BRF	Behavior-Restricting Fears
NUC	Neurological Complaints	OCS	Obsessions/Compulsions	SPF	Specific Fears
COG	Cognitive Complaints	STW	Stress/Worry		

FIGURE 14 Jordan's MMPI-A-RF Score Report, continued.

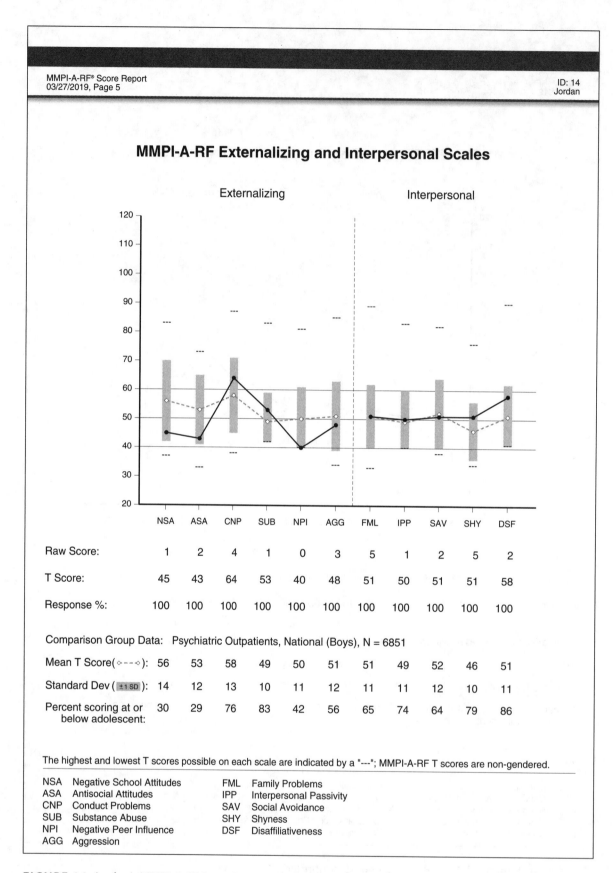

MMPI-A-RF Externalizing and Interpersonal Scales

FIGURE 14 Jordan's MMPI-A-RF Score Report, continued.

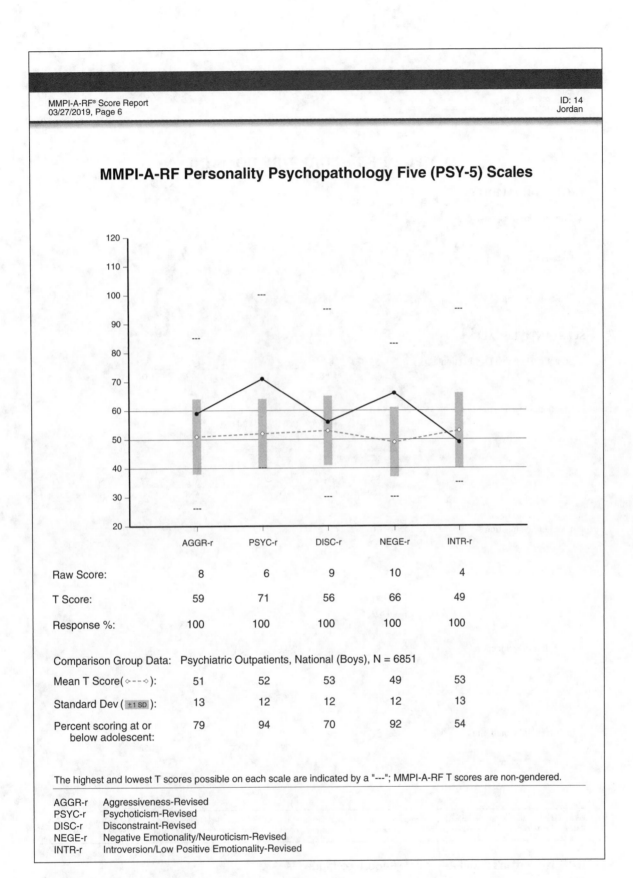

MMPI-A-RF Personality Psychopathology Five (PSY-5) Scales

	AGGR-r	PSYC-r	DISC-r	NEGE-r	INTR-r
Raw Score:	8	6	9	10	4
T Score:	59	71	56	66	49
Response %:	100	100	100	100	100

Comparison Group Data: Psychiatric Outpatients, National (Boys), N = 6851

	AGGR-r	PSYC-r	DISC-r	NEGE-r	INTR-r
Mean T Score(◇---◇):	51	52	53	49	53
Standard Dev (±1 SD):	13	12	12	12	13
Percent scoring at or below adolescent:	79	94	70	92	54

The highest and lowest T scores possible on each scale are indicated by a "---"; MMPI-A-RF T scores are non-gendered.

AGGR-r	Aggressiveness-Revised
PSYC-r	Psychoticism-Revised
DISC-r	Disconstraint-Revised
NEGE-r	Negative Emotionality/Neuroticism-Revised
INTR-r	Introversion/Low Positive Emotionality-Revised

FIGURE 14 Jordan's MMPI-A-RF Score Report, continued.

MMPI-A-RF T SCORES (BY DOMAIN)

PROTOCOL VALIDITY

Content Non-Responsiveness

0	57	65 T	58
CNS	VRIN-r	TRIN-r	CRIN

Over-Reporting

59
F-r

Under-Reporting

50	48
L-r	K-r

SUBSTANTIVE SCALES

Somatic/Cognitive Dysfunction

55	47	58	51	53	53
RC1	MLS	GIC	HPC	NUC	COG

Emotional Dysfunction

69		60	80	53	61				
EID		RCd	HLP	SFD	NFC				

53	49
RC2	INTR-r

53	65	75	59	61	57	50	66
RC7	OCS	STW	AXY	ANP	BRF	SPF	NEGE-r

Thought Dysfunction

76		70
THD		RC6

64
RC8

71
PSYC-r

Behavioral Dysfunction

56		58	45	43	64	53	40
BXD		RC4	NSA	ASA	CNP	SUB	NPI

45	48	59	56
RC9	AGG	AGGR-r	DISC-r

Interpersonal Functioning

51	68	50	51	51	58
FML	RC3	IPP	SAV	SHY	DSF

Note. This information is provided to facilitate interpretation following the recommended structure for MMPI-A-RF interpretation in Chapter 7 of the *MMPI-A-RF Administration, Scoring, Interpretation, and Technical Manual,* which provides details in the text and an outline in Table 7-1.

FIGURE 14 Jordan's MMPI-A-RF Score Report, continued.

MMPI-A-RF

Jordan's MMPI-A-RF protocol was valid but there was some evidence of a fixed True response set. Although this did not invalidate the protocol, it should be interpreted with some caution. With that in mind, there were no indications of either over- or underreporting. He appeared to understand the test items. His protocol was compared to a reference group of 6,581 male psychiatric outpatients.

Jordan's MMPI-A-RF protocol contained indications of potential risk for suicide or self-injurious behaviors reflected in elevations on RCd and HLP. However, inspection of the critical items indicates that he did not affirm any statements directly related to suicidal or self-injurious content. Nevertheless, he should be monitored and evaluated for possible suicide risk and appropriate precautions should be taken if indicated.

Jordan's scores indicate that he likely experiences significant thought dysfunction. He reports significant persecutory ideation and some unusual thought processes and perceptual experiences.

Jordan's scores also indicate that he experiences significant emotional distress. He reports feeling sad and dissatisfied with his current life circumstances and he may experience suicidal ideation, feel that life is a strain, and feel sad. He reports pervasive feelings of hopelessness and helplessness, and very likely feels hopeless, like a failure, and believes he gets a raw deal from life and cannot be helped. He may engage in self-mutilation and very likely gives up easily. He also reports being indecisive and ineffective in coping with difficulties and is likely passive and procrastinates. Jordan reports an above-average level of stress and worry, and is likely to be anxious, complain of sleeplessness, and have problems with concentration. He reports an above-average level of obsessive and compulsive symptoms. In addition, Jordan reports a high level of anger problems involving irritability and impatience and he is indeed likely angry and irritable, and is likely compulsive.

Jordan reports multiple conduct problems, may have a history of criminal charges, placement in juvenile detention, school suspension, running away from home, and poor academic performance.

Interpersonally, Jordan reports cynical beliefs concerning others, being distrustful of others, and believing that others are motivated solely by self-interest.

Diagnostically, Jordan's scores indicate the need to consider a possible thought disorder, depression-related psychopathology, a stress-related disorder, obsessive-compulsive disorder, and conduct disorder.

Treatment planning should focus on Jordan's helplessness and hopelessness and the related risk for self-harm, dysphoric affect, his sense of inefficacy, obsessive-compulsive tendencies, stress reactivity, and lack of interpersonal trust. Further diagnostic work is needed to understand the origin of the significant persecutory ideation and unusual thought processes Jordan reported. His emotional distress may motivate Jordan to engage in treatment. However, his cynicism may interfere with development of a therapeutic relationship.

Jordan's mother completed the Conners Comprehensive Behavior Rating Scale—Parent Report Form. Scores on the Validity scales did not indicate a positive, negative, or inconsistent response style.

Clinically significant ratings were found in the areas of Emotional Distress, Separation Fears, Perfectionistic and Compulsive Behaviors, as well as Physical Symptoms. Diagnostic possibilities were Major Depressive Episode, Manic Episode, and Separation Anxiety Disorder.

Diagnosis

Jordan was given the diagnosis of Posttraumatic Stress Disorder, Unspecified Disruptive, Impulse Control, and Cannabis Use Disorder by history.

OUTCOME

The perpetrator entered into a financial settlement with Jordan and his mother.

FORENSIC CONTRIBUTIONS OF THE MMPI-A-RF

Forensic civil liability cases address central questions of whether or not there is psychological injury and, if so, was it the type of disorder that could be seen as a direct and proximate result of the act. Use of the MMPI-A-RF in civil cases has several purposes. The test can identify problematic approaches to the inventory, and more broadly the evaluation. Persons involved with civil litigation, including youth, have clear incentives for secondary gain such as financial reward, which could lead them to exaggerate or feign symptoms. The MMPI-A-RF Validity scales provide the examiner with objective data concerning this possibility. If the findings are valid, the MMPI-A-RF can identify the types of psychological problems experienced by the examinee. Most specifically, are the types of problems seen those that might be expected if a direct or proximate result of the alleged act?

In Jordan's case, many of his symptoms were consistent with posttraumatic stress disorder in males. Sexually abused males are, of course, not homogeneous. It is important to note that males differ from sexually abused females in that males often do not admit being abused and will demonstrate their psychological problems through acting-out behavior (Becker & Kerig, 2011). Given the absence of extra-test indications of thought dysfunction, the significant persecutory ideation reflected in Jordan's MMPI-A-RF scores most likely is the result of having been sexually traumatized by an important adult figure in his life.

Both Jordan's behavior and the findings on the MMPI-A-RF suggest that he has conduct problems. In the context of the emotional distress seen in Jordan's MMPI-A-RF, and consistent with the research just mentioned, his acting-out behavior can be seen as a likely consequence that helps explain and define rather than diminish the extent of the psychological problems resulting from his trauma. Finally, the MMPI-A-RF can provide important data concerning treatment needs and proposed interventions that also are an important consideration in the determination of damages.

In Jordan's case, there were no indications on the MMPI-A-RF of overreporting or exaggeration. The impairment reflected in his Substantive scale scores, as just described, would be a consideration in potential damages. The need for intensive treatment would be another consideration.

Lennie

A Youth Referred for Competency to Stand Trial

BACKGROUND

Lennie is a 14-year-old male referred by his attorney for an evaluation of his competence to stand trial. The competency statute requires that the examiner assess the ability of the youth to (1) comprehend and appreciate the charges against him; (2) understand the adversarial nature of the proceeding including the role of the judge, defense counsel, prosecuting attorney, guardian ad litem or court-appointed special assistant, and witnesses; (3) assist in his own defense and communicate with counsel; and (4) comprehend and appreciate the consequences that may be imposed as a result of the proceedings.

Lennie is charged with one count of rape—child under 13, a felony of the first degree if committed by an adult. He currently resides with his mother, while he awaits further court proceedings. He is alleged to have forced his then 3-year-old half-brother to engage in sexual behaviors.

Interview With Youth

Lennie reported that he was born in Alabama and moved to his current state of residence when he was about 5 years old. He said that his parents, who were not married, separated at that time. Lennie indicated that he has lived primarily with his mother but had briefly lived with his father to attend a different school district that had better academic rankings. It was during this time that the offense is alleged to have taken place. Consequently, he moved back in with his mother. He has had limited subsequent contact with his father.

Lennie reported a generally good relationship with his mother. He indicated that she had been engaged to a man whom Lennie alleged would physically abuse him. He was uncertain when his mother and this man broke up. He reported that he has a 5-year-old half-sister who lives with his former stepfather.

Lennie stated that he has never dated. He has one best friend, but he has not seen him since the alleged instant offense. Lennie indicated that he has played basketball and also is on his high school track team.

Lennie is presently attending an online school. He had been to traditional schools until he returned to live with his mother. He has an IEP for speech but said that he does not have a learning disability and does not receive special education other than speech therapy. Lennie denied any history of discipline problems in school, indicating that he has never been suspended or expelled. He reported that he has been frequently bullied because of his speech problems. His career goal is to become a coach.

Lennie denied any substance use or misuse. He denied any history of sexual or physical abuse. He denied any history of fire-setting or animal cruelty. He indicated that this is his first contact with the juvenile court.

Lennie stated that he has never received any type of mental health services, either inpatient or outpatient. He has never been prescribed any type of mental health medication. Lennie said that he has never been suicidal but indicated that he has cut himself in response to being bullied.

Lennie stated that he is in good general health. He is not prescribed medications of any kind. He reported that as a young child, he fell off a chair and hit his head but was not taken to an emergency room. He otherwise denied any history of head trauma, seizure, loss of consciousness, or other neurological impairment.

COLLATERAL INFORMATION

Lennie's mother reported that she was 16 years old at the time she was pregnant with Lennie. She denied using alcohol or abusing substances while pregnant and said that she received regular medical care. The otherwise nonremarkable pregnancy was complicated by a 3-week early delivery. Lennie's birthweight was low, but he was not kept in the NICU. His mother indicated that Lennie was a colicky baby who experienced acid reflux. His developmental milestones were achieved nonremarkably, but he has had an IEP for a speech impediment. The mother reported that she lived with nonparental relatives during her youth and that Lennie was born in a different state from the one in which they now reside. Although she lived with his father for 3 years, they never married. Lennie's mother said that she moved with Lennie to be with her family. She described his father as "in and out" of Lennie's life and has never been consistent in seeing Lennie. She reported that she has a younger son with another man, whom she described as "mean" to her and to Lennie. She indicated that Lennie's speech impediment caused him to be bullied in elementary and middle school and to not fit in socially with his peers.

Lennie's mother said that he lived with his father for about 6 months but left after the alleged offense. She described Lennie as being depressed and anxious. She said that he has few friends and rarely leaves the house. She has observed no incidents of self-injurious behavior or suicidal threats or behaviors. He has exhibited neither markedly unusual nor bizarre behaviors nor rapid changes in mood. Lennie's mother reported that she has a family history of bipolar disorder and schizophrenia. Lennie has never been in any type of mental health services.

Lennie's mother completed a developmental history questionnaire that provided essentially the same information as above. It was reported that he struggles with self-care and has to be prompted often to bathe or brush his teeth. She also reported that he has attended seven different schools and began receiving speech therapy in the first grade. She noted that around the fourth grade, he started to become overweight, which has been a challenge for him.

School records indicate that Lennie was absent four times and tardy twice in the current school year. His grades were D's and F's with one C. There is no record of an IEP, 504 Plan, or ETR.

Current Behavioral Status

Lennie appeared to be socially immature. He had a marked speech impediment but could be understood. His hygiene and grooming were adequate. He displayed no unusual mannerisms and maintained direct eye contact throughout the examination. His speech was normal in tone, rhythm, initially low in volume, and normal in pacing. His approach to the evaluation was cooperative and he completed all tasks requested of him. He appeared to be quite anxious.

Overall, Lennie's flow of conversation and thought was without any noticeable abnormalities. His verbalizations were goal directed and responsive to the examiner's questions. He did not exhibit disturbances of thought typically associated with serious mental illnesses such as rambling, circumstantial ideation, fragmented ideation, flight of ideas, poverty of speech, or perseveration. There were no disturbances in the form of his thinking; he did not have loose associations or tangential thinking and his cognitions appeared to be well organized. Lennie exhibited no behavioral evidence of visual, gustatory, olfactory, or tactile hallucinations. Nor was there any evidence of hearing or responding to hallucinations during any of the examinations. He also denied and did not evidence any delusional thinking or grandiosity. Accordingly, there appears to be no evidence in the content of Lennie's thought indicating serious mental illness.

Lennie's affect was appropriate and consistent with his self-reported "stressed" emotional state. He rated his present level of emotional distress as a 3 out of a possible 10, citing his legal situation as his primary stress. Lennie denied some symptoms typically associated with depression such as limited appetite or sleep problems. However, he reported periodic feelings of hopelessness, which is a factor for suicide risk in adolescents. However, he denied present suicidal ideation, intent, or plan. He denied homicidal thoughts. He said that he often "cries" about his situation. Lennie reported that he is not able to enjoy the things that he once did, suggesting anhedonia, a symptom often seen in depression. He also reported problems with concentration and irritability, which are also symptoms commonly seen in depression. He denied any history of bipolar disorder or manic episodes such as marked agitation, extreme loss of the need for sleep, or rapid mood swings.

Lennie reported a history of anxiety, which he said began when he was bullied at school and made worse by his legal circumstances. He denied any specific, nonnormative phobias as well as any intrusive obsessive thinking or compulsive behavior. He denied any history of "flashbacks," intrusive thoughts, or other psychological consequences of trauma exposure. He reported a history of having nightmares of dying and waking up feeling very anxious.

Lennie was alert and responsive to his environment. He was oriented to time, place, person, and situation. He demonstrated a capacity for abstract thinking. To illustrate, he could identify relationships between related concepts beyond a basic level. This was also demonstrated in his ability to interpret commonly used proverbs. His fund of general information indicated likely intact intellectual functioning as reflected in his responses to questions of general knowledge commonly known by youth his age.

Lennie's immediate recall was intact, with the ability to recall five digits forward and three reversed. His short-term recall was intact as demonstrated by his ability to recall three of three items from memory after a 10-minute distraction. His insight and judgment did appear to be limited as determined by both his history and his responses to situational questions.

Cognitive

On the K-BIT 2, Lennie achieved a Vocabulary score of 95, a Nonverbal standard score of 93. His overall Composite IQ standard score was 93. He was also administered the Slosson Oral Reading Test, using the third edition norms. His score indicates that Lennie reads at the 11th-grade level.

MMPI-A-RF

Lennie produced a valid and interpretable MMPI-A-RF protocol that was compared to both the normative reference sample of 805 boys and the comparison group of 326 Mid-Atlantic Forensic Predisposition boys. He appeared to understand the test items and responded appropriately to their content. There were no indications of either under- or overreporting of problems. His score on L-r was considerably lower than that of most adolescents tested under similar circumstances, with only 9% of the comparison group sample scoring at or below Lennie on this scale. Thus, Lennie was less inclined than other predisposition boys to attempt to portray himself in a positive manner.

Lennie reports significant emotional distress. The elevation on the Higher-Order scale of Emotional/Internalizing Dysfunction is significantly above both the normative sample and the comparison sample, with 99% of the latter sample scoring at or below Lennie on this scale. He produced elevated scores on scales associated with suicide risk, possible suicidal gestures, and self-injurious behavior. In his interview, Lennie denied present suicidal thoughts or intent, but he did acknowledge a history of self-injury. Lennie should be monitored by a mental health professional for suicidal thoughts and appropriate precautions taken if indicated.

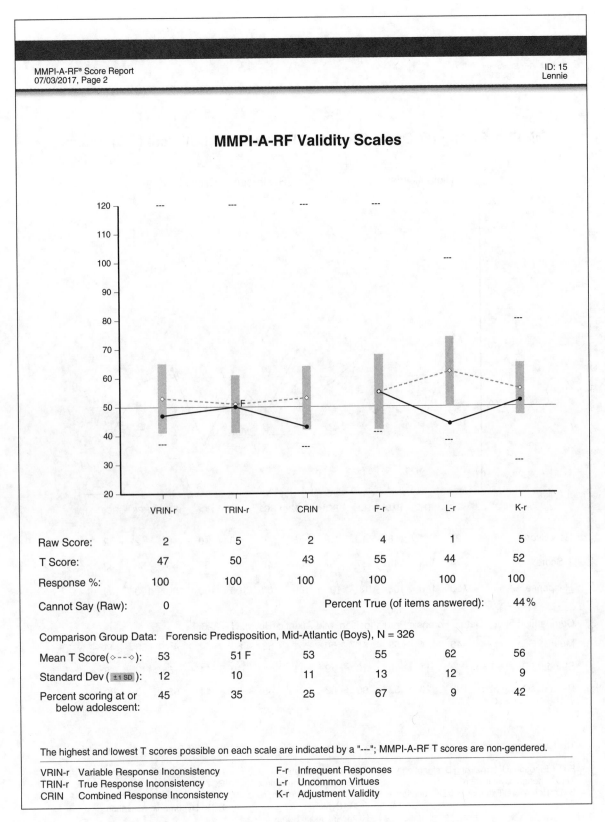

MMPI-A-RF Validity Scales

	VRIN-r	TRIN-r	CRIN	F-r	L-r	K-r
Raw Score:	2	5	2	4	1	5
T Score:	47	50	43	55	44	52
Response %:	100	100	100	100	100	100

Cannot Say (Raw): 0   Percent True (of items answered): 44%

Comparison Group Data: Forensic Predisposition, Mid-Atlantic (Boys), N = 326

	VRIN-r	TRIN-r	CRIN	F-r	L-r	K-r
Mean T Score (◇---◇):	53	51 F	53	55	62	56
Standard Dev (±1 SD):	12	10	11	13	12	9
Percent scoring at or below adolescent:	45	35	25	67	9	42

The highest and lowest T scores possible on each scale are indicated by a "---"; MMPI-A-RF T scores are non-gendered.

VRIN-r	Variable Response Inconsistency	F-r	Infrequent Responses
TRIN-r	True Response Inconsistency	L-r	Uncommon Virtues
CRIN	Combined Response Inconsistency	K-r	Adjustment Validity

FIGURE 15 Lennie's MMPI-A-RF Score Report.

MMPI-A-RF Higher-Order (H-O) and Restructured Clinical (RC) Scales

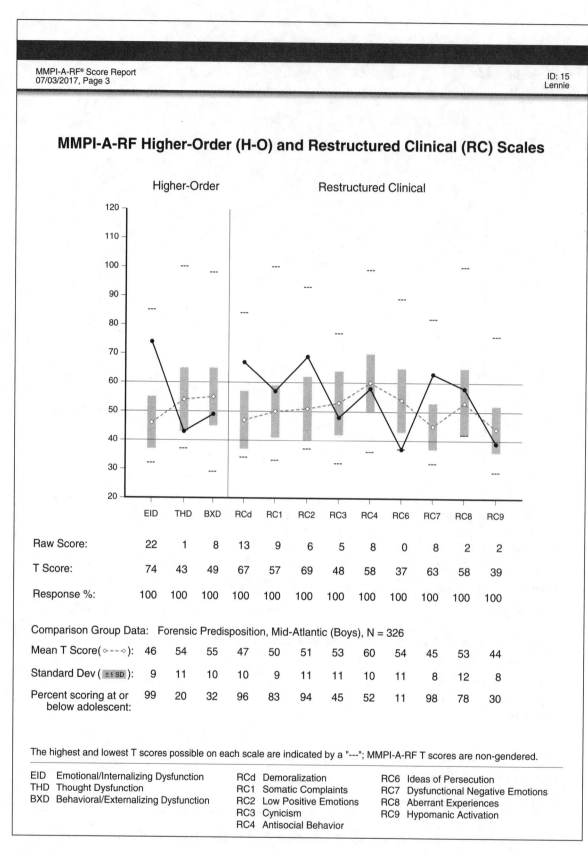

	EID	THD	BXD	RCd	RC1	RC2	RC3	RC4	RC6	RC7	RC8	RC9
Raw Score:	22	1	8	13	9	6	5	8	0	8	2	2
T Score:	74	43	49	67	57	69	48	58	37	63	58	39
Response %:	100	100	100	100	100	100	100	100	100	100	100	100

Comparison Group Data: Forensic Predisposition, Mid-Atlantic (Boys), N = 326

Mean T Score(◇---◇):	46	54	55	47	50	51	53	60	54	45	53	44
Standard Dev (±1 SD):	9	11	10	10	9	11	11	10	11	8	12	8
Percent scoring at or below adolescent:	99	20	32	96	83	94	45	52	11	98	78	30

The highest and lowest T scores possible on each scale are indicated by a "---"; MMPI-A-RF T scores are non-gendered.

EID Emotional/Internalizing Dysfunction	RCd Demoralization	RC6 Ideas of Persecution
THD Thought Dysfunction	RC1 Somatic Complaints	RC7 Dysfunctional Negative Emotions
BXD Behavioral/Externalizing Dysfunction	RC2 Low Positive Emotions	RC8 Aberrant Experiences
	RC3 Cynicism	RC9 Hypomanic Activation
	RC4 Antisocial Behavior	

FIGURE 15 Lennie's MMPI-A-RF Score Report, continued.

222

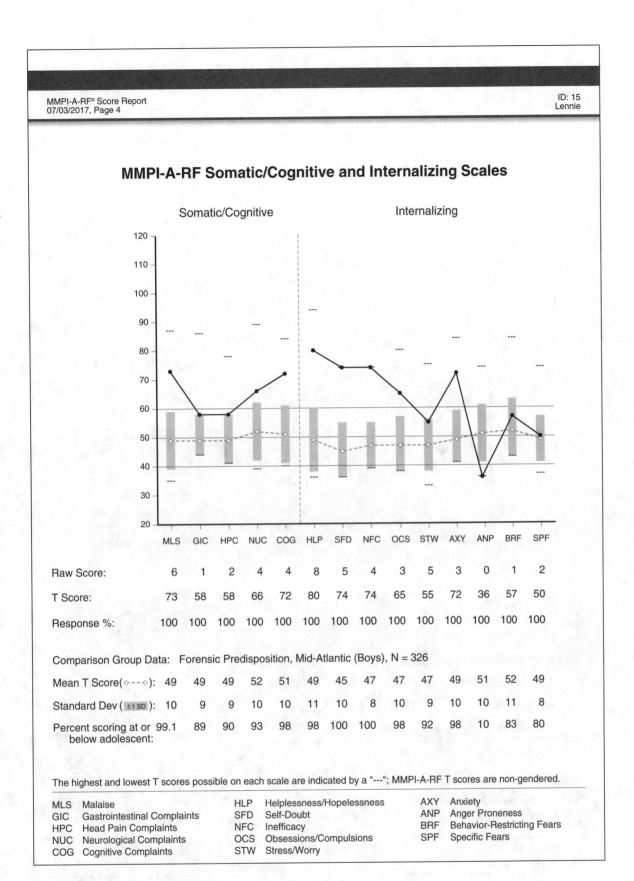

MMPI-A-RF Somatic/Cognitive and Internalizing Scales

Somatic/Cognitive   Internalizing

	MLS	GIC	HPC	NUC	COG	HLP	SFD	NFC	OCS	STW	AXY	ANP	BRF	SPF
Raw Score:	6	1	2	4	4	8	5	4	3	5	3	0	1	2
T Score:	73	58	58	66	72	80	74	74	65	55	72	36	57	50
Response %:	100	100	100	100	100	100	100	100	100	100	100	100	100	100

Comparison Group Data: Forensic Predisposition, Mid-Atlantic (Boys), N = 326

Mean T Score(◇--◇):	49	49	49	52	51	49	45	47	47	47	49	51	52	49
Standard Dev (±1 SD):	10	9	9	10	10	11	10	8	10	9	10	10	11	8
Percent scoring at or below adolescent:	99.1	89	90	93	98	98	100	100	98	92	98	10	83	80

The highest and lowest T scores possible on each scale are indicated by a "---"; MMPI-A-RF T scores are non-gendered.

MLS	Malaise	HLP	Helplessness/Hopelessness	AXY	Anxiety
GIC	Gastrointestinal Complaints	SFD	Self-Doubt	ANP	Anger Proneness
HPC	Head Pain Complaints	NFC	Inefficacy	BRF	Behavior-Restricting Fears
NUC	Neurological Complaints	OCS	Obsessions/Compulsions	SPF	Specific Fears
COG	Cognitive Complaints	STW	Stress/Worry		

FIGURE 15 Lennie's MMPI-A-RF Score Report, continued.

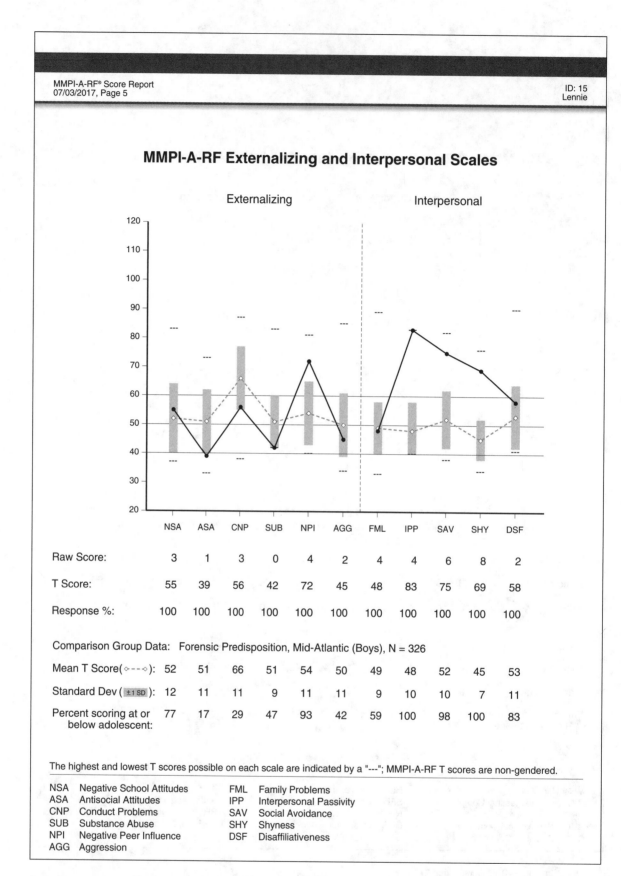

MMPI-A-RF Externalizing and Interpersonal Scales

Externalizing   Interpersonal

	NSA	ASA	CNP	SUB	NPI	AGG	FML	IPP	SAV	SHY	DSF
Raw Score:	3	1	3	0	4	2	4	4	6	8	2
T Score:	55	39	56	42	72	45	48	83	75	69	58
Response %:	100	100	100	100	100	100	100	100	100	100	100

Comparison Group Data: Forensic Predisposition, Mid-Atlantic (Boys), N = 326

Mean T Score(◇- - -◇):	52	51	66	51	54	50	49	48	52	45	53
Standard Dev (±1 SD):	12	11	11	9	11	11	9	10	10	7	11
Percent scoring at or below adolescent:	77	17	29	47	93	42	59	100	98	100	83

The highest and lowest T scores possible on each scale are indicated by a "---"; MMPI-A-RF T scores are non-gendered.

NSA	Negative School Attitudes		FML	Family Problems
ASA	Antisocial Attitudes		IPP	Interpersonal Passivity
CNP	Conduct Problems		SAV	Social Avoidance
SUB	Substance Abuse		SHY	Shyness
NPI	Negative Peer Influence		DSF	Disaffiliativeness
AGG	Aggression			

FIGURE 15 Lennie's MMPI-A-RF Score Report, continued.

224

MMPI-A-RF Personality Psychopathology Five (PSY-5) Scales

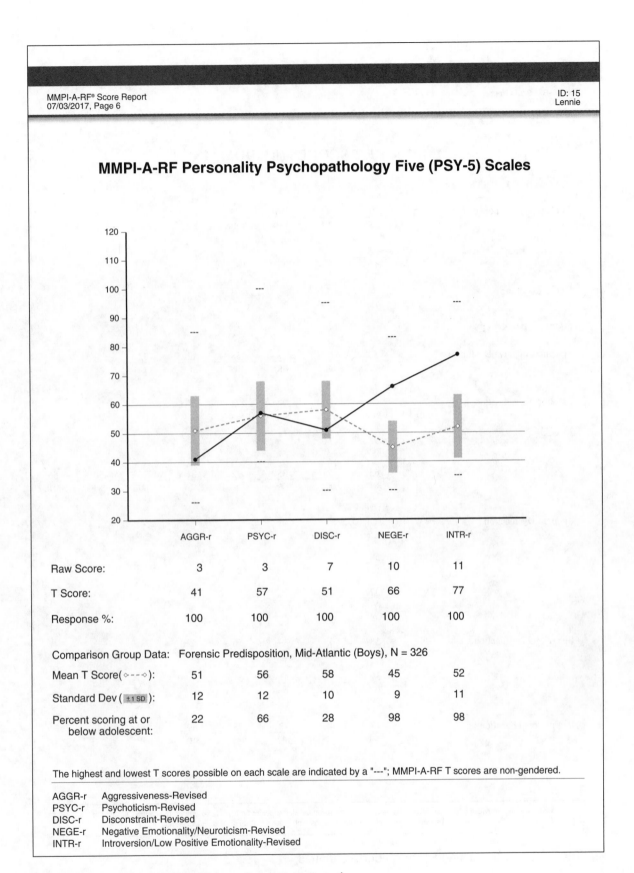

	AGGR-r	PSYC-r	DISC-r	NEGE-r	INTR-r
Raw Score:	3	3	7	10	11
T Score:	41	57	51	66	77
Response %:	100	100	100	100	100

Comparison Group Data: Forensic Predisposition, Mid-Atlantic (Boys), N = 326

Mean T Score(◇---◇):	51	56	58	45	52
Standard Dev (±1 SD):	12	12	10	9	11
Percent scoring at or below adolescent:	22	66	28	98	98

The highest and lowest T scores possible on each scale are indicated by a "---"; MMPI-A-RF T scores are non-gendered.

AGGR-r   Aggressiveness-Revised
PSYC-r   Psychoticism-Revised
DISC-r   Disconstraint-Revised
NEGE-r   Negative Emotionality/Neuroticism-Revised
INTR-r   Introversion/Low Positive Emotionality-Revised

FIGURE 15 Lennie's MMPI-A-RF Score Report, continued.

225

MMPI-A-RF T SCORES (BY DOMAIN)

PROTOCOL VALIDITY

Content Non-Responsiveness

0	47	50	43
CNS	VRIN-r	TRIN-r	CRIN

Over-Reporting

55
F-r

Under-Reporting

44	52
L-r	K-r

SUBSTANTIVE SCALES

Somatic/Cognitive Dysfunction

57	73	58	58	66	72
RC1	MLS	GIC	HPC	NUC	COG

Emotional Dysfunction

74		67	80	74	74			
EID		RCd	HLP	SFD	NFC			

		69	77					
		RC2	INTR-r					

		63	65	55	72	36	57	50	66
		RC7	OCS	STW	AXY	ANP	BRF	SPF	NEGE-r

Thought Dysfunction

43		37
THD		RC6

		58
		RC8

		57
		PSYC-r

Behavioral Dysfunction

49		58	55	39	56	42	72
BXD		RC4	NSA	ASA	CNP	SUB	NPI

		39	45	41	51
		RC9	AGG	AGGR-r	DISC-r

Interpersonal Functioning

48	48	83	75	69	58
FML	RC3	IPP	SAV	SHY	DSF

Note. This information is provided to facilitate interpretation following the recommended structure for MMPI-A-RF interpretation in Chapter 7 of the *MMPI-A-RF Administration, Scoring, Interpretation, and Technical Manual*, which provides details in the text and an outline in Table 7-1.

FIGURE 15 Lennie's MMPI-A-RF Score Report, continued.

Lennie reports a significant lack of positive emotions, a pronounced lack of interest in activities he once enjoyed (anhedonia). He is likely to be very pessimistic, to lack energy, and to display vegetative symptoms of depression. Review of the Restructured Clinical scales indicates levels of demoralization (RCd), Low Positive Emotions (RC2), and Dysfunctional Negative Experiences (RC7) that are considerably above the mean of the reference group of forensic predisposition males as well as the normative sample. This would suggest that in comparison to other youth in a forensic setting, Lennie experiences considerably more symptoms in these areas.

Lennie describes himself as feeling very sad and dissatisfied with his current life circumstances. It is likely that he feels overwhelmed and dysphoric and experiences significant hopelessness about his future. He feels that he has been treated poorly in life and that his problems cannot be helped. Lennie tends to give up easily, has considerable feelings of self-doubt. He feels useless and inferior. His thinking and behavior are self-defeating, and he cannot make decisions owing to substantial indecisiveness. He is ineffective in coping with his emotions and the stresses in his life. He tends to ruminate about his problems and perceived failings. Lennie's anxiety is pervasive and consuming. He feels considerable remorse and guilt about his behaviors and choices. He most likely has nightmares. Lennie also reports an above-average level of obsessive and compulsive symptoms. These symptoms are likely significant enough to cause problems in his thinking. Lennie does not report problems with anger.

Lennie reports concerns about being in poor physical health and may often feel fatigued and report having low energy. He likely has problems with sleep and complains of vague neurological symptoms of an unknown origin. He is at risk for developing physical symptoms in response to stress. Lennie also reports a diffuse pattern of problems with his thinking and cognitive functioning. He likely experiences considerable difficulty with concentration and attention and slow speech.

Lennie does not report disordered thinking of the type associated with poor ties with reality such as delusional thinking. He also does not report aberrant perceptual experiences such as hallucinations or illusions.

Lennie reports associating with a negative peer group and he is at risk for oppositional and rule-breaking behavior. His responses are similar to youth whose behavioral problems have brought them into contact with courts or school authorities. He is therefore at risk for substance abuse as well as running away from home, although he did not report engaging in these behaviors.

Interpersonally, Lennie is passive, submissive, and easily dominated by or influenced by others. He reports avoiding social situations and being very uncomfortable around others. Lennie is very likely introverted, socially isolated, and awkward. He likely has been (as indicated in his record) bullied by peers and remains at risk to be bullied by others. He is shy, uncomfortable around the opposite sex, easily embarrassed, and very socially uncomfortable.

Lennie's MMPI-A-RF scores indicate the need to consider diagnosing him with internalizing disorders such as anxiety and depression as well as obsessions-compulsions and somatoform or similar disorders.

Behaviorally, test results indicate that Lennie is at risk for externalizing disorders such as ADHD, substance abuse, and conduct disorder.

Finally, his protocol is similar to adolescents diagnosed with social anxiety or other disorders of social avoidance.

Lennie's scores indicate that in light of his level of emotional distress he may be motivated for treatment. However, owing to his malaise, it may be difficult for him to initially engage in treatment. He should be seen for evaluation of possible need for antidepressant medication and should be monitored for any indications of suicidal thoughts or self-injurious behaviors. The MMPI-A-RF identified possible cognitive problems including poor attention and concentration, as well as possible behavioral problems. Consequently, he should be further evaluated for a possible neurocognitive disorder such as ADHD.

Personality and Emotional Functioning—Parent Report

Lennie's mother completed the Conners Comprehensive Behavior Rating Scale—a norm-referenced assessment of emotional and behavioral problems in youth. The instrument contains Validity scales and there were no indications of either under- or overreporting of problems or of inconsistent responding. The CBRS has two primary components. One addresses major problem areas (the Content scales) and the other addresses statistical similarities to selected DSM-5 diagnoses.

Lennie's mother's scores showed considerable elevation (T scores equal to or greater than 70) in the areas of Emotional Distress and Social Problems as well as physical symptoms. These findings are consistent with Lennie's self-report on the MMPI-A-RF as well as the findings of his clinical interview.

Regarding DSM-5 diagnoses, Lennie's mother rated him as very elevated on the symptom scales of Major Depressive Episode and Generalized Anxiety Disorder. These findings are also consistent with the MMPI-A-RF and Lennie's clinical interview.

Diagnosis

Lennie was given diagnoses of Unspecified Depressive Disorder, Unspecified Anxiety Disorder, and Unspecified Disruptive, Impulse Control and Conduct Disorder. He was also given a rule out of Attention Deficit Hyperactivity Disorder. Finally, he was diagnosed with a Language Disorder by history.

Competency Inquiry

Lennie was interviewed using the Juvenile Adjudicative Competence Interview (Grisso, 2005). The JACI is a structured set of questions that assess the youth's understanding, appreciation, and reasoning in decisions concerning rights waiver, within content areas that pertain directly to the legal standard for competence to stand trial. Based primarily upon work of the MacArthur Research Network on Adolescent Development and Juvenile Justice, the instrument does not provide a "score" and is not a norm-based assessment or test, but rather an interview guide.

EXPERIENCE AND LEGAL CONTEXT OF EXAMINATION

Lennie has had limited experience with court. He was able to indicate why he was charged and provided an understandable and internally consistent response to the allegations.

UNDERSTANDING AND APPRECIATION OF CHARGES

Lennie correctly identified the charge against him. He was able to indicate that he understood that it is quite serious. He could distinguish between a charge that was more serious ("murder") and one that was less serious ("thieving").

NATURE AND PURPOSE OF THE JUVENILE COURT TRIAL

Lennie understood that the purpose of a trial was to "decide if you are guilty or not" and also understood that going to court was more serious than being seen for a disciplinary action in school.

POSSIBLE PLEAS

Lennie correctly defined the plea of guilty (in juvenile court, admit) as "you did it" and the plea of not guilty (in juvenile court, deny) as "you didn't do it." He was aware that if a person pleaded guilty, a consequence could follow ("you could get locked up") and that if a not guilty plea was entered then there would be more proceedings ("you get more trial"). He also demonstrated an understanding of the difference between actual guilt and an initial plea of not guilty, or denial.

GUILT AND PUNISHMENT/PENALTIES

Lennie knew that if he is adjudicated, he could be incarcerated, put into placement, or put on probation. He demonstrated adequate appreciation of knowing that incarceration was a more severe consequence than probation.

ROLE OF COURTROOM PERSONNEL

Lennie knew the roles of the various courtroom personnel. He knew that the prosecutor was against him ("try to prove me guilty") and that the prosecutor would advocate the side of the police over his version. He knew the advocate role of the defense attorney ("defend me"). He also knew the importance of telling his version of the offense to counsel. Lennie knew what a probation officer did ("keep track of you—drug test you"). He also knew that in a trial or hearing the probation officer differed from his attorney because his attorney would "protect me." He knew that a judge or magistrate was "in charge— has more authority" and would decide "guilty or not guilty," as well as impose sentence. He knew that a judge or magistrate was "not supposed to" have a predetermined decision as to responsibility. He was incorrect in responding that if the jurist asked him if he was culpable that he would have to answer. This, however, is a common error seen in adolescents.

ABILITY TO ASSIST COUNSEL

Lennie knew the importance of telling his side to his attorney. He did not know her name. When given various scenarios of how to assist his attorney, Lennie consistently responded that he did not know what to do.

ABILITY TO MAKE DECISIONS

Lennie did not know the meaning of a plea bargain or plea agreement. When it was explained to him, he was able to correctly repeat this back in his own words. At the end of the interview, the concept was revisited and Lennie was able to provide a correct description of a plea bargain. This indicated that, at least in the short term, Lennie was able to learn, retain, and recall this concept. He also knew that rejecting a plea offer was somewhat like gambling and could result in a more serious consequence.

When asked how he thought he could best assist his attorney, Lennie began to cry and said that he couldn't think of how. Similarly, when asked what he thought he might plead if it were up to him, Lennie became upset and said that he should be punished.

Lennie was asked to consider various scenarios in which he would have to make decisions about his case. He again became visibly upset and had difficulty explaining what he would do.

Opinions

MENTAL ILLNESS, INTELLECTUAL DISABILITY, DEVELOPMENTAL DISABILITY, LACK OF MENTAL CAPACITY

The examiner found that Lennie was significantly depressed. The depression appeared to be pervasive and in acute need of treatment. His MMPI-A-RF results pointed to risk of suicide, although he denied such intent during his interview. Lennie was, however, emotionally very fragile. His defenses were brittle, and he had minimal coping skills. For that reason, it was the examiner's opinion that Lennie was mentally ill. He was not intellectually disabled, nor did he have a developmental disability. He did not lack mental capacity. Lennie had a language (expressive) disability but this did not seriously impair him in responding to the examiner's inquiries. However, his expressive impairment could worsen his depression and anxiety, as he was not able to adequately express himself.

CAPACITY TO COMPREHEND AND APPRECIATE
THE CHARGES AGAINST HIM

It was further the examiner's opinion that Lennie comprehended and appreciated the charges against him.

CAPACITY TO UNDERSTAND THE ADVERSARIAL NATURE
OF THE PROCEEDING, INCLUDING THE ROLE OF THE JUDGE,
DEFENSE COUNSEL, PROSECUTING ATTORNEY, GUARDIAN
AD LITEM OR SPECIAL ASSISTANT, AND WITNESS

Lennie had adequate knowledge of the roles of the major courtroom personnel.

CAPACITY TO COMPREHEND AND APPRECIATE THE
CONSEQUENCES THAT MAY BE IMPOSED

Lennie had adequate comprehension and appreciation of the consequences that may be imposed.

CAPACITY TO ASSIST IN HIS OWN DEFENSE
AND COMMUNICATING WITH COUNSEL

It was the examiner's opinion that Lennie was seriously impaired by his depression and anxiety. He was not able to manage his emotions and was in acute need of treatment. Owing to his depression, Lennie was easily overwhelmed, unable to adequately assert his own best interest, and unable to fully attend and comprehend. He was also at risk to psychologically decompensate and experience suicidal thoughts, suicidal behavior, or engage in self-defeating and possibly self-injurious behaviors.

ACCOMMODATIONS NECESSARY TO SUPPORT COMPETENCE

It was the examiner's opinion that Lennie's impairment was so significantly depressed and anxious that no reasonable accommodations provided by the court would be sufficient to support his competence.

PROBABILITY OF COMPETENCY ATTAINMENT

The examiner opined further that with proper treatment, Lennie could attain competence within the 12-month period allowed for by statute. Lennie's attainment needs were primarily clinical. Although he would benefit from educational programing for competency remediation, the principal focus of treatment should be on his depression and anxiety and the functional impact of these problems upon his competence. The examiner opined further that Lennie will require both individual therapy and assessment for his depression.

LEAST RESTRICTIVE SETTING FOR COMPETENCY ATTAINMENT

It was the examiner's opinion that the least restrictive setting for the competency attainment program for Lennie would be an outpatient program. Because Lennie was charged with an offense involving sexual behavior problems, the examiner recommended that he be appropriately supervised while he is receiving attainment programming.

OUTCOME

The court found Lennie to be not competent but able to attain competency. He was referred to an outpatient competency attainment program that provided both psychoeducational and mental health services.

FORENSIC CONTRIBUTIONS OF THE MMPI-A-RF

Competency to stand trial (or proceed) has become an increasingly frequent evaluation for juvenile court psychologists. Although juvenile competency standards are generally based on the adult court equivalents, many states have adopted provisions in the law specific to juveniles. This case illustrates that point. Adult competency evaluations do not require assessment of factors such as developmental capacity. The MMPI-A-RF aids the examiner in identifying potential psychological problems that can interfere with the youth's ability to assist counsel or understand court proceedings. In Lennie's case, the MMPI-A-RF data played an important role in the assessment of his competency to stand trial. Lennie did not have a serious deficiency in the knowledge required for competency. But the MMPI-A-RF identified significant psychological problems that produced functional impairment. In addition to his documented clinical history as well as his interview presentation, the MMPI-A-RF provided the court objective data that supported the examiner's finding of a mental illness and its resulting functional impairment.

The MMPI-A-RF can also provide insight into an adolescent's personality functioning in areas such as dependency, and into passivity, which can be used in assessing aspects of developmental capacity. The MMPI-A-RF can be used to identify problem areas that need to be addressed in competency attainment if a youth is found not competent. Also, the MMPI-A-RF can provide an assessment of a youth's functioning after competency attainment programming and recommendations to the court concerning maintaining competence.

Ralph

An Adolescent Evaluated for Bindover/Waiver to the Adult Criminal Justice System

BACKGROUND

Ralph is a 17-year-old male who was referred for a bindover or waiver evaluation to assess his amenability for treatment in the juvenile justice system. He was charged with one count each of robbery and criminal damaging and was held in the juvenile detention center pending further court proceedings. He was 16 years old at the time of the alleged offenses, which occurred after he ran away from a court-ordered placement. He had a lengthy history of prior juvenile justice contacts and multiple placements in detention but had never been placed in a state juvenile correctional facility. He was seen in the local juvenile detention facility.

Interview With Youth

Ralph reported a very complicated social history. He said that he never lived with his birth mother, whom he said was addicted to drugs and also mentally ill. Ralph said that a woman, Mary, took him in when he was 10 weeks old and he lived with her until he was about 14. Until he was 8, he thought that Mary was his birth mother. However, she informed him at that time that she was not his mother but was his "guardian" (although this was never legally formalized). At the same time, he also learned about the identity of his birth father. From ages 8 to 11, Ralph acted out significantly, and eventually he ran away. He said that he was placed in foster care and then at age 14 lived with his father. Ralph said that his father never explained to him the reasons that he had not been in his life prior to this time. Ralph reported that when he was 14, he was placed in three foster homes, then returned to Mary, then was placed again with a foster parent and then placed by the court with a paternal uncle. He denied any history of being physically or sexually abused but said that he was "beat on" a bit by Mary when he was younger.

Ralph reported that he was first before the court at the age of 14 for criminal damaging, for which he was placed on probation. He has remained on probation since that time and acknowledged that he has not been compliant and that he also failed drug tests. At the age of 15, he was charged with robbery. He has been presently detained for 6 months. He acknowledged running away from the authorities and that during this time, he was charged with the instant alleged offenses. He indicated that he has never been in the state juvenile correctional facility.

Ralph estimated that he has been in about eight fights, claiming that he has never caused physical injury. He denied any history of animal cruelty. He stated that he sees himself as a "follower" and said that he regrets his prior offenses—"because I know how it feels."

Ralph said that he does not have a developed sense of who he is as a person. Asked about how he feels about himself, Ralph responded, "I hate myself." He acknowledged being easily frustrated and that he does not think of long-term implications of his behaviors.

Ralph reported that at the facility, he is "on watch all the time because I tried to hang myself." He feels that he has made some progress in managing what he described as long-term anger and depression. Ralph indicated that he has been in mental health counseling "ever since I was young." He conveyed that he has been diagnosed with depression and ADHD. He was once psychiatrically hospitalized after his suicide attempt in the detention center. He said that he has been on "a lot" of medications, including antidepressants such as Wellbutrin, Zoloft, and Prozac. He has also been placed on Risperdal as well as Ritalin and Concerta for his ADHD. He said that he is not taking any medication at the time of the evaluation, but he has requested to see the mental health staff at the detention center.

Ralph reported that his mother has been diagnosed with a mood disorder and also has a history of substance abuse. He said that he believes that she has not used substances for the past 3 years.

Ralph indicated that he began smoking marijuana and drinking alcohol at the age of 12. He said that he stopped both when he was 15 because of probation violations and drug testing. He has experimented once with cocaine. He believes that his substance abuse has negatively impacted him and that when he got into trouble, he was typically under the influence.

Ralph denied any significant neurological history and specifically denied any history of head trauma, seizures, concussions, or loss of consciousness, but said that he once had sutures in his scalp after being pushed through a window and falling. He said that he is in good overall health.

COLLATERAL INFORMATION

Juvenile court records indicate that Ralph has had prior contacts for robbery, vandalism, unruly behavior, and school truancy. The vandalism charges were the result of setting dumpsters on fire while with a group of other youth. He had been placed on probation for each.

Ralph's biological mother could not be located. His "guardian" refused all efforts to interview her about Ralph's early development. His father said that he has 12 children from multiple relationships and that although Ralph lived with him, they did not have a close relationship and that Ralph often ran away from home.

School records indicated that Ralph has received special educational services since kindergarten under the category of Other Health Impaired and Emotional Disability. Psychoeducational testing has consistently found him to be of average intelligence with no evidence of any learning disability. He has had multiple suspensions for fighting and classroom disruption and two instances of bringing a knife to school but has never been expelled. He also has never been held back or repeated a grade.

Ralph was diagnosed with ADHD at the age of 7 and has been prescribed a variety of psychostimulant medications. He attempted suicide by hanging once while in detention. The detention staff found him unconscious and he was taken to an emergency room and subsequently transferred to a psychiatric hospital. He was held for 2 weeks. The discharge diagnosis was Disruptive Mood Dysregulation Disorder; Cannabis Dependence Uncomplicated; Conduct Disorder Adolescent Onset.

Current Behavioral Status

Ralph was appropriately groomed, with adequate hygiene. He was dressed in detention-issued clothing and appeared to be about his stated age. He evidenced no unusual behavioral mannerisms. There were no overt indications of loosening of associations, flight of ideas, or tangentiality. His psychomotor activity was nonremarkable. He showed no evidence of gross or fine motor dysfunction.

Ralph's speech was normal in tone, pacing, and volume. His attention span was adequate. His manner of social interaction was friendly, polite, and cooperative. Ralph presented with an appropriate and expressive affect to a mood that he described as "depressed," rating his subjective level of emotional distress as a "9 or 10" out of a possible 10.

Ralph denied and demonstrated no behavioral evidence of current visual, gustatory, olfactory, or tactile hallucinations and further showed no behavioral evidence of hearing or responding to hallucinations during any of the examinations. He denied and did not evidence specific delusional thinking or grandiosity. Accordingly, there appeared to be no evidence in the content of Ralph's thought or perceptual processes that would typically be seen with seriously mentally ill adolescents.

Ralph reported that he often has mood swings and problems with his temper. He denied a rapid or quick temper, saying that he usually has a "slow burn." When upset, his thoughts will race, but otherwise he denied other symptoms associated with bipolar disorder such as manic episodes or reckless spending as well as an inflated mood or grandiosity. He reported significant sleep problems as well as unplanned weight loss but denied other symptoms commonly associated with depression such as feelings of hopelessness (a significant risk factor for suicide in adolescents), inability to enjoy things, and poor concentration. Ralph reported frequent irritability and a decrease in sexual interest, which can be associated with depression. He also reported episodic suicidal ideation but denied actual intent or plan. He also denied homicidal ideation.

Ralph denied experiencing any specific, nonnormative phobias. He also denied any significantly intrusive obsessive thinking or markedly compulsive behavior. He denied any history of flashbacks, intrusive thoughts, dissociative episodes, or other psychological consequences of trauma exposure, but indicated that he sometimes has nightmares of his childhood.

Ralph was alert and responsive to his environment. He was oriented to time, place, person, and situation. His fund of general information suggested generally intact intellectual functioning but with limited general knowledge. His concentration was not noticeably variable as evidenced by a lack of any marked fluctuations in his attention and focus in the conversation with the examiner. As a more formal test, he was able to correctly perform serial subtractions by 3 from 30 but made some errors in calculations.

Ralph's memory functions were clinically intact. His immediate recall of digits was demonstrated to be five forward and four reversed, which is not indicative of substantial impairment in immediate memory or attention. His short-term memory was successfully demonstrated by his ability to recall three of three items from memory after a 10-minute distraction. His long-term memory was demonstrated to be intact by his ability to state the above-cited general information questions as well as details from his psychosocial history in a generally consistent manner with supporting records.

Ralph was not limited in his ability for abstract thinking as illustrated by his ability to identify similarities between increasingly complex concepts. His insight and judgment were appraised as being less than typical for his age as demonstrated both by his history as well as his responses to situational questions.

On the KBIT-2, Ralph achieved a Vocabulary score of 81. His Nonverbal score was 76. His overall Composite IQ was 75.

Ralph was also given the Slosson Oral Reading Test. His score indicated that he reads at the eighth-grade level, which is below his actual academic grade level.

MMPI-A-RF

Ralph's MMPI-A-RF protocol was valid. He appeared to be able to understand the test items and responded appropriately to their content. There were no indications of either overreporting or underreporting of problems. His protocol was compared to a reference group of 326 Mid-Atlantic Forensic Predisposition boys.

Of immediate note was that Ralph responded affirmatively to items with explicit suicidal content and he had elevated scores on scales associated with increased risk for suicide. Risk for suicidal behavior should therefore be monitored closely.

Ralph reported that he has a number of physical problems including poor energy, fatigue, sleep problems, and concentration problems. He also reports a diffuse pattern of cognitive difficulties and will likely have difficulties with paying attention and concentrating.

Ralph's scores indicate he is experiencing considerable emotional distress that is likely perceived as a crisis. He reports feeling sad and dissatisfied with his current life circumstance. He is likely to feel that life is a strain and to

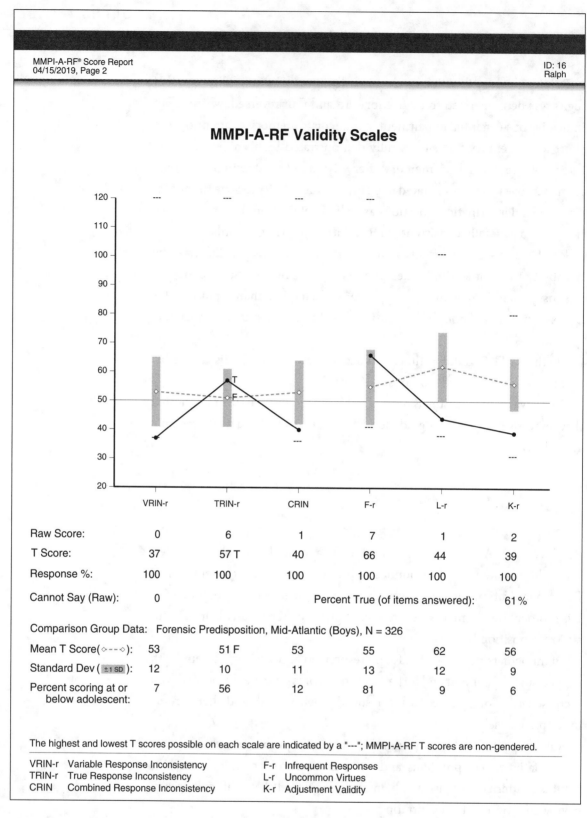

MMPI-A-RF Validity Scales

	VRIN-r	TRIN-r	CRIN	F-r	L-r	K-r
Raw Score:	0	6	1	7	1	2
T Score:	37	57 T	40	66	44	39
Response %:	100	100	100	100	100	100

Cannot Say (Raw): 0   Percent True (of items answered): 61%

Comparison Group Data: Forensic Predisposition, Mid-Atlantic (Boys), N = 326

Mean T Score(◇---◇):	53	51 F	53	55	62	56
Standard Dev (±1 SD):	12	10	11	13	12	9
Percent scoring at or below adolescent:	7	56	12	81	9	6

The highest and lowest T scores possible on each scale are indicated by a "---"; MMPI-A-RF T scores are non-gendered.

VRIN-r	Variable Response Inconsistency	F-r	Infrequent Responses
TRIN-r	True Response Inconsistency	L-r	Uncommon Virtues
CRIN	Combined Response Inconsistency	K-r	Adjustment Validity

FIGURE 16 Ralph's MMPI-A-RF Score Report. Copyright 2016 by the Regents of the University of Minnesota. All rights reserved.

MMPI-A-RF Higher-Order (H-O) and Restructured Clinical (RC) Scales

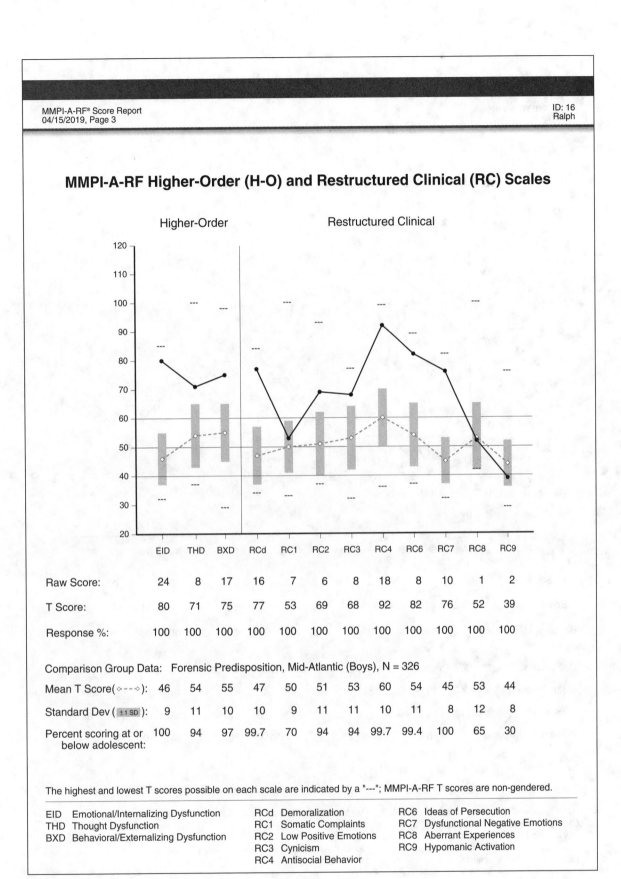

	EID	THD	BXD	RCd	RC1	RC2	RC3	RC4	RC6	RC7	RC8	RC9
Raw Score:	24	8	17	16	7	6	8	18	8	10	1	2
T Score:	80	71	75	77	53	69	68	92	82	76	52	39
Response %:	100	100	100	100	100	100	100	100	100	100	100	100

Comparison Group Data: Forensic Predisposition, Mid-Atlantic (Boys), N = 326

	EID	THD	BXD	RCd	RC1	RC2	RC3	RC4	RC6	RC7	RC8	RC9
Mean T Score(◇- - -◇):	46	54	55	47	50	51	53	60	54	45	53	44
Standard Dev (±1 SD):	9	11	10	10	9	11	11	10	11	8	12	8
Percent scoring at or below adolescent:	100	94	97	99.7	70	94	94	99.7	99.4	100	65	30

The highest and lowest T scores possible on each scale are indicated by a "---"; MMPI-A-RF T scores are non-gendered.

EID	Emotional/Internalizing Dysfunction	RCd	Demoralization	
THD	Thought Dysfunction	RC1	Somatic Complaints	RC6 Ideas of Persecution
BXD	Behavioral/Externalizing Dysfunction	RC2	Low Positive Emotions	RC7 Dysfunctional Negative Emotions
		RC3	Cynicism	RC8 Aberrant Experiences
		RC4	Antisocial Behavior	RC9 Hypomanic Activation

FIGURE 16 Ralph's MMPI-A-RF Score Report, continued.

241

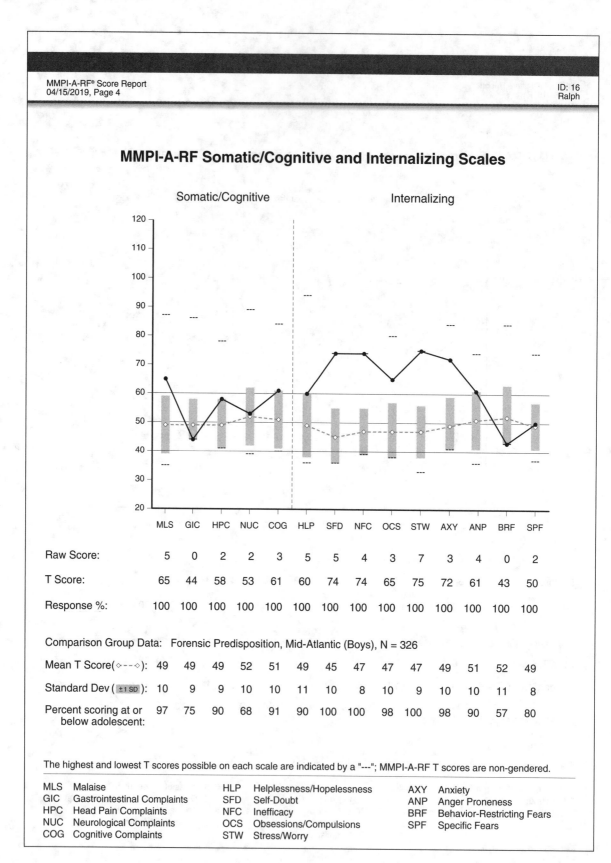

MMPI-A-RF Somatic/Cognitive and Internalizing Scales

	MLS	GIC	HPC	NUC	COG	HLP	SFD	NFC	OCS	STW	AXY	ANP	BRF	SPF
Raw Score:	5	0	2	2	3	5	5	4	3	7	3	4	0	2
T Score:	65	44	58	53	61	60	74	74	65	75	72	61	43	50
Response %:	100	100	100	100	100	100	100	100	100	100	100	100	100	100

Comparison Group Data: Forensic Predisposition, Mid-Atlantic (Boys), N = 326

	MLS	GIC	HPC	NUC	COG	HLP	SFD	NFC	OCS	STW	AXY	ANP	BRF	SPF
Mean T Score(◇---◇):	49	49	49	52	51	49	45	47	47	47	49	51	52	49
Standard Dev (±1 SD):	10	9	9	10	10	11	10	8	10	9	10	10	11	8
Percent scoring at or below adolescent:	97	75	90	68	91	90	100	100	98	100	98	90	57	80

The highest and lowest T scores possible on each scale are indicated by a "---"; MMPI-A-RF T scores are non-gendered.

MLS	Malaise	HLP	Helplessness/Hopelessness	AXY	Anxiety
GIC	Gastrointestinal Complaints	SFD	Self-Doubt	ANP	Anger Proneness
HPC	Head Pain Complaints	NFC	Inefficacy	BRF	Behavior-Restricting Fears
NUC	Neurological Complaints	OCS	Obsessions/Compulsions	SPF	Specific Fears
COG	Cognitive Complaints	STW	Stress/Worry		

FIGURE 16 Ralph's MMPI-A-RF Score Report, continued.

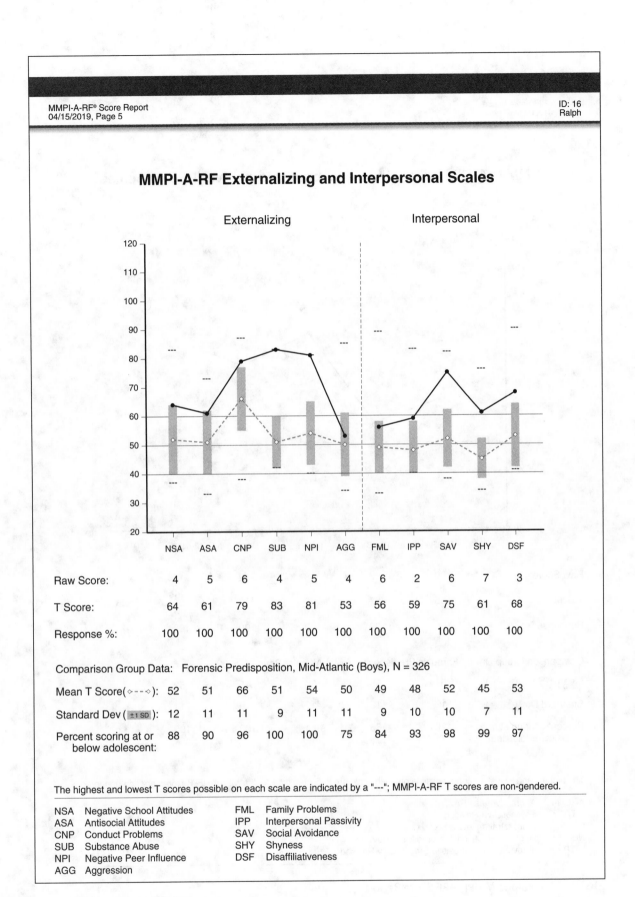

MMPI-A-RF Externalizing and Interpersonal Scales

Externalizing   Interpersonal

	NSA	ASA	CNP	SUB	NPI	AGG	FML	IPP	SAV	SHY	DSF
Raw Score:	4	5	6	4	5	4	6	2	6	7	3
T Score:	64	61	79	83	81	53	56	59	75	61	68
Response %:	100	100	100	100	100	100	100	100	100	100	100

Comparison Group Data: Forensic Predisposition, Mid-Atlantic (Boys), N = 326

	NSA	ASA	CNP	SUB	NPI	AGG	FML	IPP	SAV	SHY	DSF
Mean T Score(◇--◇):	52	51	66	51	54	50	49	48	52	45	53
Standard Dev (±1 SD):	12	11	11	9	11	11	9	10	10	7	11
Percent scoring at or below adolescent:	88	90	96	100	100	75	84	93	98	99	97

The highest and lowest T scores possible on each scale are indicated by a "---"; MMPI-A-RF T scores are non-gendered.

NSA	Negative School Attitudes	FML	Family Problems
ASA	Antisocial Attitudes	IPP	Interpersonal Passivity
CNP	Conduct Problems	SAV	Social Avoidance
SUB	Substance Abuse	SHY	Shyness
NPI	Negative Peer Influence	DSF	Disaffiliativeness
AGG	Aggression		

FIGURE 16 Ralph's MMPI-A-RF Score Report, continued.

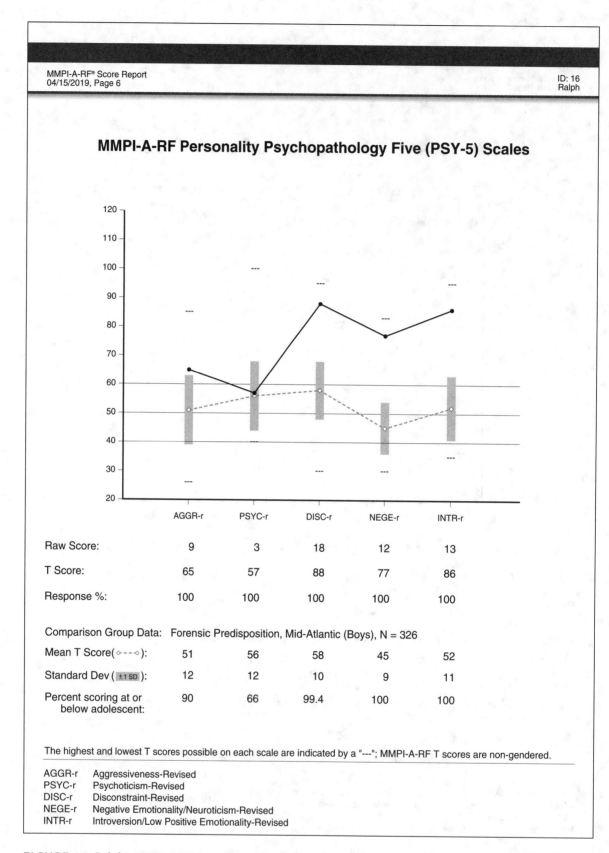

MMPI-A-RF Personality Psychopathology Five (PSY-5) Scales

	AGGR-r	PSYC-r	DISC-r	NEGE-r	INTR-r
Raw Score:	9	3	18	12	13
T Score:	65	57	88	77	86
Response %:	100	100	100	100	100

Comparison Group Data: Forensic Predisposition, Mid-Atlantic (Boys), N = 326

	AGGR-r	PSYC-r	DISC-r	NEGE-r	INTR-r
Mean T Score(◇- - -◇):	51	56	58	45	52
Standard Dev (±1 SD):	12	12	10	9	11
Percent scoring at or below adolescent:	90	66	99.4	100	100

The highest and lowest T scores possible on each scale are indicated by a "---"; MMPI-A-RF T scores are non-gendered.

AGGR-r   Aggressiveness-Revised
PSYC-r   Psychoticism-Revised
DISC-r   Disconstraint-Revised
NEGE-r   Negative Emotionality/Neuroticism-Revised
INTR-r   Introversion/Low Positive Emotionality-Revised

FIGURE 16   Ralph's MMPI-A-RF Score Report, continued.

MMPI-A-RF T SCORES (BY DOMAIN)

PROTOCOL VALIDITY

Content Non-Responsiveness

0	37	57 T	40
CNS	VRIN-r	TRIN-r	CRIN

Over-Reporting

66
F-r

Under-Reporting

44	39
L-r	K-r

SUBSTANTIVE SCALES

Somatic/Cognitive Dysfunction

53	65	44	58	53	61
RC1	MLS	GIC	HPC	NUC	COG

Emotional Dysfunction

80
EID

77	60	74	74
RCd	HLP	SFD	NFC

69	86
RC2	INTR-r

76	65	75	72	61	43	50	77
RC7	OCS	STW	AXY	ANP	BRF	SPF	NEGE-r

Thought Dysfunction

71
THD

82
RC6

52
RC8

57
PSYC-r

Behavioral Dysfunction

75
BXD

92	64	61	79	83	81
RC4	NSA	ASA	CNP	SUB	NPI

39	53	65	88
RC9	AGG	AGGR-r	DISC-r

Interpersonal Functioning

56	68	59	75	61	68
FML	RC3	IPP	SAV	SHY	DSF

Note. This information is provided to facilitate interpretation following the recommended structure for MMPI-A-RF interpretation in Chapter 7 of the *MMPI-A-RF Administration, Scoring, Interpretation, and Technical Manual*, which provides details in the text and an outline in Table 7-1.

FIGURE 16 Ralph's MMPI-A-RF Score Report, continued.

report feeling depressed and anxious. He is likely to experience problems with attention and concentration. He is also likely to complain of low energy and fatigue. Ralph reports self-doubt, feelings of uselessness, and low self-esteem. He is likely self-defeating and self-degrading. He also reports being indecisive and ineffective in coping with difficulties and is likely to procrastinate. In addition, he reports feeling hopeless and helpless and is likely to feel he gets a raw deal out of life and cannot be helped. He is likely to engage in self-injurious behavior and to give up easily.

Ralph also reports an above-average level of negative emotional experiences including anxiety, irritability, remorse, and apprehensiveness. He is likely to have nightmares and to be insecure. He reports an above-average level of stress and worry as well as an above-average level of obsessive and compulsive symptoms. He is indeed likely to be compulsive and to experience problems with thinking. Ralph also reports a high level of anger problems involving irritability and impatience, and he is likely to be angry and irritable and to engage in acting-out behaviors.

Ralph's scores also indicate significant thought dysfunction. Specifically, he reports prominent persecutory ideation that likely includes paranoid ideation. He is likely to experience hallucinations and other psychotic symptoms.

Ralph's scores also indicate significant externalizing-acting-out behaviors. He reports a broad range of acting-out behaviors such as substance abuse, school behavior problems, and family conflict. He is very likely to engage in conduct-disordered behaviors, rule breaking, oppositional behavior, and fighting. He also likely has a history of juvenile detention placements, criminal charges, alcohol and/or drug use, running away from home, and school suspensions. Ralph does in fact report problematic use of alcohol and drugs, including marijuana, and multiple conduct problems. He also reports significant problems stemming from affiliation with a socially undesirable peer group, holding various antisocial attitudes, and a higher than average number of negative school attitudes. He is likely to have academic problems, to experience test anxiety, and to have poor study skills. More generally, and contributing to many of his problems, Ralph very likely has extremely poor impulse control.

Interpersonally, Ralph reports avoiding some social situations and events, being shy, easily embarrassed, feeling uncomfortable around others, and some dislike of being around people. He is likely bullied by peers, has few or no friends, is socially withdrawn and isolated, feels socially awkward, and is introverted and uncomfortable with the opposite sex. Ralph also reports holding cynical beliefs concerning others, being distrustful of others, and believing that others are motivated only by their own self-interest.

Ralph's MMPI-A-RF scores indicate the need to consider a broad range of diagnoses including various internalizing disorders such as depression, anxiety, and posttraumatic stress disorder, as well as externalizing disorders such as conduct, and substance use disorders as well as other disorders related to undercontrolled behavior. His scores also indicate a need to consider disorders related to persecutory beliefs.

Prognosis for treatment is guarded in light of Ralph's antisocial behavioral proclivities and cynical attitudes. However, the acute emotional distress he is experiencing could motivate Ralph to initially engage in treatment.

Diagnosis

Ralph was given diagnoses of Disruptive Mood Dysregulation Disorder, Conduct Disorder Adolescent Onset, Unspecified Trauma and Stressor Related Disorder, Cannabis Use Disorder Unspecified, and Alcohol Use Disorder Unspecified.

Amenability to Treatment

Ralph was also assessed utilizing the Risk Sophistication Treatment Inventory (Salekin, 2004), a semistructured interview and rating scale used to assess juvenile offenders ages 9–18 in the following areas: (1) risk for dangerousness, (2) sophistication–maturity, and (3) treatment amenability.

On the Risk for Dangerousness scale Ralph's raw score of 9 resulted in a T score of 31, at the 3rd percentile in the low range. On the Sophistication-Maturity scale, his raw score of 17 resulted in a T score of 64 that was in the 64th percentile and in the high range. On the Treatment Amenability scale, his raw score of 18 resulted in a T score of 60 at the 83rd percentile (high range).

Overall, Ralph was seen as having both negative and positive factors for amenability. Those factors that argued against amenability included his history of poor compliance in the community, a history of early onset behavioral problems, the MMPI-A-RF finding of strong tendencies for antisocial behavior and his history of limited attachments and caregiver disruption and rejection.

Those factors that indicated he was amenable to treatment in the juvenile justice system included his high rating on the RSTI-I for treatment amenability and low risk of violence on the RST-I and the treatability of his mood disorder. Consideration was also given to the fact that he had never been placed in a juvenile correctional facility other than detention and had not been provided programming specific to his needs.

The examiner's opinion was that Ralph had a moderate to high amenability to treatment in the juvenile justice system. This opinion was based on consideration of the following countervailing factors.

Factors that suggest that Ralph is not amenable to treatment:

1. He is 17 years old and, as a result, the time remaining in the juvenile justice system is limited.
2. He has not been compliant with community-based treatment and has had behavioral problems in detention.
3. He has a history of poor school achievement and behavioral problems.
4. He has only limited attachments and a history of traumatic caregiver disruption.
5. The MMPI-A-RF indicated psychological characteristics of youth who have conduct-disordered behaviors, oppositional-defiant tendencies, and distrust of others. It also indicated that Ralph was at significant risk for treatment noncompliance and that his acting-out tendencies may disrupt treatment. Finally, the MMPI-A-RF data indicate that his low positive emotionality, interpersonal suspiciousness, tendencies for disaffiliation from others and cynicism may make initiation of a therapeutic relationship difficult.
6. He has a history of poor impulse control.
7. He has been before the court on multiple cases.

Factors indicating that Ralph is amenable to treatment in the juvenile justice system:

1. He was rated in the high range for treatment amenability on the RSTI, an evidence-based instrument specifically developed for this purpose.
2. He was rated in the low range in the Risk for Dangerousness subscale of the RSTI.[3]

3. He is of sufficient intelligence to understand and implement treatment.

4. There is no record of early onset violent or markedly antisocial behavior.

5. On the MMPI-A-RF, Ralph was neither defensive (underreporting) or overreporting problems and appeared to have responded accurately to the test items. This could suggest that he will be reasonably forthright in treatment efforts.

6. He has significant emotional distress that may motivate him to receive treatment. Youth, by virtue of their age and developmental status, have far greater likelihood of change than older adult offenders. Research has consistently shown that many violent behaviors, including homicide, do not carry over throughout the lifespan. Research also indicates that only a small proportion of youth who show delinquent behavior persist in that behavior through adulthood (Moffit, 1993). Adolescent criminal behavior more often than not is the result of association with negative peers or behaviors that reflect normative experimentation with risky behavior rather than any deep-seated moral deficiency. The vast majority of adolescents desist from criminal behaviors as they mature.

7. Research has found that transfer to criminal court increases the likelihood of recidivism for many youths who have been transferred (Bishop et al., 1996) although there are differential effects in some youth (Loughran, 2010).

OUTCOME

Both the prosecutor and the defense attorney stipulated to the findings of the examination. Ralph was retained in the juvenile justice system. He was placed in a juvenile correctional setting that provided mental health services.

FORENSIC CONTRIBUTIONS OF THE MMPI-A-RF

Bindover evaluations, sometimes termed waiver or transfer, are examinations of great consequence in juvenile court. The question addressed is the amenability of the adolescent to remaining in the juvenile justice system. As in the case of all forensic examinations, the ultimate issue, that of amenability, is the determination of the court. However, most statutes require a psychological evaluation to inform the court about the youth's present functioning as well as other areas such as future risk, treatment needs, and responsiveness as well as the sophistication and maturity of the adolescent. Some states specify that certain offenses, when committed by a youth of a particular age, result in a mandatory transfer but allow for discretionary transfers in other offenses and ages.

As illustrated by Ralph's case, the MMPI-A-RF addresses both potential diagnostic considerations as well as personality characteristics that can assist in the psychological determination of amenability. Ralph was found to have problems that could be responsive to treatment but would clearly require intensive interventions. The MMPI-A-RF provided information to the court about the potential for Ralph's engagement in treatment, his likely response as well as treatment challenges. The ultimate determination of amenability is made by the court. However, the MMPI-A-RF, along with specialized instruments such as the RST-I, can serve as an integral part of the assessment process.

NOTES

THE FORENSIC CASES

1. In certain cases, especially preadjudication, it is not advisable for the same examiner to evaluate codefendants. In this specific case, the evaluation was postadjudication and the court discussed the matter with all parties concerned, including legal counsel for each youth. All parties agreed to the same examiner, who also verified this with the court and each evaluee and family.

2. The CBRS-P can be completed by nonbiological primary caregivers (Conners, 2008, p. 22). However, the court should be aware that the normative sample was based upon ratings by the parents of the youth and this does represent a deviation from that sample. For that reason, these data should be reviewed with this caution in mind.

3. With the caveat that the alleged offense was a sexually oriented offense that requires a different, postadjudicative risk assessment.

REFERENCES

Alexander, M. A. (1999). Sexual offender treatment efficacy revisited. *Sexual Abuse: A Journal of Research and Treatment, 11*, 101–116.

American Educational Research Association. (2014). *Standards for educational and psychological testing.*

American Psychological Association. (2013). Specialty guidelines for forensic psychology. *American Psychologist, 68*(1), 7–19. https://doi.org/10.1037/a0029889

Archer, R. P. (2017). *Assessing adolescent psychopathology: MMPI-A/MMPI-A-RF* (4th ed.). Routledge Press.

Archer, R. P., Handel R. W., Ben-Porath, Y. S., & Tellegen, A. (2016a). *Minnesota Multiphasic Personality Inventory-Adolescent-Restructured Form (MMPI-A-RF): Manual for administration, scoring, interpretation, and technical manual.* University of Minnesota Press.

Archer, R. P., Handel R. W., Ben-Porath Y. S., & Tellegen, A. (2016b). *MMPI-A-RF user's guide for reports.* University of Minnesota Press.

Association for Treatment of Sexual Abusers (ASTA). (2012). *Adolescents who have engaged in sexually abusive behavior: Effective policies and practices.* http://www.atsa.com/adolescents-engaged-in-sexually-abusive-behavior

Becker, S. P., & Kerig, P. K. (2011). Posttraumatic stress symptoms are associated with the frequency and severity of delinquency among detained boys. *Journal of Clinical and Child and Adolescent Psychology, 40*, 765–771.

Ben-Porath, Y. S. (2013). Assessing personality and psychopathology with self-report inventories. In J. R. Graham & J. A. Naglieri (Eds.), *Handbook of psychology: Assessment psychology* (2nd ed., Vol. 10). John Wiley & Sons.

Ben-Porath, Y. S., & Tellegen, A. (2008/2011). *Minnesota Multiphasic Personality Inventory-2-Restructured Form (MMPI-2-RF): Manual for administration, scoring, and interpretation.* University of Minnesota Press.

Bishop, D. M., Frazier, C. E., Lanza-Kaduce, L., & Winner, L. (1996). The transfer of juveniles to criminal court: Does it make a difference? *Crime and Delinquency, 42*(2), 171–191.

Borduin, C. M., Henggeler, S. W., Blaske, D. M., & Stain, R. J. (1990). Multisystemic treatment of adolescent sexual offenders. *International Journal of Offender Therapy and Comparative Criminology, 35*, 105–114.

Borum, R., Bartel, P., & Forth, A. (2006). *SAVRY: Structured assessment of violence risk in youth: Professional manual.* Psychological Assessment Resources.

Briere, J. (1996). *Trauma symptom checklist professional manual.* Psychological Assessment Resources.

Bushman, B. J., Newman, K., Calvert, S. L., Downey, G., Dredze, M., Gottfredson, M., & Webster, D. W. (2016). Youth violence: What we know and what we need to know. *American Psychologist, 71*(1), 17–39.

Butcher, J. N., Williams, C. L., Graham, J. R., Archer, R. P., Tellegen, A., Ben-Porath, Y. S., & Kaemmer, B. (1992). *MMPI-A: Minnesota Multiphasic Personality Inventory-Adolescent: Manual for administration, scoring, and interpretation.* University of Minnesota Press.

Caldwell, M. F. (2010). Study characteristics and recidivism base rates in juvenile sex offender recidivism. *International Journal of Offender Therapy and Comparative Criminology, 54,* 197–212.

Capwell, D. F. (1945a). Personality patterns of adolescent girls: I. Girls who show improvement in IQ. *Journal of Applied Psychology, 29*(3), 212–228. https://doi.org /10.1037/h0062853

Capwell, D. F. (1945b). Personality patterns of adolescent girls: II. Delinquents and non-delinquents. *Journal of Applied Psychology, 29*(4), 289–297. https://doi.org/10.1037 /h0054701

Conners, C. K. (2008). *Manual for the Conners comprehensive behavior rating scales.* Multi-Health Systems.

Dahlstrom, W. G., Welsh, G. S., & Dahlstrom, L. E. (1972). *An MMPI handbook: Clinical interpretation* (rev ed., Vol. 1). University of Minnesota Press.

Ehrenworth, N. V., & Archer, R. P. (1985). A comparison of clinical accuracy ratings of interpretive approaches for adolescent MMPI responses. *Journal of Personality Assessment, 49*(4), 413–421. https://doi.org/10:1207/sl5327752jpa4904_9

Forby, J. D., Ben-Porath, Y. S., & Davis, D. L. (2000). A comparison of sexually abused and non-sexually abused adolescents in a clinical treatment facility using the MMPI-A. *Child Abuse and Neglect, 24*(4), 557–568.

Frumkin, I. B. (2000). Competency to waive Miranda rights: Clinical and legal issues. *Mental and Physical Disabilities Law Reporter, 4,* 326–331.

Frumkin, I. B. (2014). Report on juvenile Miranda waiver capacity. In K. Heilbrun, D. DeMatteo, S. Brooks-Holliday, & C. LaDuke (Eds.), *Forensic mental health assessment: A casebook* (2nd ed.). Oxford University Press.

Goldstein, N. E., Zelle, H., & Grisso, T. (2011). *Miranda rights comprehension instruments (MRCI) manual.* Professional Resource Press.

Grisso, T. (2005). *Evaluating juvenile's adjudicative competence: A guide for clinical practice.* Professional Resource Press.

Harkness, A. R., McNulty, J. L., & Ben-Porath, Y. S. (1995). The Personality Psychopathology Five (PSY-5): Constructs and MMPI-2 scales. *Psychological Assessment, 7*(10), 104–114.

Hathaway, S. R., & McKinley, J. C. (1943). *The Minnesota Multiphasic Personality Schedule.* University of Minnesota Press.

Hathaway, S. R., & Monachesi, E. D. (1963). *Adolescent personality and behavior.* University of Minnesota Press.

Janus, M. D., de Groot, C., & Toepfer, S. M. (1998). The MMPI-A and 13-year-old inpatients: How young is too young? *Assessment, 5*(4), 321–332. https://doi.org/10.1177/107319119800500402

Landes, S. J., & Linehan, M. M. (2015). Dissemination and implementation of dialectical behavior therapy. In R. K. McHugh & D. H. Barlow (Eds.), *Dissemination and implementation of evidence-based psychological treatments.* Oxford University Press. https://doi.org/10.1093/med:psych/9780195389050.003.0010

Loughran, T. A. (2010). Differential effects of adult court transfer on juvenile offender recidivism. *Law and Human Behavior, 34,* 476–488.

Marks, P. A., Seeman, W., & Haller, D. L. (1974). *The actuarial use of the MMPI with adolescents and adults.* Williams and Wilkins.

McNulty, J. L., Harkness, A. R., Ben-Porath, Y. S., & Williams, C. L. (1997). Assessing the Personality Psychopathology Five (PSY-5) in adolescents: New MMPI-A scales. *Psychological Assessment, 9*(3), 250–259. https://doi.org/10.1037/1040–3590.9.3.250

Meloy, J. R., & Hoffmann, J. (2014). *International handbook of threat assessment.* Oxford University Press.

Meloy, J. R., & O'Toole, M. E. (2011). The concept of leakage in threat assessment. *Behavioral Sciences and the Law, 29,* 513–527.

Moffit, T. (1993). Adolescent limited and life course persistent antisocial behavior: A developmental taxonomy. *Psychological Bulletin, 100,* 675–701.

Odgers, C. L., Moretti, M. M., & Reppucci, N. D. (2005). Examining the science and practice of violence risk assessment with female adolescents. *Law and Human Behavior, 29*(1), 7–27.

Oldenburg, J. C. (1997). *The relation between age and MMPI-A scale scores and correlates in a clinical population* [Unpublished doctoral dissertation]. Kent State University.

Prentky, R. (2017). *Risk assessment of juvenile sex offenders.* American Academy of Forensic Psychology.

Prentky, R., & Righthand, S. (2003). *Juvenile sex offender assessment protocol manual.* U.S. Department of Justice, Office of Juvenile Justice and Delinquency Prevention.

Salekin, R. T. (2004). *RSTI, risk-sophistication-treatment inventory; risk for dangerousness sophistication-maturity treatment amenability: Professional manual.* Psychological Assessment Resources.

Schubert, C. A., Mulvey, E. P., Loughran, T. A., Fagan, J., Chassin, L. A., Piquero, A. R., & Cauffman, E. (2010). Predicting outcomes for youth transferred to adult court. *Law and Human Behavior, 34*(6), 460–475. https://doi.org/10.1007/s10979-009-9209-5

Sexton, T. L., & Alexander, J. F. (2000). *Functional family therapy.* U.S. Department of Justice, Office of Justice Programs, Office of Juvenile Justice and Delinquency Prevention.

Tellegen, A., & Ben-Porath, Y. S. (2008, 2011). *Minnesota Multiphasic Personality Inventory-2-Restructured Form (MMPI-2-RF): Technical manual.* University of Minnesota Press.

Trickett, P. K., Noll, J. G., & Putnam, F. W. (2011). The impact of sexual abuse on female development: Lessons from a multigenerational, longitudinal research study. *Development and Psychopathology, 23*(2), 453–476.

Wijk, A. V., Vermeiren, R., Loeber, R., Hart-Kerkhoffs, L., Doreleijers, T., & Bullens, R. (2006). Juvenile sex offenders compared to non-sex offenders. *Trauma, Violence, & Abuse, 7*(4), 227–243. https://doi.org/10.1177/1524838006292519

Worling, J. R. (2013). What were we thinking? Five erroneous assumptions that have fueled specialized interventions for adolescents who have sexually offended. *International Journal of Behavioral Consultation and Therapy, 8*(3–4), 80–88. http://dx.doi.org/10.1037/h0100988

Worling, J. (2017). Protective + risk observations for eliminating sexual offense recidivism (PROFESOR). https://www.profesor.ca

Worling, J. R., & Curwin, T. (2000). Adolescent sexual offender recidivism: Success of specialized treatment and implication for risk prediction. *Child Abuse and Neglect, 24,* 965–982.

INDEX

Page numbers in italics refer to figures or tables.

DANIEL L. DAVIS, PhD, ABPP, is a psychologist in private practice in Columbus, Ohio. He is board certified by the American Board of Professional Psychology in forensic psychology. He has more than 40 years of practice in forensic psychology as well as assessment and therapy with adolescents and adults. He has served as a senior forensic psychologist for the Netcare Forensic Center, the clinical director of the Buckeye Ranch, and the supervising psychologist of the Timothy B. Moritz Forensic Unit of the Ohio Department of Mental Health. He also served as the clinical director of the Central Ohio Cluster of Mental Health Services of the Ohio Department of Rehabilitation and Correction.

YOSSEF S. BEN-PORATH, PhD, ABPP, is professor of psychological sciences at Kent State University and a board-certified clinical psychologist. He received his doctoral training at the University of Minnesota and has been involved extensively in MMPI research for the past 30 years. He is a codeveloper of the MMPI-2-RF and MMPI-A-RF and coauthor of numerous test manuals, books, book chapters, and articles on the MMPI instruments. He is editor-in-chief of the journal *Psychological Assessment* and a member of APA's Committee on Psychological Tests and Assessment. His clinical practice involves supervision of assessments at Kent State's Psychological Clinic, consultation to agencies that screen candidates for public safety positions, and provision of consultation and expert witness services in forensic cases.